hawkeye

L.A. WOMAN

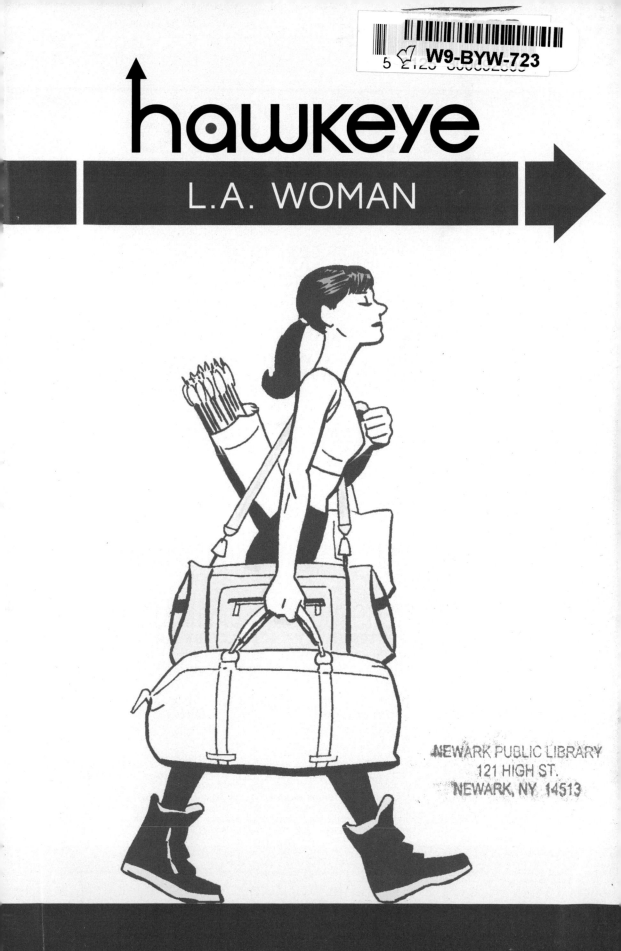

hawkeye

L.A. WOMAN

MATT FRACTION
WRITER

ANNUAL #1

JAVIER PULIDO
ARTIST & COVER

MATT HOLLINGSWORTH
COLOR ARTIST

VC'S CLAYTON COWLES
LETTERER

ISSUES #14, #16, #18 & #20

ANNIE WU
ARTIST

MATT HOLLINGSWORTH
COLOR ARTIST

CHRIS ELIOPOULOS
LETTERER

DAVID AJA
COVER ART

DEVIN LEWIS
ASSISTANT EDITOR

TOM BRENNAN
ASSOCIATE EDITOR

STEPHEN WACKER & SANA AMANAT
EDITORS

COLLECTION EDITOR: **JENNIFER GRÜNWALD** • ASSISTANT EDITOR: **SARAH BRUNSTAD**
ASSOCIATE MANAGING EDITOR: **ALEX STARBUCK** • EDITOR, SPECIAL PROJECTS: **MARK D. BEAZLEY**
SENIOR EDITOR, SPECIAL PROJECTS: **JEFF YOUNGQUIST**
SVP PRINT, SALES & MARKETING: **DAVID GABRIEL** • BOOK DESIGN: **JEFF POWELL**

EDITOR IN CHIEF: **AXEL ALONSO** • CHIEF CREATIVE OFFICER: **JOE QUESADA**
PUBLISHER: **DAN BUCKLEY** • EXECUTIVE PRODUCER: **ALAN FINE**

HAWKEYE VOL. 3: L.A. WOMAN. Contains material originally published in magazine form as HAWKEYE #14, #16, #18, #20 and ANNUAL #1. First printing 2014. ISBN# 978-0-7851-8390-7. Published by MARVEL WORLDWIDE, INC., a subsidiary of MARVEL ENTERTAINMENT, LLC. OFFICE OF PUBLICATION: 135 West 50th Street, New York, NY 10020. Copyright © 2013 and 2014 Marvel Characters, Inc. All rights reserved. All characters featured in this issue and the distinctive names and likenesses thereof, and all related indicia are trademarks of Marvel Characters, Inc. No similarity between any of the names, characters, persons, and/or institutions in this magazine with those of any living or dead person or institution is intended, and any such similarity which may exist is purely coincidental. **Printed in Canada.** ALAN FINE, EVP - Office of the President, Marvel Worldwide, Inc. and EVP & CMO Marvel Characters B.V.; DAN BUCKLEY, Publisher & President - Print, Animation & Digital Divisions; JOE QUESADA, Chief Creative Officer; TOM BREVOORT, SVP of Publishing; DAVID BOGART, SVP of Operations & Procurement, Publishing; C.B. CEBULSKI, SVP of Creator & Content Development; DAVID GABRIEL, SVP Print, Sales & Marketing; JIM O'KEEFE, VP of Operations & Logistics; DAN CARR, Executive Director of Publishing Technology; SUSAN CRESPI, Editorial Operations Manager; ALEX MORALES, Publishing Operations Manager; STAN LEE, Chairman Emeritus. For information regarding advertising in Marvel Comics or on Marvel.com, please contact Niza Disla, Director of Marvel Partnerships, at ndisla@marvel.com. For Marvel subscription inquiries, please call 800-217-9158. **Manufactured between 6/20/2014 and 7/28/2014 by SOLISCO PRINTERS, SCOTT, QC, CANADA.**

10 9 8 7 6 5 4 3 2 1

PREVIOUSLY...

KATE BISHOP, A.K.A. HAWKEYE IS ACTUALLY
THE GREATEST SHARPSHOOTER KNOWN TO MAN.

(SHUT-UP, BARTON.)

SHE'S PRACTICALLY AN AVENGER.

THIS IS WHAT HAPPENS WHEN SHE GETS SICK OF
THE OTHER HAWKEYE'S DRAMA AND HEADS OUT
TO L.A.

THE DOG WENT WITH HER.

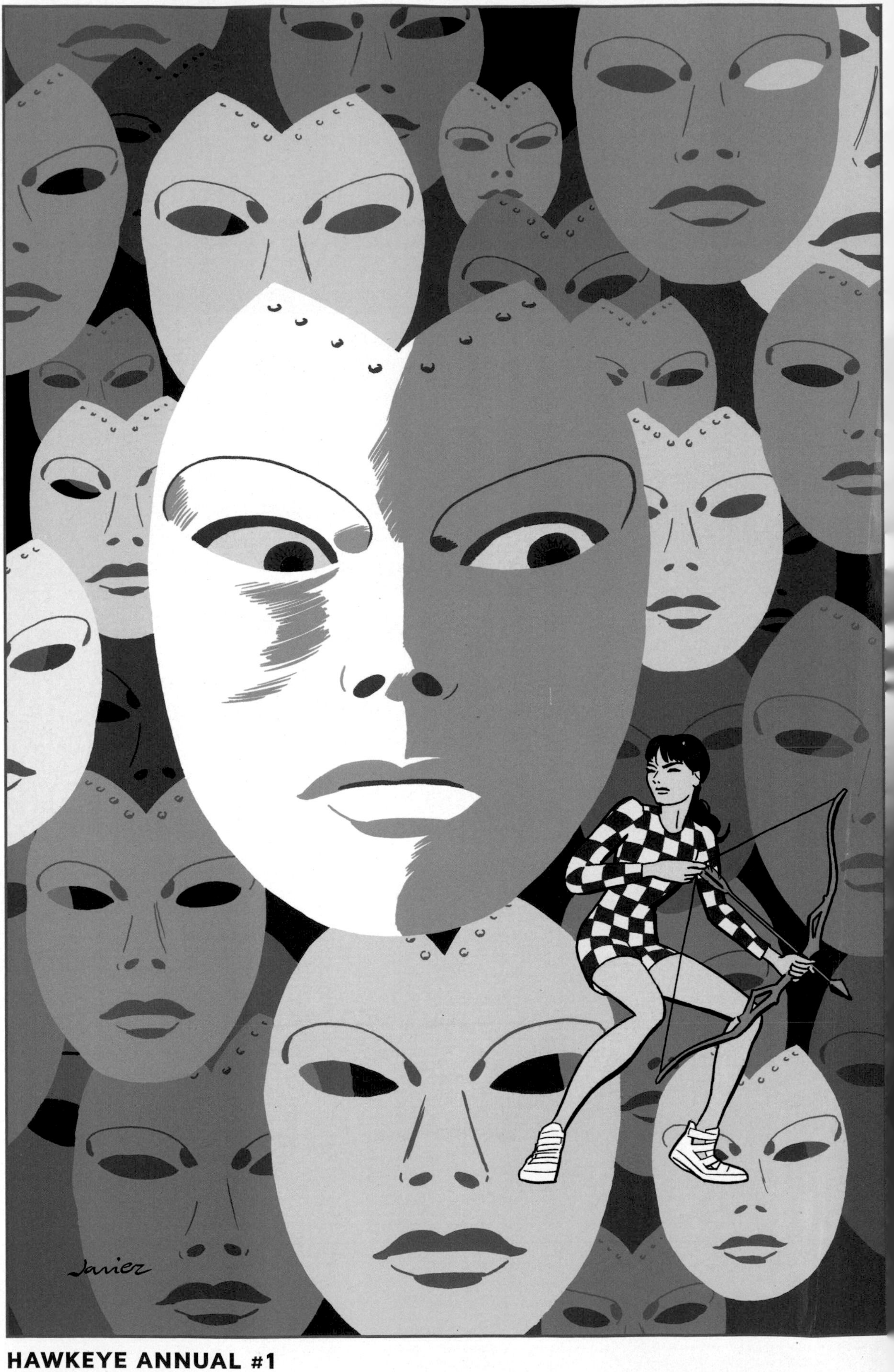
Javier

HAWKEYE ANNUAL #1

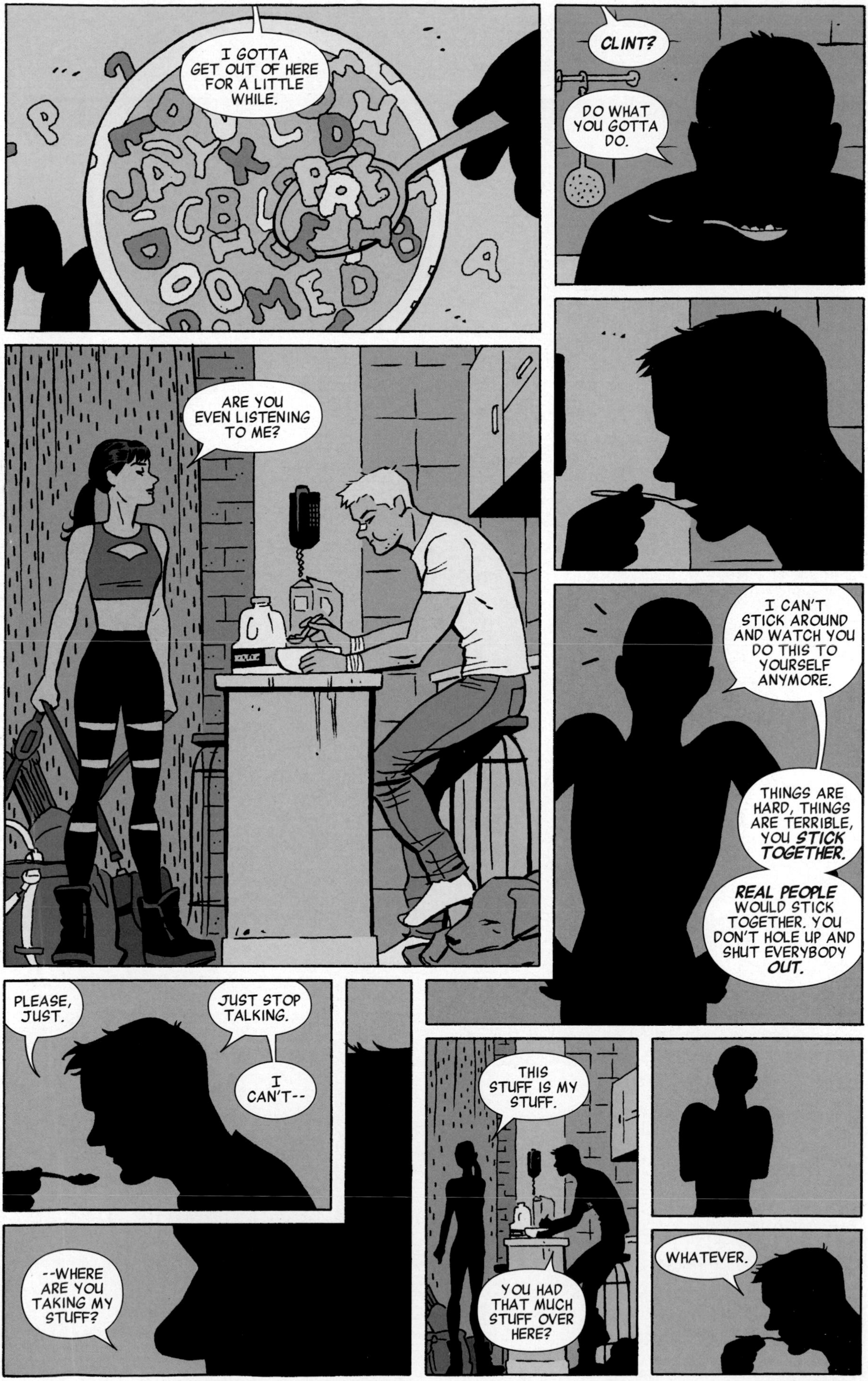
I GOTTA GET OUT OF HERE FOR A LITTLE WHILE.
DOOMED
CLINT?
DO WHAT YOU GOTTA DO.
ARE YOU EVEN LISTENING TO ME?
I CAN'T STICK AROUND AND WATCH YOU DO THIS TO YOURSELF ANYMORE.
THINGS ARE HARD, THINGS ARE TERRIBLE, YOU STICK TOGETHER.
REAL PEOPLE WOULD STICK TOGETHER. YOU DON'T HOLE UP AND SHUT EVERYBODY OUT.
PLEASE, JUST.
JUST STOP TALKING.
I CAN'T--
--WHERE ARE YOU TAKING MY STUFF?
THIS STUFF IS MY STUFF.
YOU HAD THAT MUCH STUFF OVER HERE?
WHATEVER.

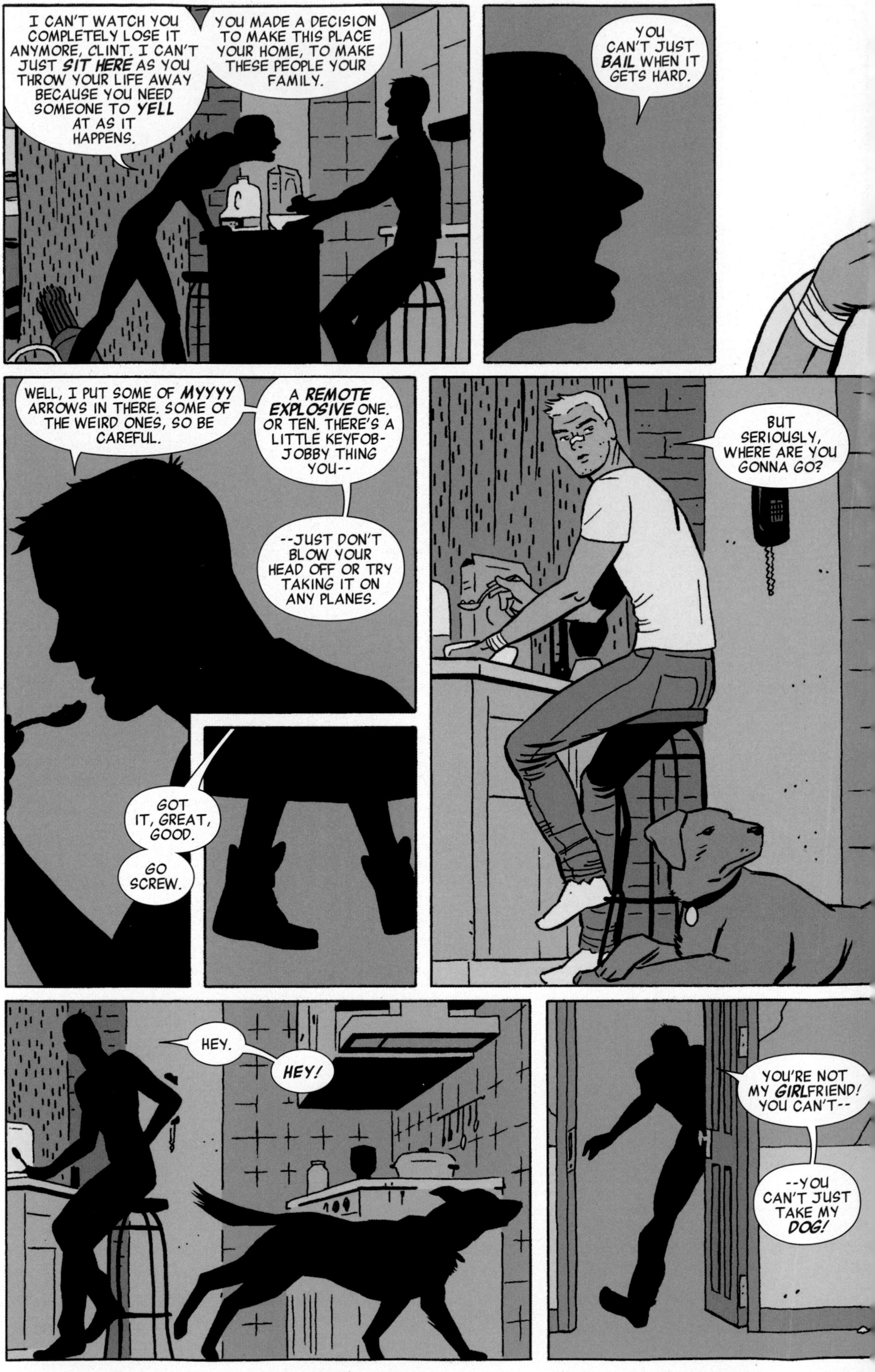
I CAN'T WATCH YOU COMPLETELY LOSE IT ANYMORE, CLINT. I CAN'T JUST SIT HERE AS YOU THROW YOUR LIFE AWAY BECAUSE YOU NEED SOMEONE TO YELL AT AS IT HAPPENS.
YOU MADE A DECISION TO MAKE THIS PLACE YOUR HOME, TO MAKE THESE PEOPLE YOUR FAMILY.
YOU CAN'T JUST BAIL WHEN IT GETS HARD.
WELL, I PUT SOME OF MYYYY ARROWS IN THERE. SOME OF THE WEIRD ONES, SO BE CAREFUL.
A REMOTE EXPLOSIVE ONE. OR TEN. THERE'S A LITTLE KEYFOB-JOBBY THING YOU--
--JUST DON'T BLOW YOUR HEAD OFF OR TRY TAKING IT ON ANY PLANES.
GOT IT, GREAT, GOOD.
GO SCREW.
BUT SERIOUSLY, WHERE ARE YOU GONNA GO?
HEY.
HEY!
YOU'RE NOT MY GIRLFRIEND! YOU CAN'T--
--YOU CAN'T JUST TAKE MY DOG!

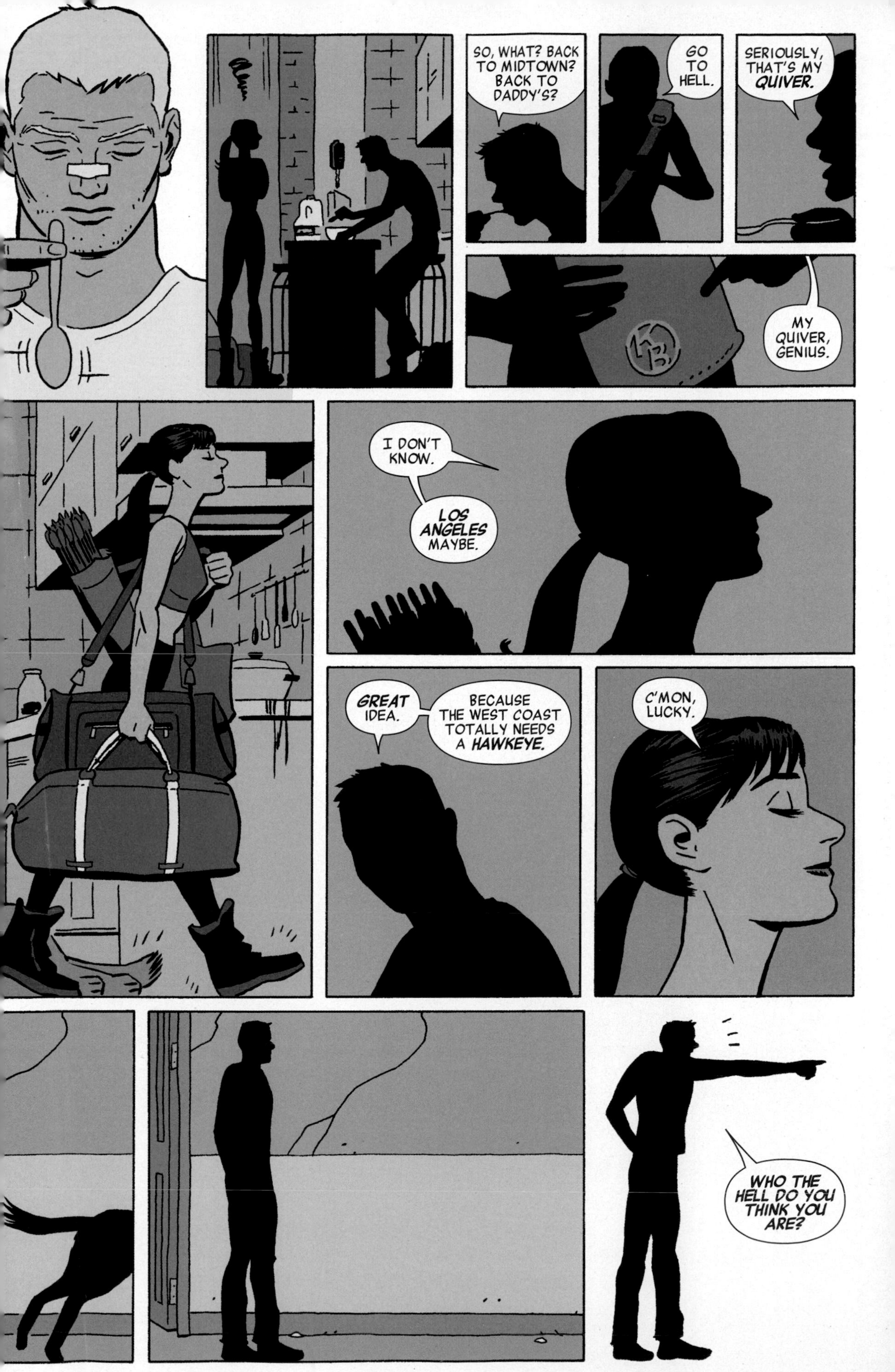
SO, WHAT? BACK TO MIDTOWN? BACK TO DADDY'S?
GO TO HELL.
SERIOUSLY, THAT'S MY QUIVER.
MY QUIVER, GENIUS.
I DON'T KNOW.
LOS ANGELES MAYBE.
GREAT IDEA.
BECAUSE THE WEST COAST TOTALLY NEEDS A HAWKEYE.
C'MON, LUCKY.
WHO THE HELL DO YOU THINK YOU ARE?

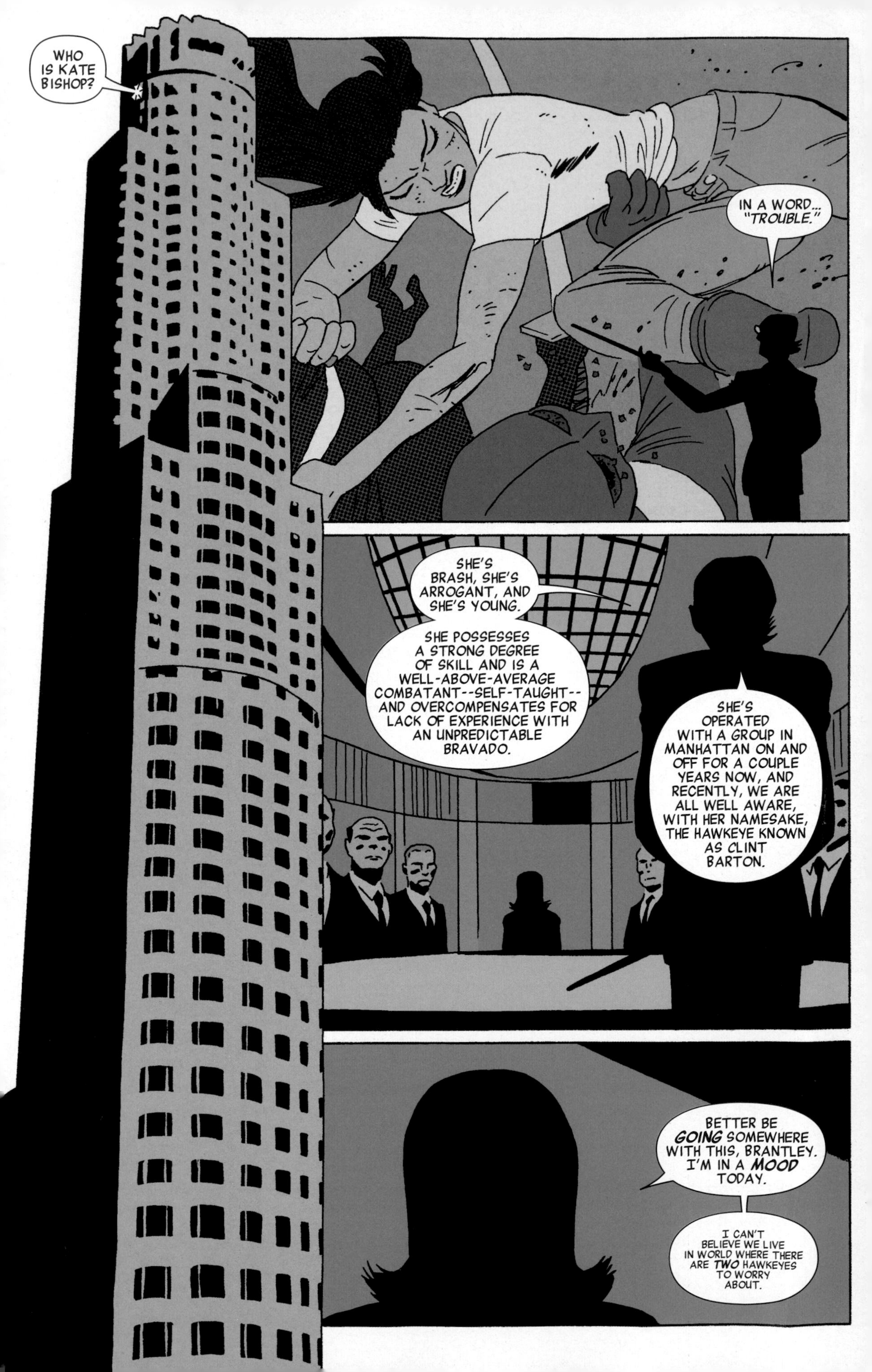
WHO IS KATE BISHOP?
IN A WORD... "TROUBLE."
SHE'S BRASH, SHE'S ARROGANT, AND SHE'S YOUNG.
SHE POSSESSES A STRONG DEGREE OF SKILL AND IS A WELL-ABOVE-AVERAGE COMBATANT--SELF-TAUGHT--AND OVERCOMPENSATES FOR LACK OF EXPERIENCE WITH AN UNPREDICTABLE BRAVADO.
SHE'S OPERATED WITH A GROUP IN MANHATTAN ON AND OFF FOR A COUPLE YEARS NOW, AND RECENTLY, WE ARE ALL WELL AWARE, WITH HER NAMESAKE, THE HAWKEYE KNOWN AS CLINT BARTON.
BETTER BE GOING SOMEWHERE WITH THIS, BRANTLEY. I'M IN A MOOD TODAY.
I CAN'T BELIEVE WE LIVE IN WORLD WHERE THERE ARE TWO HAWKEYES TO WORRY ABOUT.

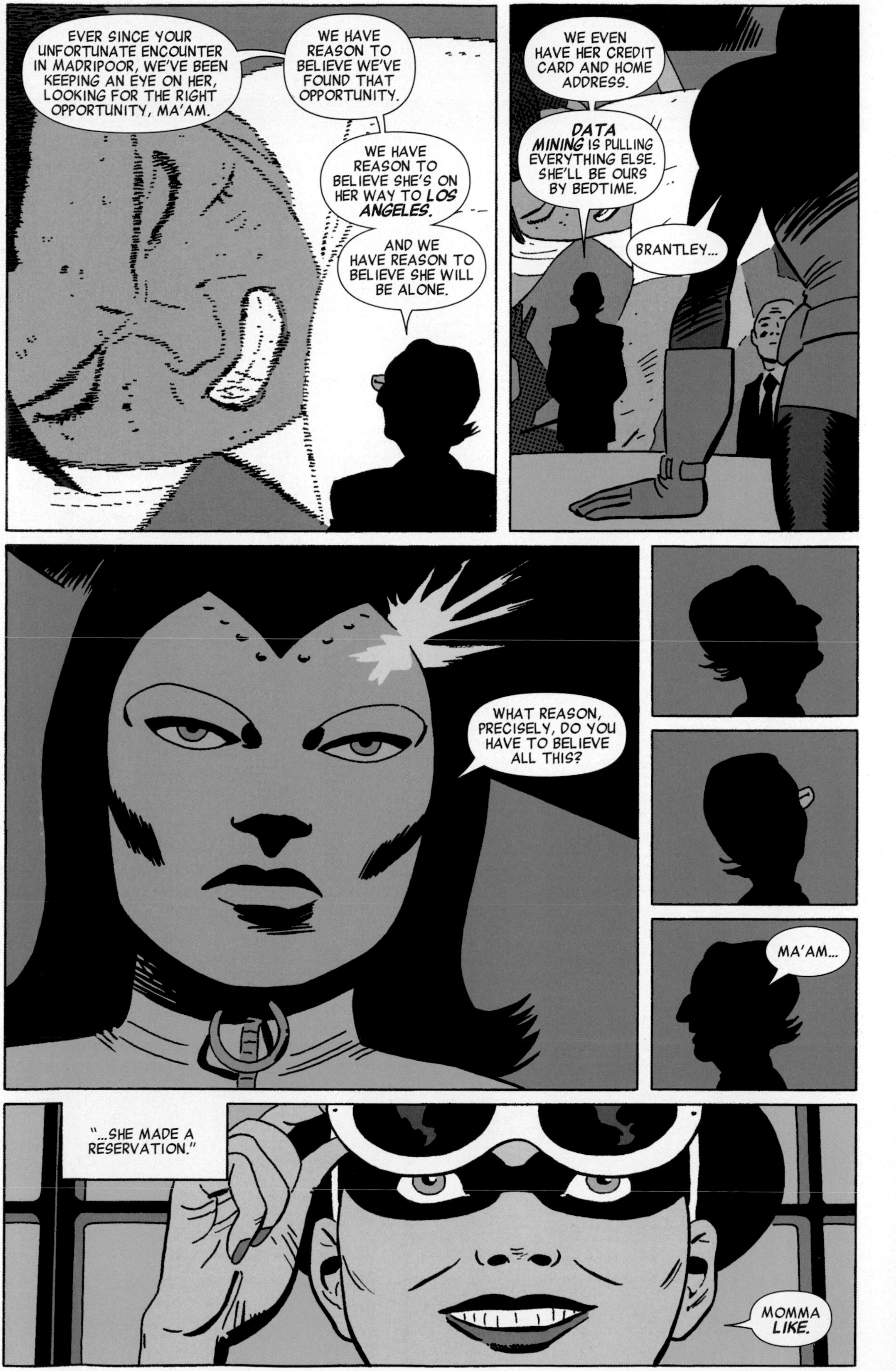
EVER SINCE YOUR UNFORTUNATE ENCOUNTER IN MADRIPOOR, WE'VE BEEN KEEPING AN EYE ON HER, LOOKING FOR THE RIGHT OPPORTUNITY, MA'AM.
WE HAVE REASON TO BELIEVE WE'VE FOUND THAT OPPORTUNITY.
WE HAVE REASON TO BELIEVE SHE'S ON HER WAY TO LOS ANGELES.
AND WE HAVE REASON TO BELIEVE SHE WILL BE ALONE.
WE EVEN HAVE HER CREDIT CARD AND HOME ADDRESS.
DATA MINING IS PULLING EVERYTHING ELSE. SHE'LL BE OURS BY BEDTIME.
BRANTLEY...
WHAT REASON, PRECISELY, DO YOU HAVE TO BELIEVE ALL THIS?
MA'AM...
"...SHE MADE A RESERVATION."
MOMMA LIKE.

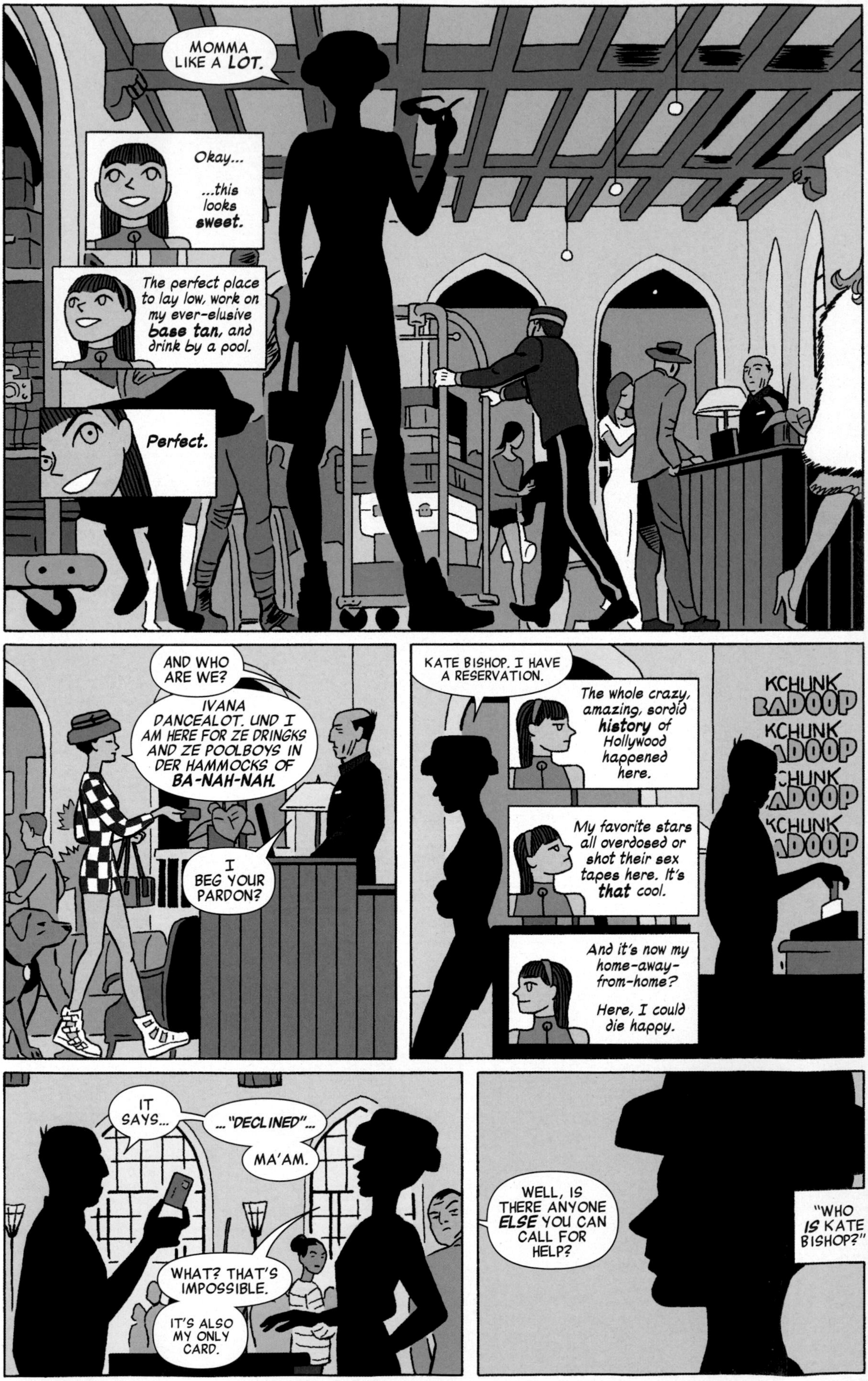
MOMMA LIKE A LOT.
Okay...
...this looks sweet.
The perfect place to lay low, work on my ever-elusive base tan, and drink by a pool.
Perfect.
AND WHO ARE WE?
IVANA DANCEALOT. UND I AM HERE FOR ZE DRINGKS AND ZE POOLBOYS IN DER HAMMOCKS OF BA-NAH-NAH.
I BEG YOUR PARDON?
KATE BISHOP. I HAVE A RESERVATION.
The whole crazy, amazing, sordid history of Hollywood happened here.
KCHUNK BADOOP KCHUNK BADOOP KCHUNK BADOOP KCHUNK BADOOP
My favorite stars all overdosed or shot their sex tapes here. It's that cool.
And it's now my home-away-from-home?
Here, I could die happy.
IT SAYS...
..."DECLINED"...
MA'AM.
WHAT? THAT'S IMPOSSIBLE.
IT'S ALSO MY ONLY CARD.
WELL, IS THERE ANYONE ELSE YOU CAN CALL FOR HELP?
"WHO IS KATE BISHOP?"

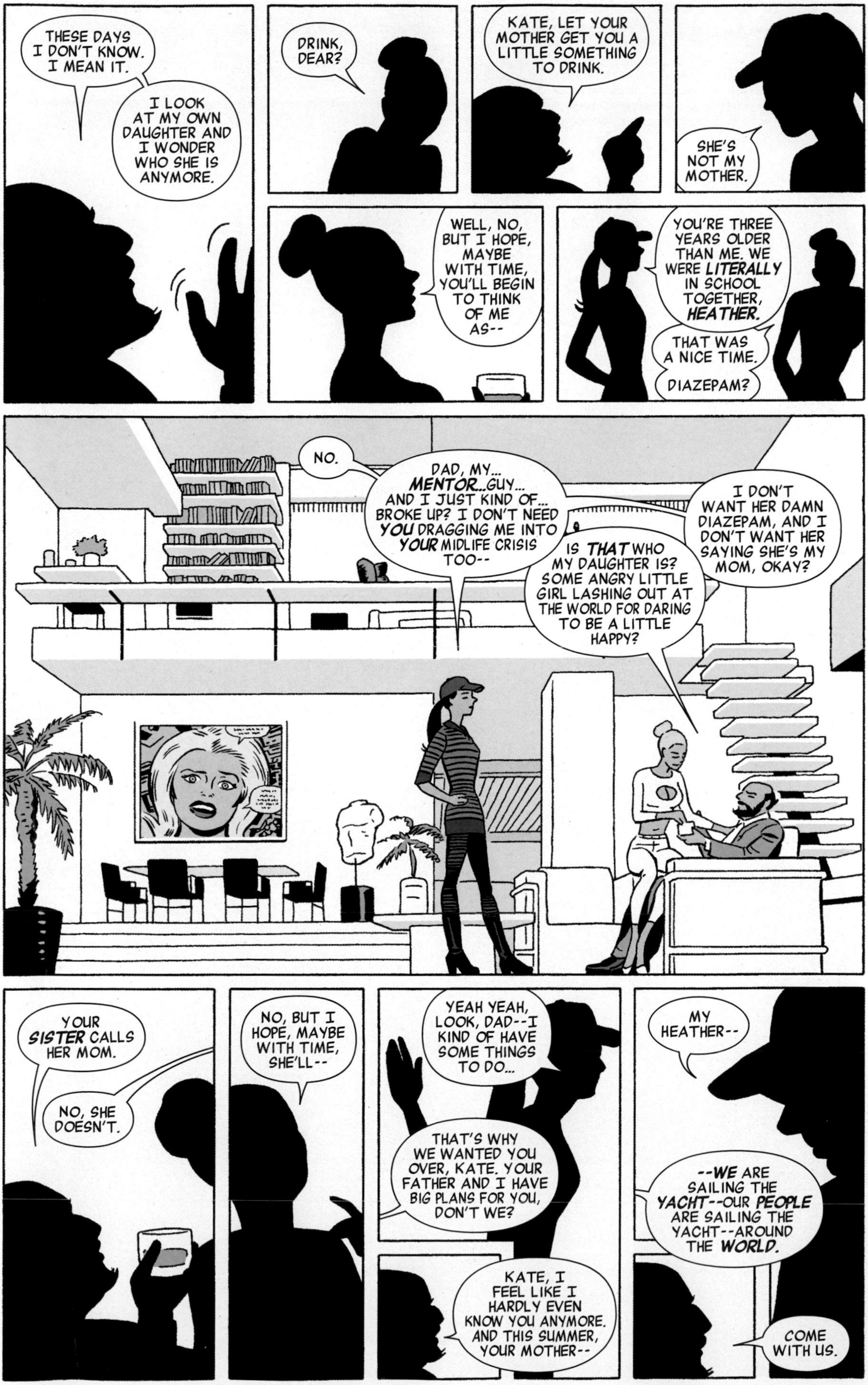
THESE DAYS I DON'T KNOW. I MEAN IT.
I LOOK AT MY OWN DAUGHTER AND I WONDER WHO SHE IS ANYMORE.
DRINK, DEAR?
KATE, LET YOUR MOTHER GET YOU A LITTLE SOMETHING TO DRINK.
SHE'S NOT MY MOTHER.
WELL, NO, BUT I HOPE, MAYBE WITH TIME, YOU'LL BEGIN TO THINK OF ME AS--
YOU'RE THREE YEARS OLDER THAN ME. WE WERE LITERALLY IN SCHOOL TOGETHER, HEATHER.
THAT WAS A NICE TIME.
DIAZEPAM?
NO.
DAD, MY... MENTOR...GUY... AND I JUST KIND OF... BROKE UP? I DON'T NEED YOU DRAGGING ME INTO YOUR MIDLIFE CRISIS TOO--
I DON'T WANT HER DAMN DIAZEPAM, AND I DON'T WANT HER SAYING SHE'S MY MOM, OKAY?
IS THAT WHO MY DAUGHTER IS? SOME ANGRY LITTLE GIRL LASHING OUT AT THE WORLD FOR DARING TO BE A LITTLE HAPPY?
YOUR SISTER CALLS HER MOM.
NO, SHE DOESN'T.
NO, BUT I HOPE, MAYBE WITH TIME, SHE'LL--
YEAH YEAH, LOOK, DAD--I KIND OF HAVE SOME THINGS TO DO...
THAT'S WHY WE WANTED YOU OVER, KATE. YOUR FATHER AND I HAVE BIG PLANS FOR YOU, DON'T WE?
KATE, I FEEL LIKE I HARDLY EVEN KNOW YOU ANYMORE. AND THIS SUMMER, YOUR MOTHER--
MY HEATHER--
--WE ARE SAILING THE YACHT--OUR PEOPLE ARE SAILING THE YACHT--AROUND THE WORLD.
COME WITH US.

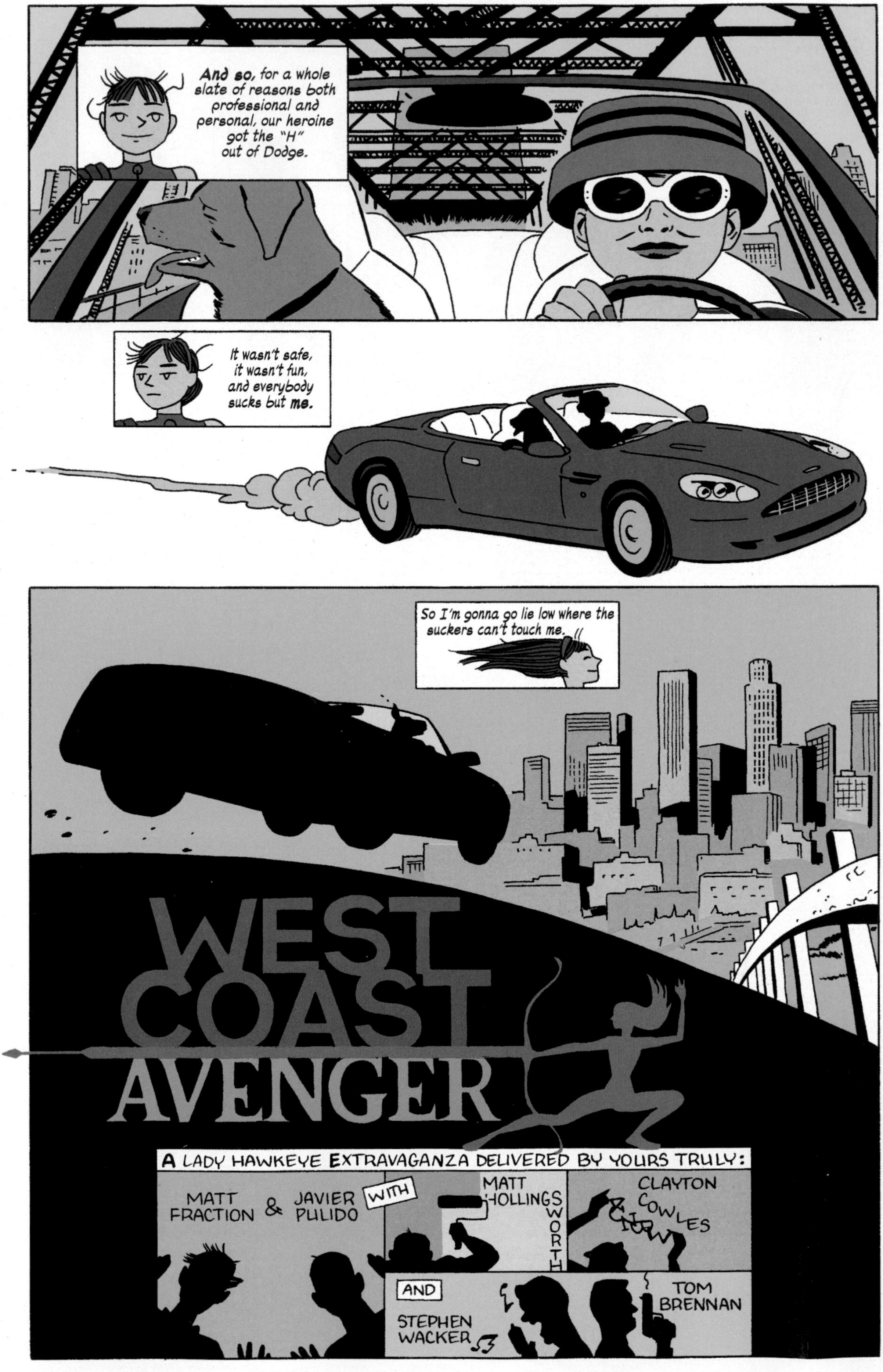
And so, for a whole slate of reasons both professional and personal, our heroine got the "H" out of Dodge.
It wasn't safe, it wasn't fun, and everybody sucks but me.
So I'm gonna go lie low where the suckers can't touch me.
WEST COAST AVENGER
A LADY HAWKEYE EXTRAVAGANZA DELIVERED BY YOURS TRULY:
MATT FRACTION & JAVIER PULIDO
WITH
MATT HOLLINGSWORTH
CLAYTON COWLES
AND
STEPHEN WACKER
TOM BRENNAN

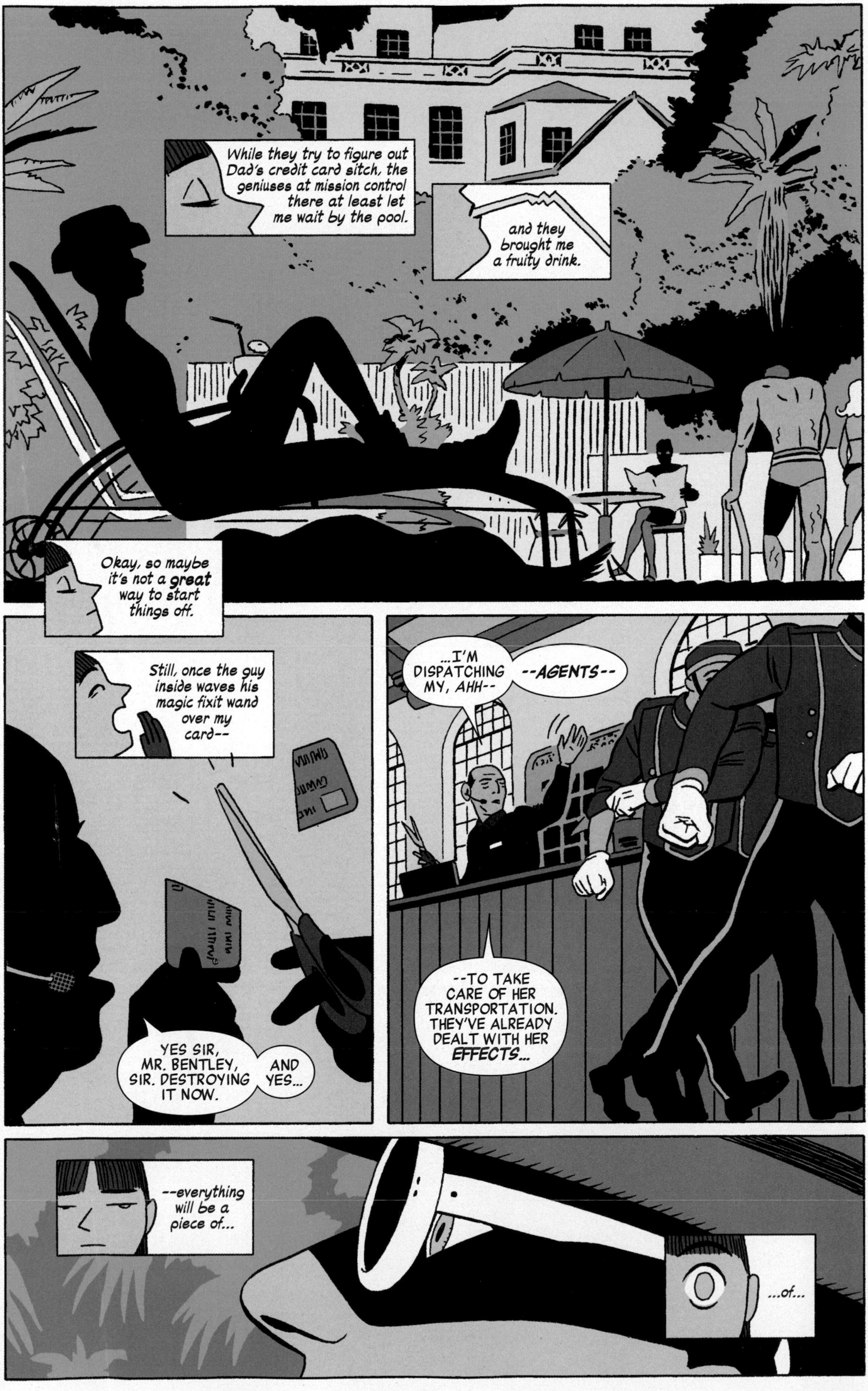
While they try to figure out Dad's credit card sitch, the geniuses at mission control there at least let me wait by the pool.
and they brought me a fruity drink.
Okay, so maybe it's not a **great** way to start things off.
Still, once the guy inside waves his magic fixit wand over my card--
YES SIR, MR. BENTLEY, SIR. DESTROYING IT NOW.
AND YES...
...I'M DISPATCHING MY, AHH--
--AGENTS--
--TO TAKE CARE OF HER TRANSPORTATION. THEY'VE ALREADY DEALT WITH HER EFFECTS...
--everything will be a piece of...
...of...

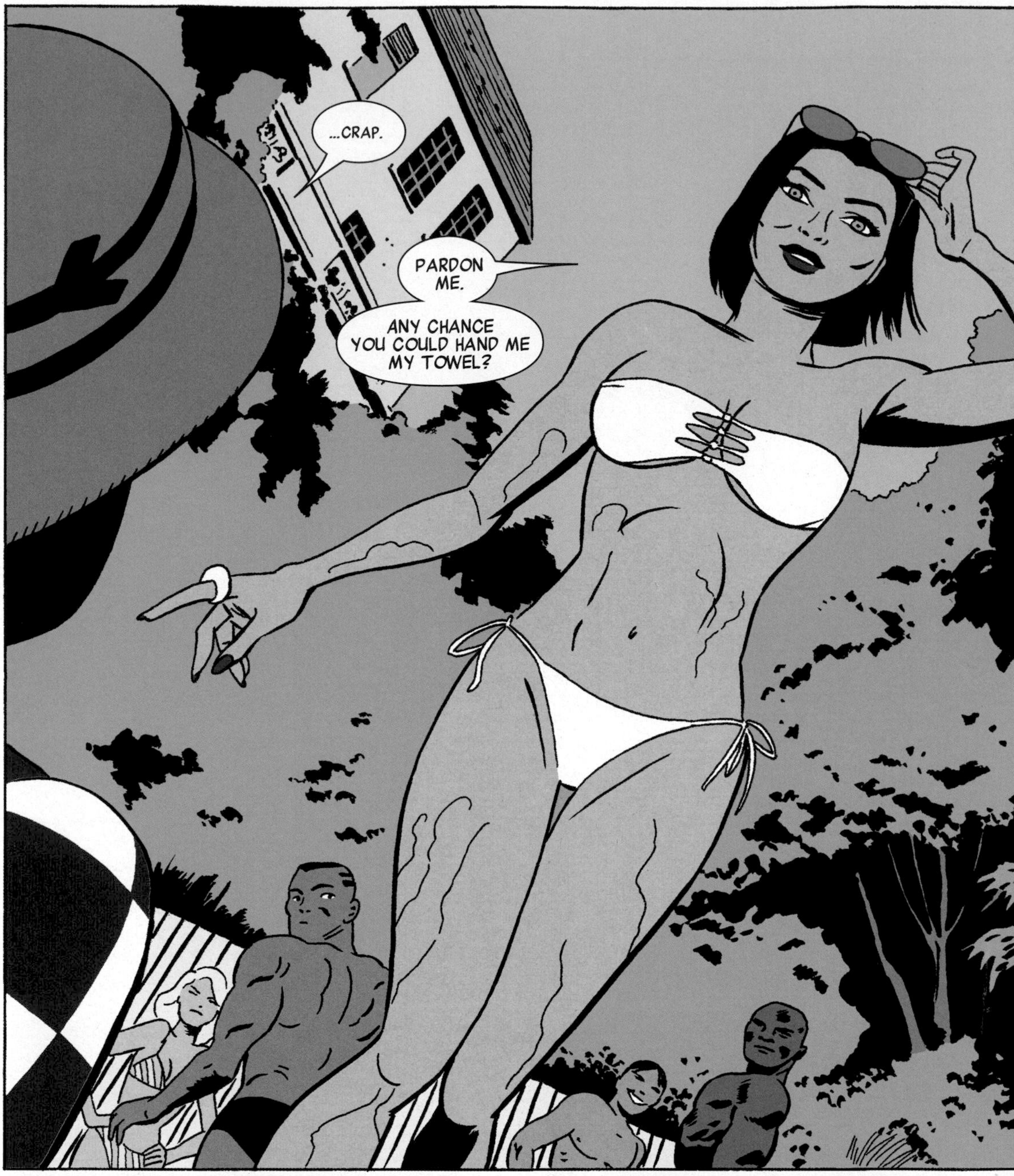
...CRAP.
PARDON ME.
ANY CHANCE YOU COULD HAND ME MY TOWEL?

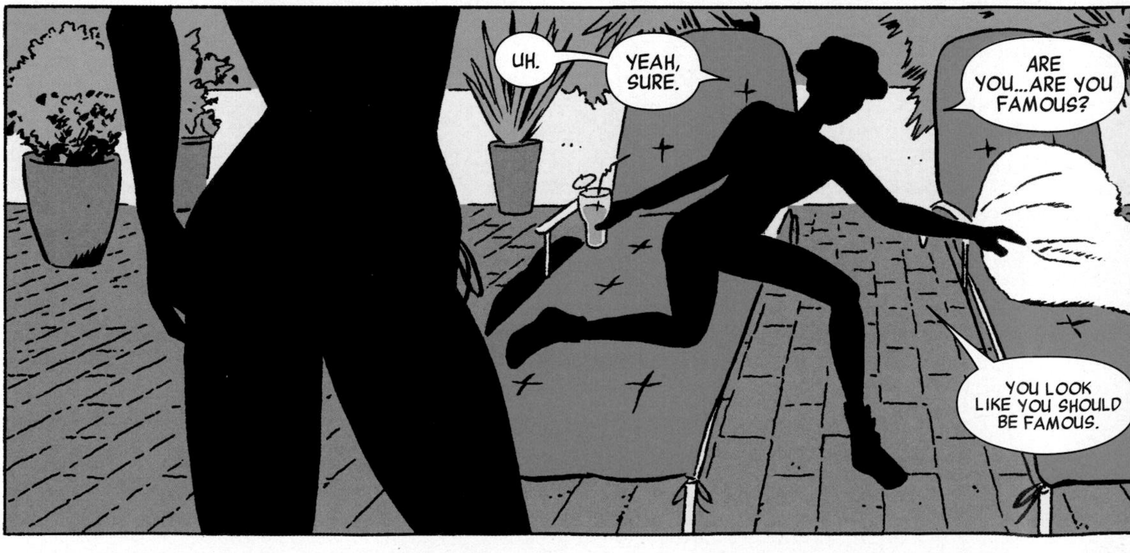
UH.
YEAH, SURE.
...
ARE YOU...ARE YOU FAMOUS?
YOU LOOK LIKE YOU SHOULD BE FAMOUS.

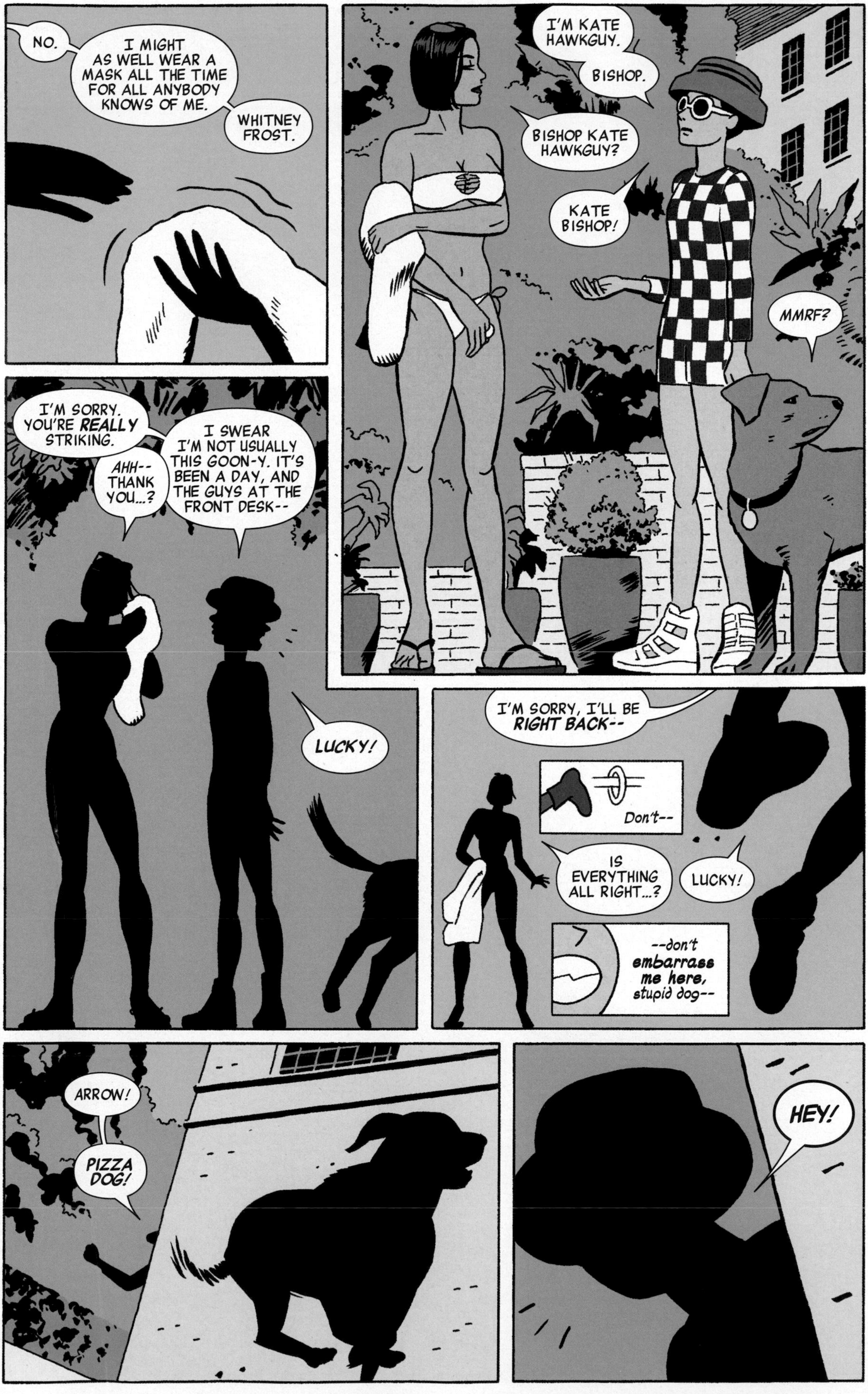
NO.
I MIGHT AS WELL WEAR A MASK ALL THE TIME FOR ALL ANYBODY KNOWS OF ME.
WHITNEY FROST.
I'M KATE HAWKGUY.
BISHOP.
BISHOP KATE HAWKGUY?
KATE BISHOP!
MMRF?
I'M SORRY. YOU'RE **REALLY** STRIKING.
AHH-- THANK YOU...?
I SWEAR I'M NOT USUALLY THIS GOON-Y. IT'S BEEN A DAY, AND THE GUYS AT THE FRONT DESK--
LUCKY!
I'M SORRY, I'LL BE **RIGHT BACK**--
Don't--
IS EVERYTHING ALL RIGHT...?
LUCKY!
--don't **embarrass me here,** stupid dog--
ARROW!
PIZZA DOG!
HEY!

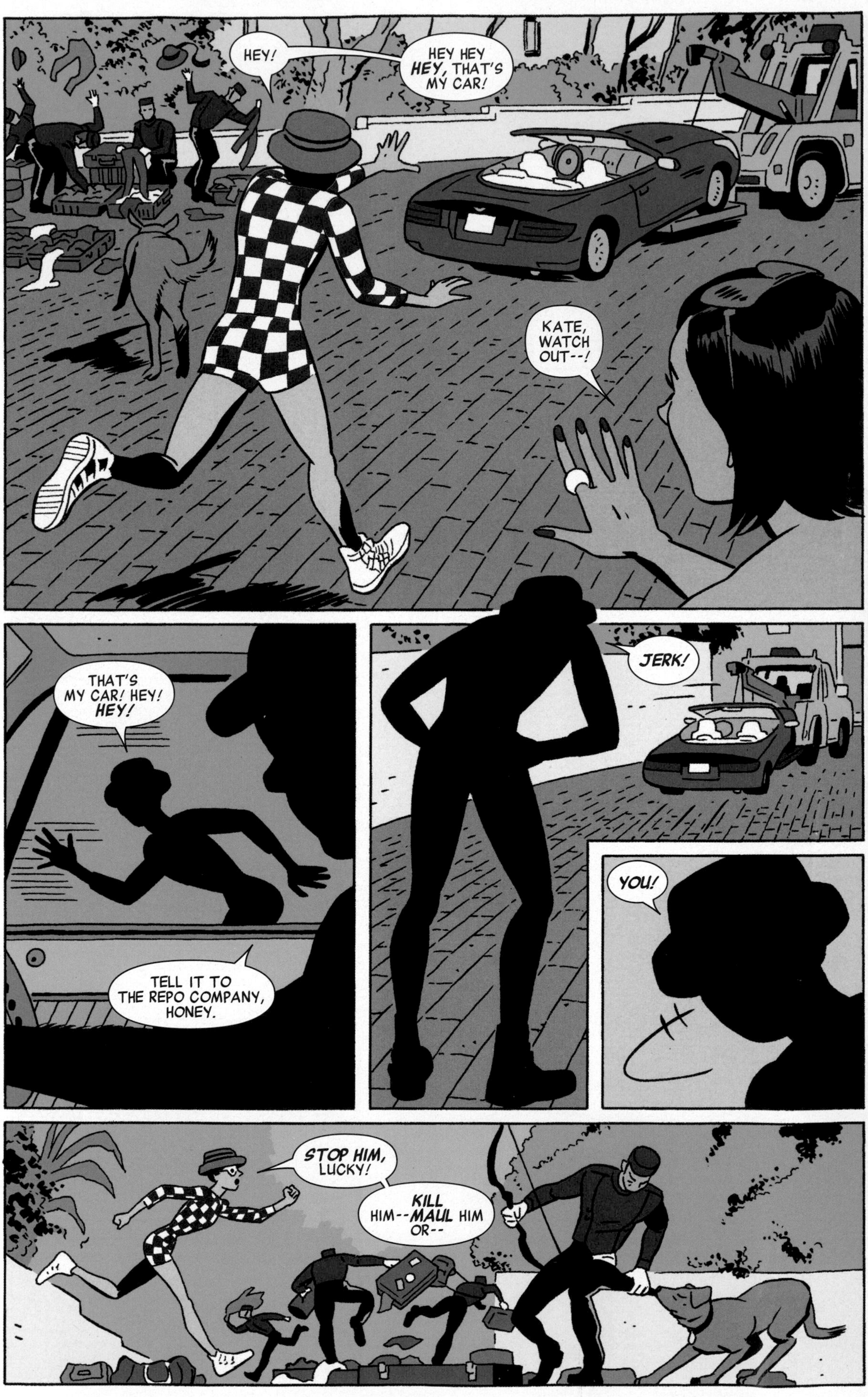
HEY!
HEY HEY HEY, THAT'S MY CAR!
KATE, WATCH OUT--!
THAT'S MY CAR! HEY! HEY!
TELL IT TO THE REPO COMPANY, HONEY.
JERK!
YOU!
STOP HIM, LUCKY!
KILL HIM--MAUL HIM OR--

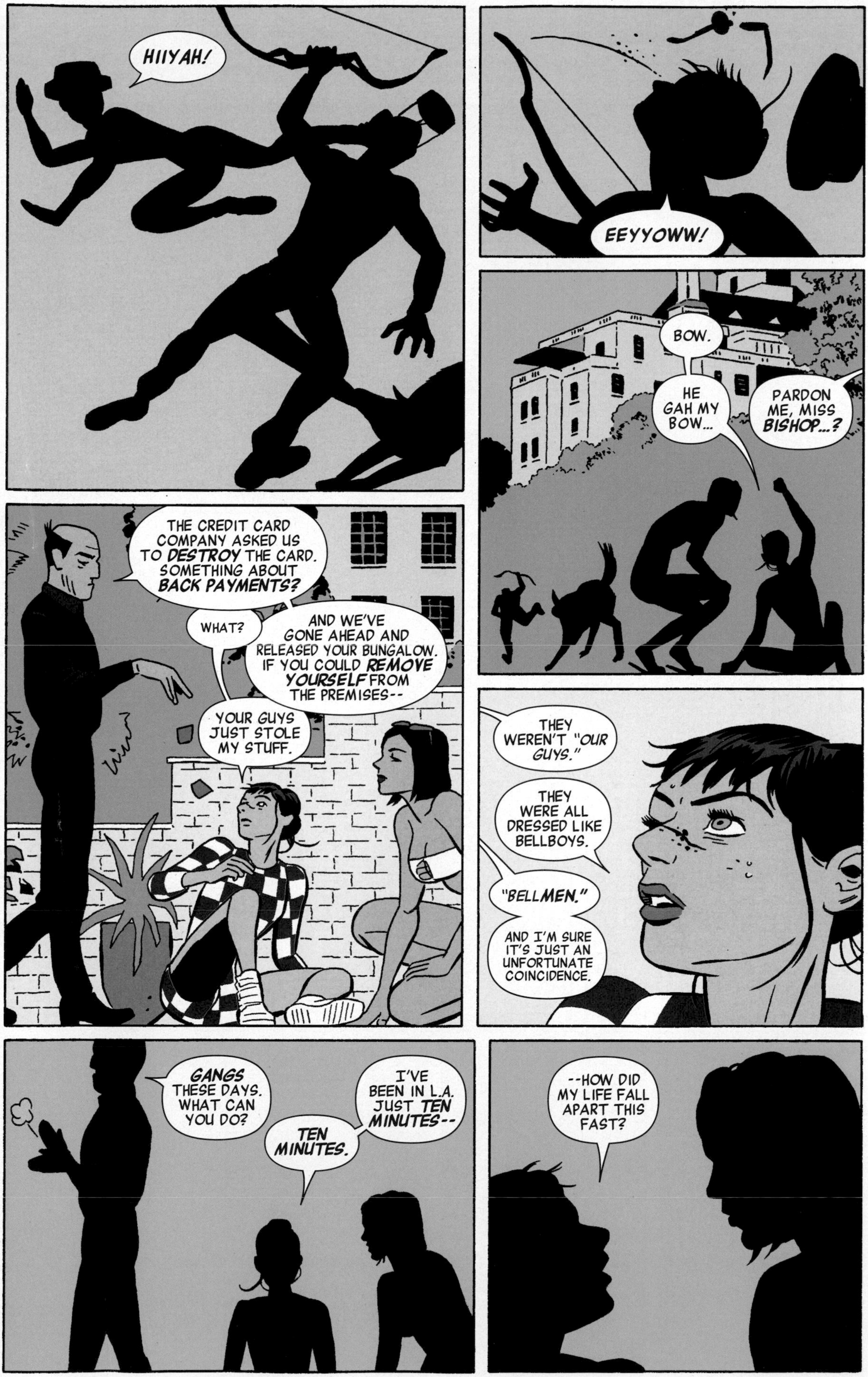
HIIYAH!
EEYYOWW!
BOW.
HE GAH MY BOW...
PARDON ME, MISS BISHOP...?
THE CREDIT CARD COMPANY ASKED US TO DESTROY THE CARD. SOMETHING ABOUT BACK PAYMENTS?
WHAT?
AND WE'VE GONE AHEAD AND RELEASED YOUR BUNGALOW. IF YOU COULD REMOVE YOURSELF FROM THE PREMISES--
YOUR GUYS JUST STOLE MY STUFF.
THEY WEREN'T "OUR GUYS."
THEY WERE ALL DRESSED LIKE BELLBOYS.
"BELLMEN."
AND I'M SURE IT'S JUST AN UNFORTUNATE COINCIDENCE.
GANGS THESE DAYS. WHAT CAN YOU DO?
I'VE BEEN IN L.A. JUST TEN MINUTES--
TEN MINUTES.
--HOW DID MY LIFE FALL APART THIS FAST?

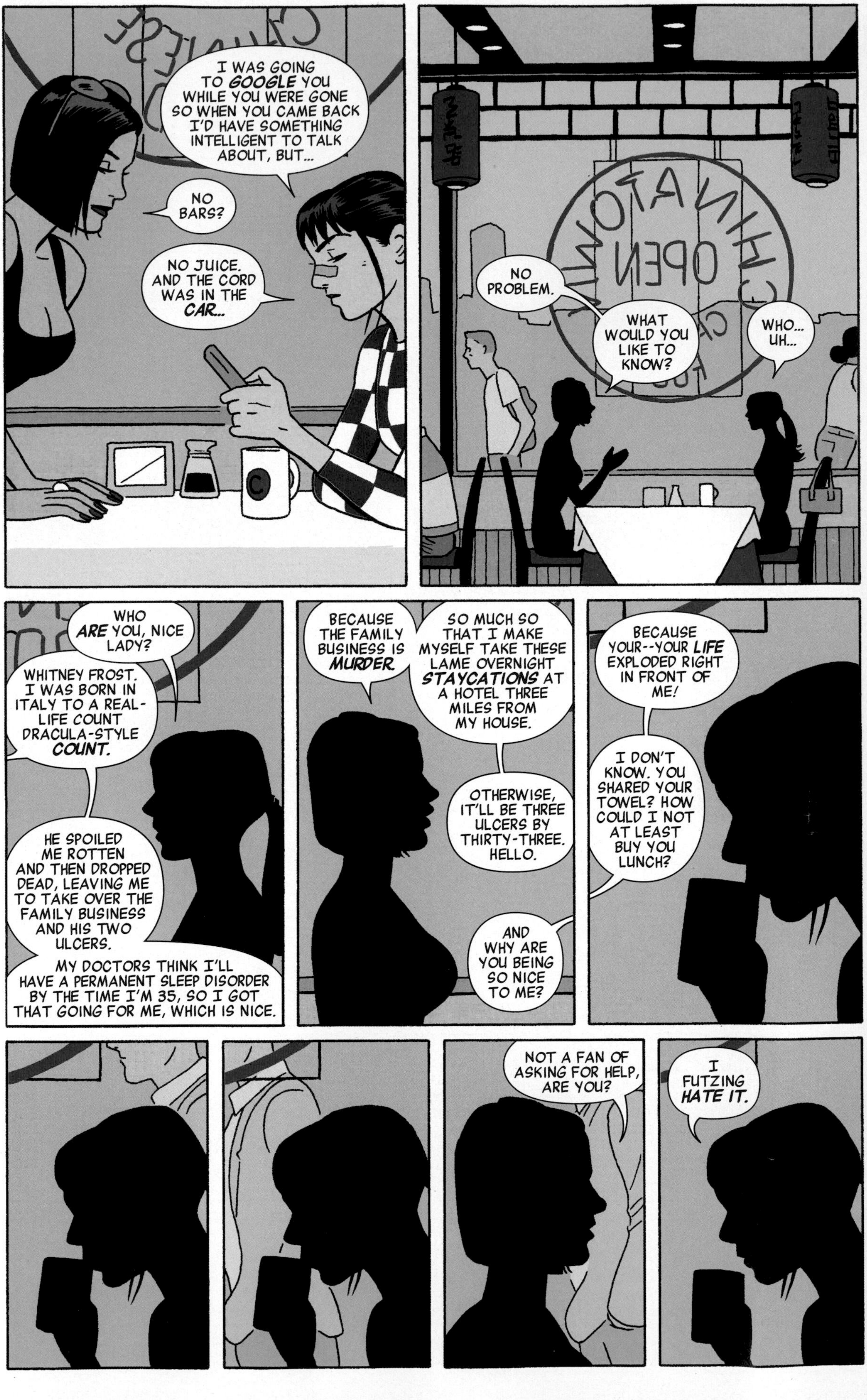
I WAS GOING TO GOOGLE YOU WHILE YOU WERE GONE SO WHEN YOU CAME BACK I'D HAVE SOMETHING INTELLIGENT TO TALK ABOUT, BUT...
NO BARS?
NO JUICE. AND THE CORD WAS IN THE CAR...
NO PROBLEM.
WHAT WOULD YOU LIKE TO KNOW?
WHO... UH...
WHO ARE YOU, NICE LADY?
WHITNEY FROST. I WAS BORN IN ITALY TO A REAL-LIFE COUNT DRACULA-STYLE COUNT.
HE SPOILED ME ROTTEN AND THEN DROPPED DEAD, LEAVING ME TO TAKE OVER THE FAMILY BUSINESS AND HIS TWO ULCERS.
MY DOCTORS THINK I'LL HAVE A PERMANENT SLEEP DISORDER BY THE TIME I'M 35, SO I GOT THAT GOING FOR ME, WHICH IS NICE.
BECAUSE THE FAMILY BUSINESS IS MURDER.
SO MUCH SO THAT I MAKE MYSELF TAKE THESE LAME OVERNIGHT STAYCATIONS AT A HOTEL THREE MILES FROM MY HOUSE.
OTHERWISE, IT'LL BE THREE ULCERS BY THIRTY-THREE. HELLO.
AND WHY ARE YOU BEING SO NICE TO ME?
BECAUSE YOUR--YOUR LIFE EXPLODED RIGHT IN FRONT OF ME!
I DON'T KNOW. YOU SHARED YOUR TOWEL? HOW COULD I NOT AT LEAST BUY YOU LUNCH?
NOT A FAN OF ASKING FOR HELP, ARE YOU?
I FUTZING HATE IT.

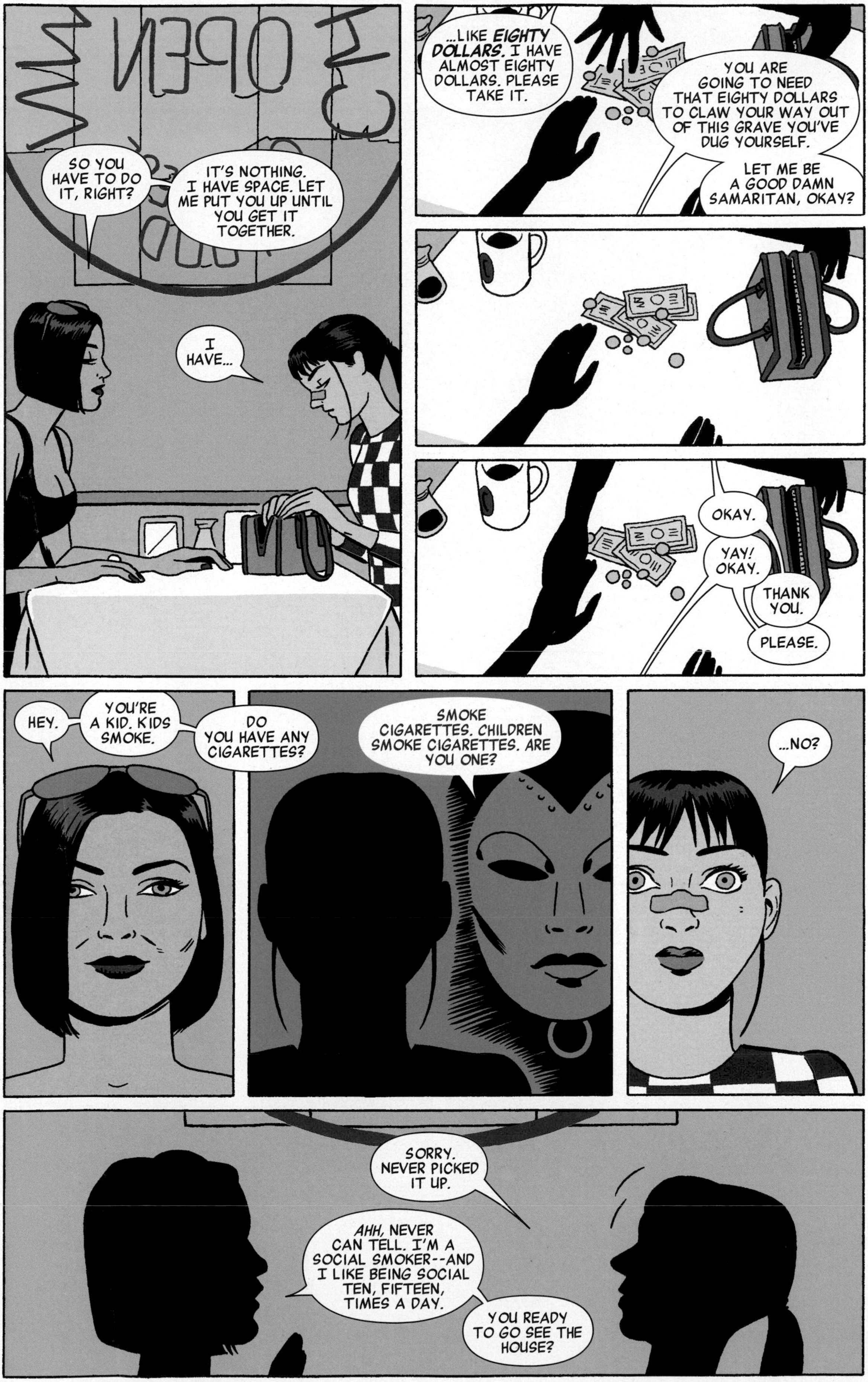
OPEN
SO YOU HAVE TO DO IT, RIGHT?
IT'S NOTHING. I HAVE SPACE. LET ME PUT YOU UP UNTIL YOU GET IT TOGETHER.
I HAVE...
...LIKE *EIGHTY DOLLARS.* I HAVE ALMOST EIGHTY DOLLARS. PLEASE TAKE IT.
YOU ARE GOING TO NEED THAT EIGHTY DOLLARS TO CLAW YOUR WAY OUT OF THIS GRAVE YOU'VE DUG YOURSELF.
LET ME BE A GOOD DAMN SAMARITAN, OKAY?
OKAY.
YAY! OKAY.
THANK YOU.
PLEASE.
HEY.
YOU'RE A KID. KIDS SMOKE.
DO YOU HAVE ANY CIGARETTES?
SMOKE CIGARETTES. CHILDREN SMOKE CIGARETTES. ARE YOU ONE?
...NO?
SORRY. NEVER PICKED IT UP.
AHH, NEVER CAN TELL. I'M A SOCIAL SMOKER--AND I LIKE BEING SOCIAL TEN, FIFTEEN, TIMES A DAY.
YOU READY TO GO SEE THE HOUSE?

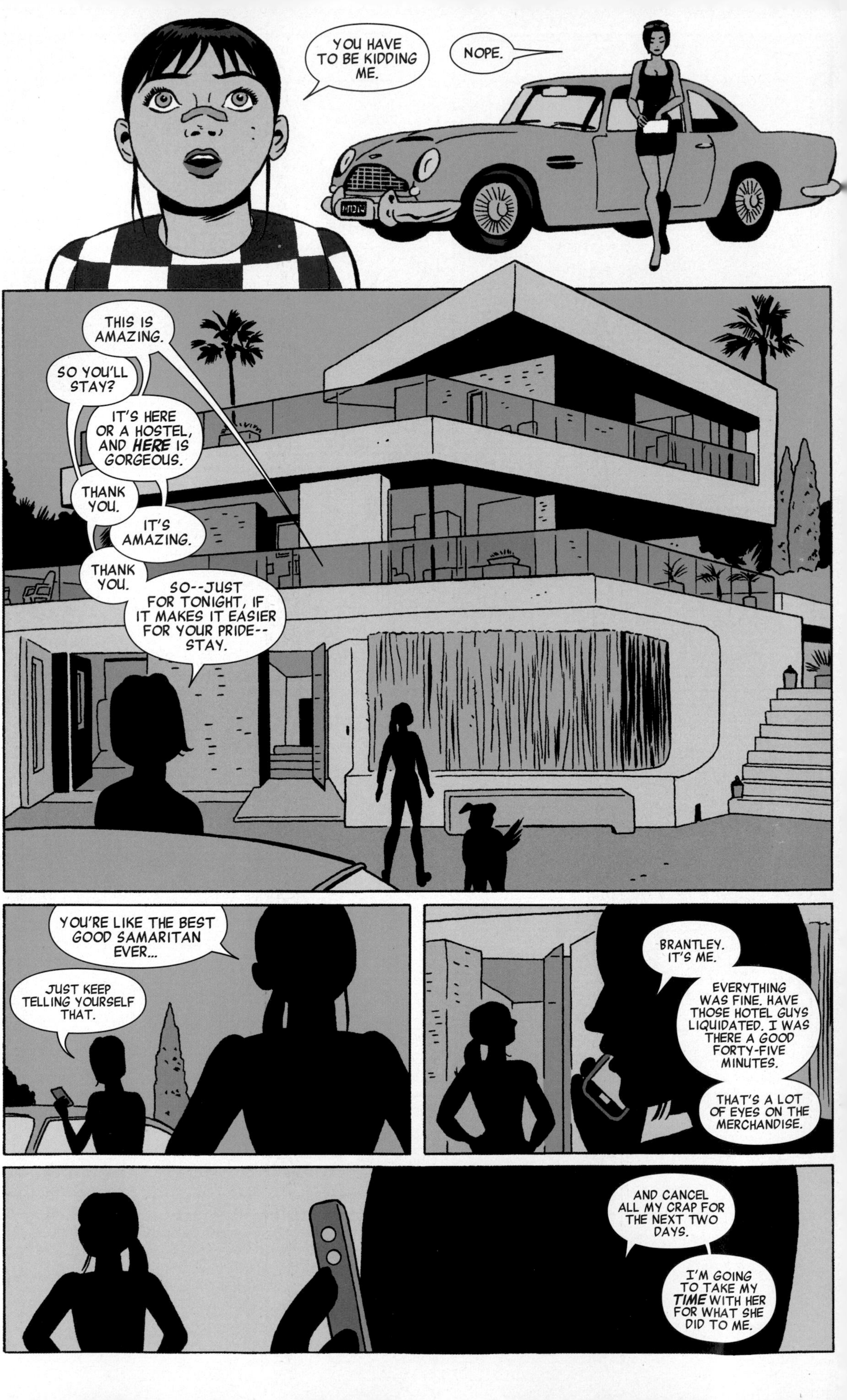
YOU HAVE TO BE KIDDING ME.
NOPE.
THIS IS AMAZING.
SO YOU'LL STAY?
IT'S HERE OR A HOSTEL, AND HERE IS GORGEOUS.
THANK YOU.
IT'S AMAZING.
THANK YOU.
SO--JUST FOR TONIGHT, IF IT MAKES IT EASIER FOR YOUR PRIDE--STAY.
YOU'RE LIKE THE BEST GOOD SAMARITAN EVER...
JUST KEEP TELLING YOURSELF THAT.
BRANTLEY. IT'S ME.
EVERYTHING WAS FINE. HAVE THOSE HOTEL GUYS LIQUIDATED. I WAS THERE A GOOD FORTY-FIVE MINUTES.
THAT'S A LOT OF EYES ON THE MERCHANDISE.
AND CANCEL ALL MY CRAP FOR THE NEXT TWO DAYS.
I'M GOING TO TAKE MY TIME WITH HER FOR WHAT SHE DID TO ME.

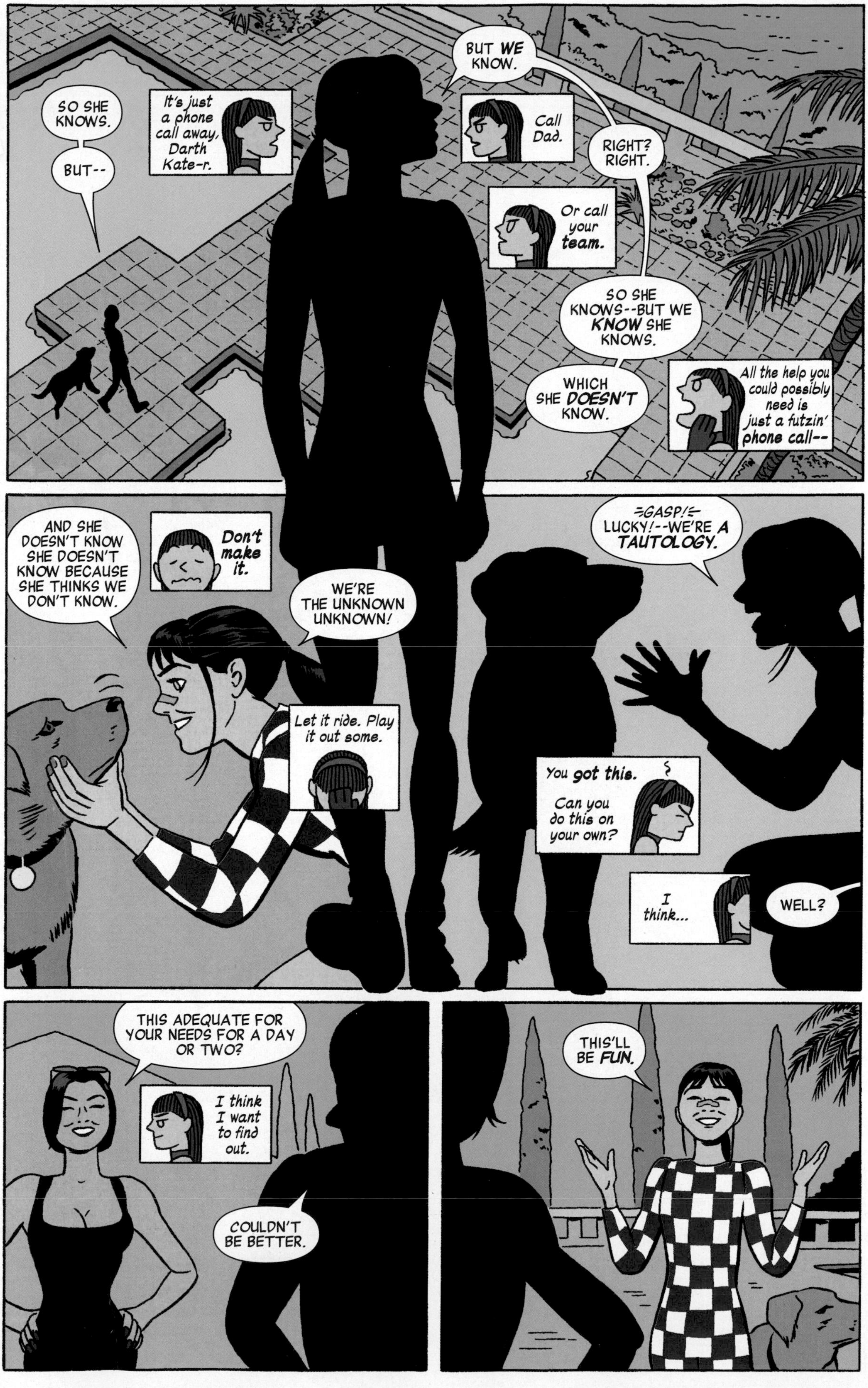
SO SHE KNOWS.
BUT--
It's just a phone call away, Darth Kate-r.
BUT WE KNOW.
Call Dad.
RIGHT? RIGHT.
Or call your team.
SO SHE KNOWS--BUT WE KNOW SHE KNOWS.
WHICH SHE DOESN'T KNOW.
All the help you could possibly need is just a futzin' phone call--
AND SHE DOESN'T KNOW SHE DOESN'T KNOW BECAUSE SHE THINKS WE DON'T KNOW.
Don't make it.
WE'RE THE UNKNOWN UNKNOWN!
GASP! LUCKY!--WE'RE A TAUTOLOGY.
Let it ride. Play it out some.
You got this.
Can you do this on your own?
I think...
WELL?
THIS ADEQUATE FOR YOUR NEEDS FOR A DAY OR TWO?
I think I want to find out.
COULDN'T BE BETTER.
THIS'LL BE FUN.

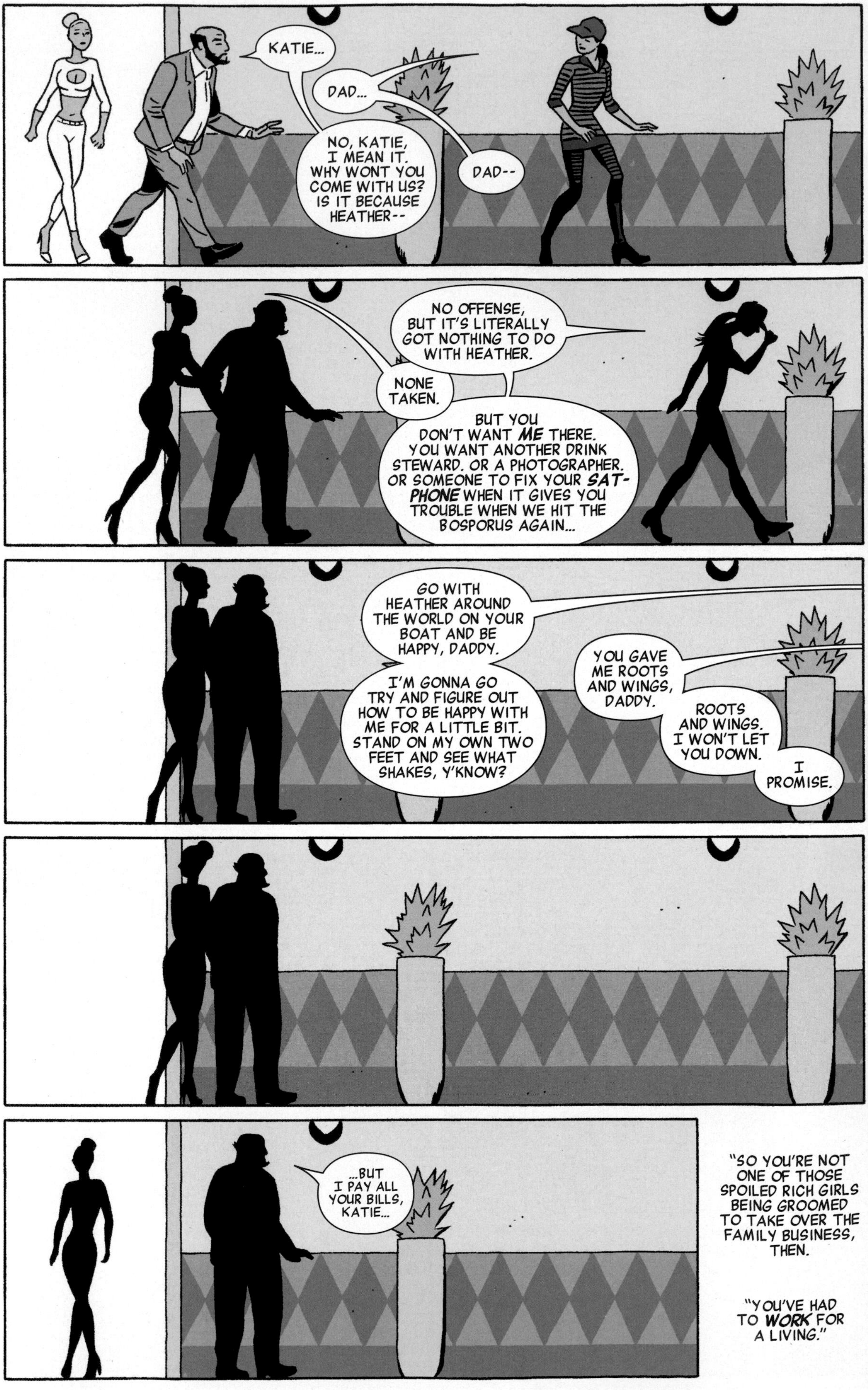
KATIE...
DAD...
NO, KATIE, I MEAN IT. WHY WONT YOU COME WITH US? IS IT BECAUSE HEATHER--
DAD--
NO OFFENSE, BUT IT'S LITERALLY GOT NOTHING TO DO WITH HEATHER.
NONE TAKEN.
BUT YOU DON'T WANT *ME* THERE. YOU WANT ANOTHER DRINK STEWARD. OR A PHOTOGRAPHER. OR SOMEONE TO FIX YOUR *SAT-PHONE* WHEN IT GIVES YOU TROUBLE WHEN WE HIT THE BOSPORUS AGAIN...
GO WITH HEATHER AROUND THE WORLD ON YOUR BOAT AND BE HAPPY, DADDY.
I'M GONNA GO TRY AND FIGURE OUT HOW TO BE HAPPY WITH ME FOR A LITTLE BIT. STAND ON MY OWN TWO FEET AND SEE WHAT SHAKES, Y'KNOW?
YOU GAVE ME ROOTS AND WINGS, DADDY.
ROOTS AND WINGS. I WON'T LET YOU DOWN.
I PROMISE.
...BUT I PAY ALL YOUR BILLS, KATIE...
"SO YOU'RE NOT ONE OF THOSE SPOILED RICH GIRLS BEING GROOMED TO TAKE OVER THE FAMILY BUSINESS, THEN.
"YOU'VE HAD TO *WORK* FOR A LIVING."

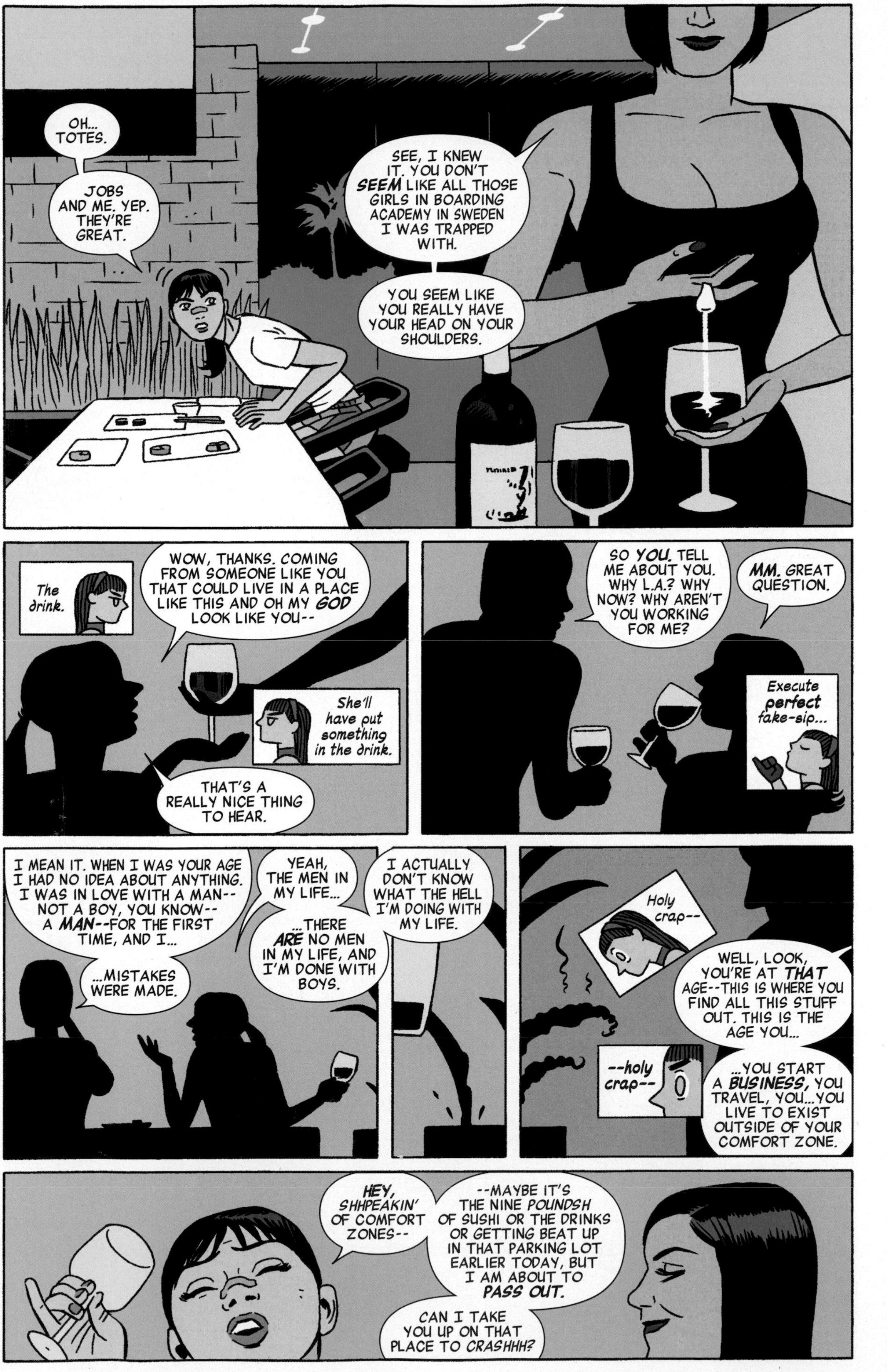
OH... TOTES.
JOBS AND ME. YEP. THEY'RE GREAT.
SEE, I KNEW IT. YOU DON'T SEEM LIKE ALL THOSE GIRLS IN BOARDING ACADEMY IN SWEDEN I WAS TRAPPED WITH.
YOU SEEM LIKE YOU REALLY HAVE YOUR HEAD ON YOUR SHOULDERS.
The drink.
WOW, THANKS. COMING FROM SOMEONE LIKE YOU THAT COULD LIVE IN A PLACE LIKE THIS AND OH MY GOD LOOK LIKE YOU--
She'll have put something in the drink.
THAT'S A REALLY NICE THING TO HEAR.
SO YOU. TELL ME ABOUT YOU. WHY L.A.? WHY NOW? WHY AREN'T YOU WORKING FOR ME?
MM. GREAT QUESTION.
Execute perfect fake-sip...
I MEAN IT. WHEN I WAS YOUR AGE I HAD NO IDEA ABOUT ANYTHING. I WAS IN LOVE WITH A MAN-- NOT A BOY, YOU KNOW-- A MAN--FOR THE FIRST TIME, AND I...
...MISTAKES WERE MADE.
YEAH, THE MEN IN MY LIFE...
...THERE ARE NO MEN IN MY LIFE, AND I'M DONE WITH BOYS.
I ACTUALLY DON'T KNOW WHAT THE HELL I'M DOING WITH MY LIFE.
Holy crap--
WELL, LOOK, YOU'RE AT THAT AGE--THIS IS WHERE YOU FIND ALL THIS STUFF OUT. THIS IS THE AGE YOU...
--holy crap--
...YOU START A BUSINESS, YOU TRAVEL, YOU...YOU LIVE TO EXIST OUTSIDE OF YOUR COMFORT ZONE.
HEY, SHHPEAKIN' OF COMFORT ZONES--
--MAYBE IT'S THE NINE POUNDSH OF SUSHI OR THE DRINKS OR GETTING BEAT UP IN THAT PARKING LOT EARLIER TODAY, BUT I AM ABOUT TO PASS OUT.
CAN I TAKE YOU UP ON THAT PLACE TO CRASHHH?

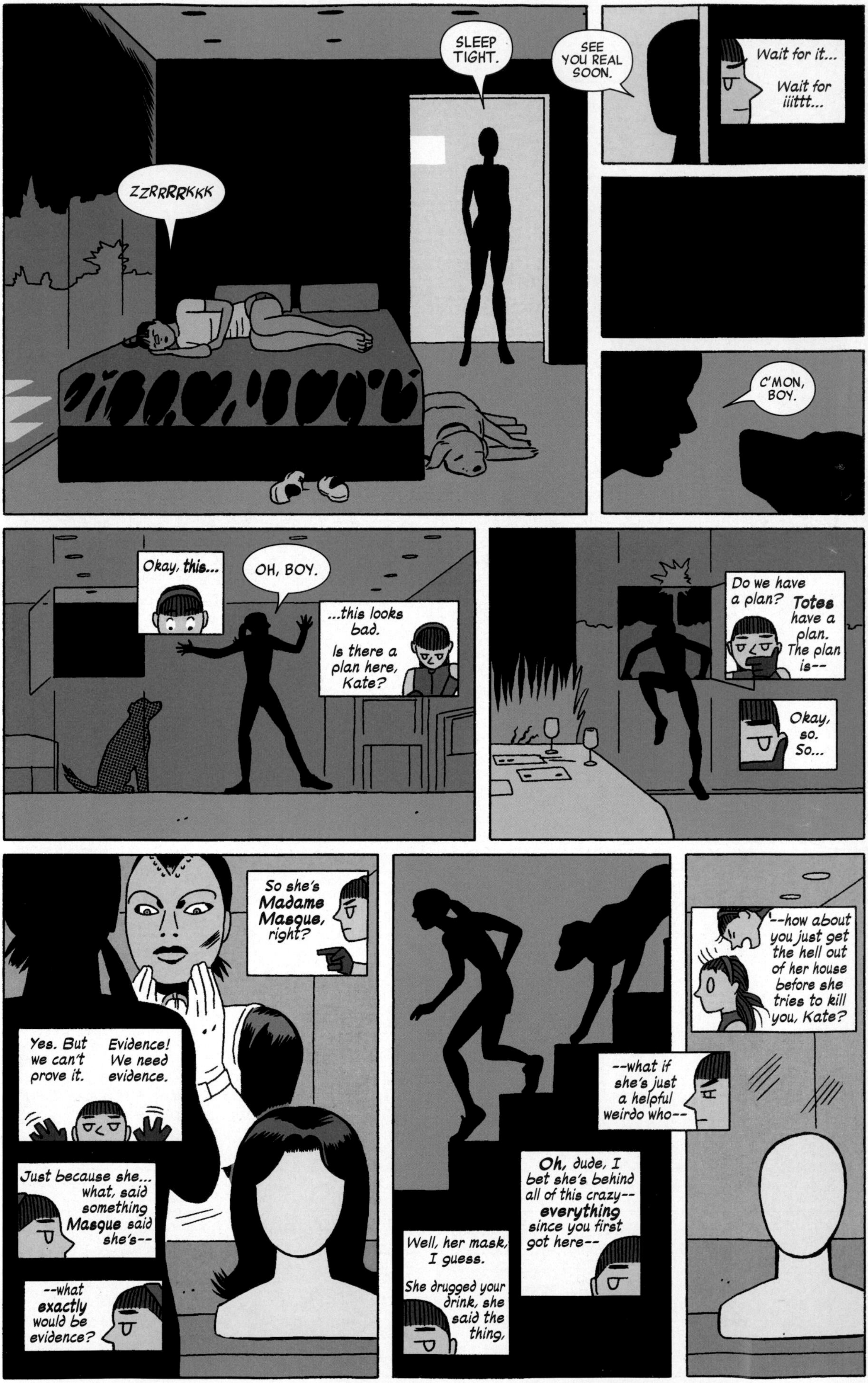
ZZRRRRKKK
SLEEP TIGHT.
SEE YOU REAL SOON.
Wait for it...
Wait for iiittt...
C'MON, BOY.
Okay, this...
OH, BOY.
...this looks bad.
Is there a plan here, Kate?
Do we have a plan?
Totes have a plan. The plan is--
Okay, so. So...
So she's Madame Masque, right?
Yes. But we can't prove it.
Evidence! We need evidence.
Just because she... what, said something Masque said she's--
--what exactly would be evidence?
Well, her mask, I guess.
She drugged your drink, she said the thing,
Oh, dude, I bet she's behind all of this crazy-- everything since you first got here--
--what if she's just a helpful weirdo who--
--how about you just get the hell out of her house before she tries to kill you, Kate?

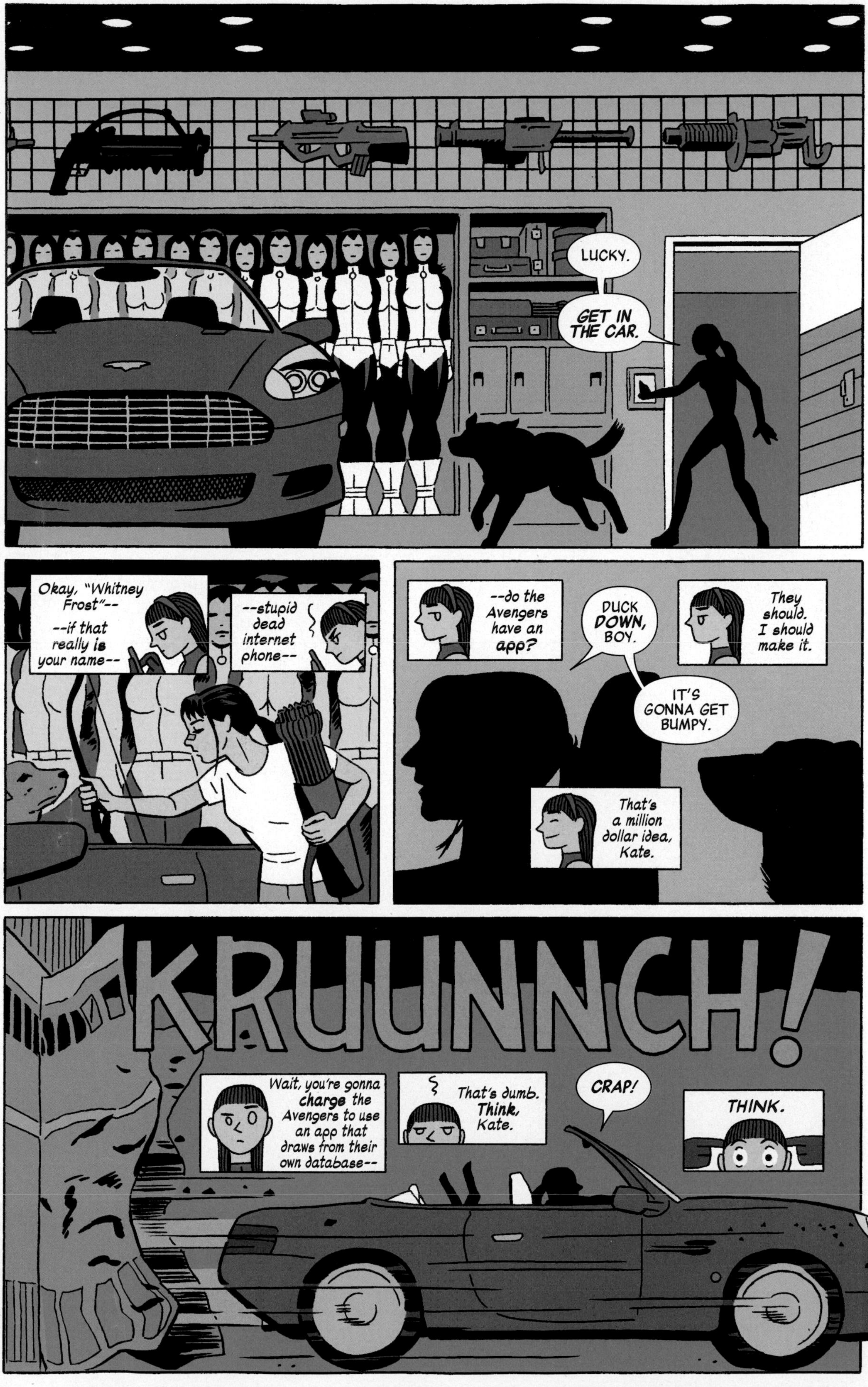
LUCKY.
GET IN THE CAR.
Okay, "Whitney Frost"-- --if that really is your name--
--stupid dead internet phone--
--do the Avengers have an app?
DUCK DOWN, BOY.
IT'S GONNA GET BUMPY.
They should. I should make it.
That's a million dollar idea, Kate.
KRUUNNCH!
Wait, you're gonna charge the Avengers to use an app that draws from their own database--
That's dumb. Think, Kate.
CRAP!
THINK.

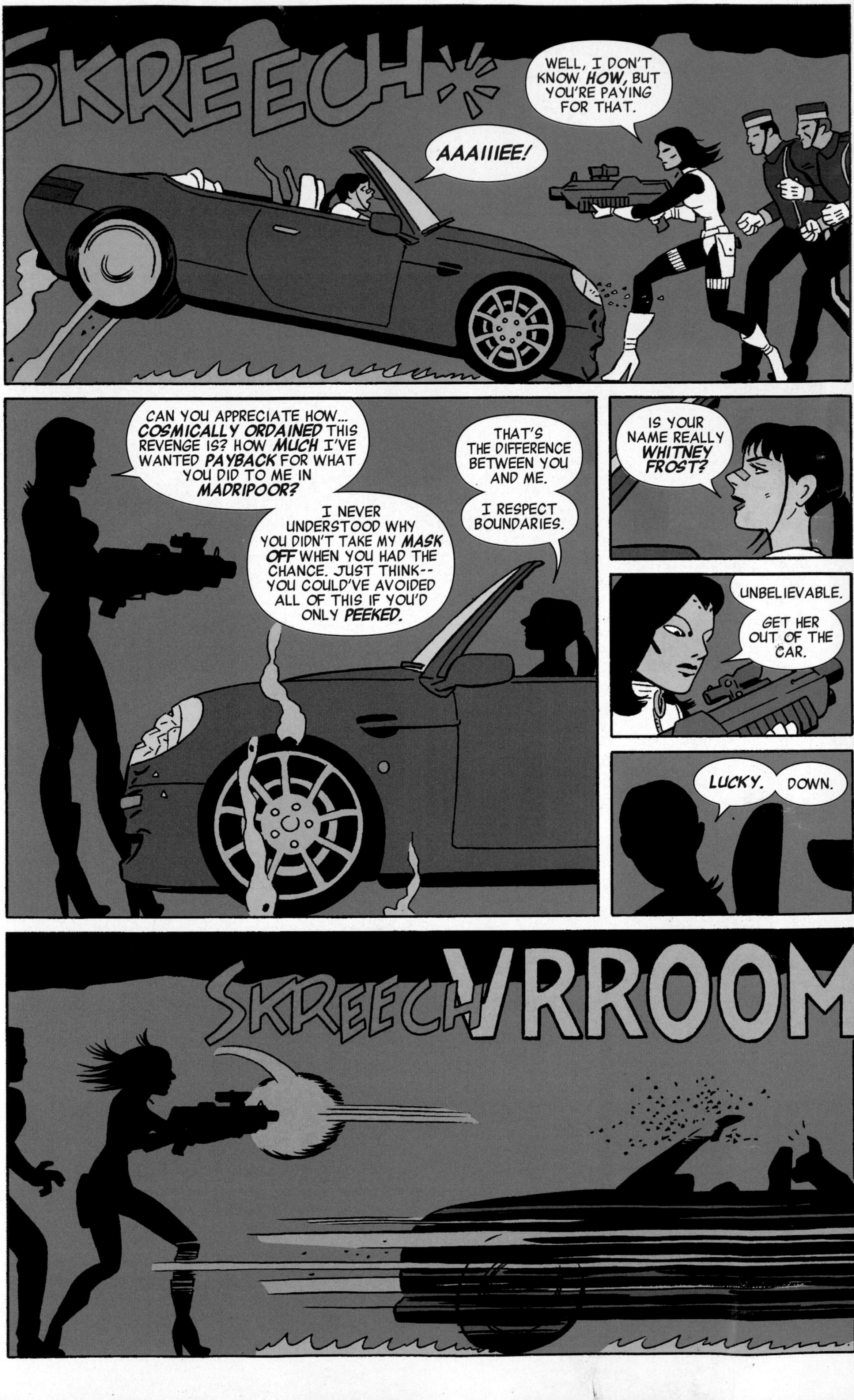
SKREECH
WELL, I DON'T KNOW HOW, BUT YOU'RE PAYING FOR THAT.
AAAIIIEE!
CAN YOU APPRECIATE HOW... COSMICALLY ORDAINED THIS REVENGE IS? HOW MUCH I'VE WANTED PAYBACK FOR WHAT YOU DID TO ME IN MADRIPOOR?
I NEVER UNDERSTOOD WHY YOU DIDN'T TAKE MY MASK OFF WHEN YOU HAD THE CHANCE. JUST THINK-- YOU COULD'VE AVOIDED ALL OF THIS IF YOU'D ONLY PEEKED.
THAT'S THE DIFFERENCE BETWEEN YOU AND ME.
I RESPECT BOUNDARIES.
IS YOUR NAME REALLY WHITNEY FROST?
UNBELIEVABLE.
GET HER OUT OF THE CAR.
LUCKY.
DOWN.
SKREECH
VRROOM

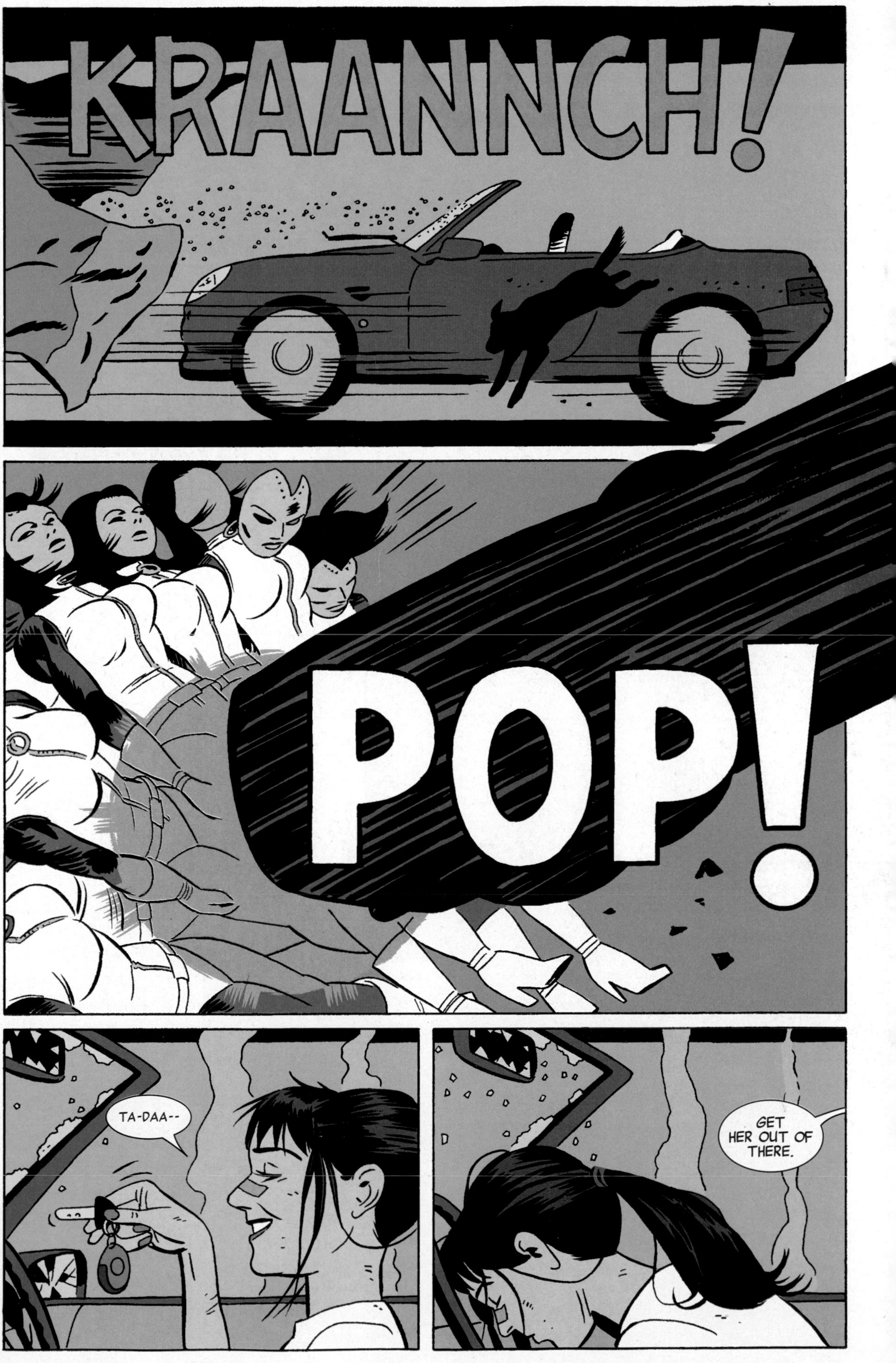
KRAANNCH!
POP!
TA-DAA--
GET HER OUT OF THERE.

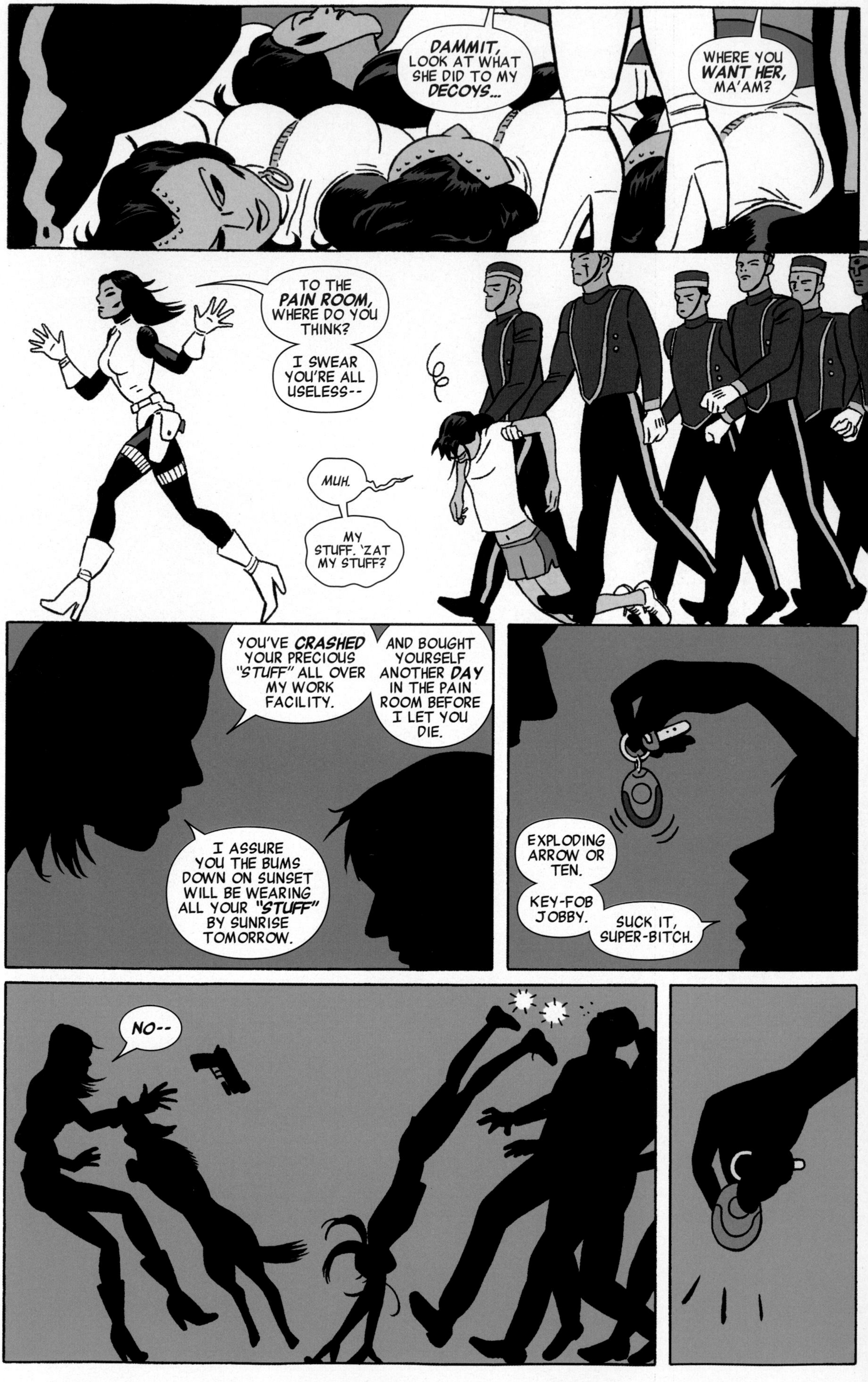
DAMMIT, LOOK AT WHAT SHE DID TO MY DECOYS...
WHERE YOU WANT HER, MA'AM?
TO THE PAIN ROOM, WHERE DO YOU THINK?
I SWEAR YOU'RE ALL USELESS--
MUH.
MY STUFF. 'ZAT MY STUFF?
YOU'VE CRASHED YOUR PRECIOUS "STUFF" ALL OVER MY WORK FACILITY.
AND BOUGHT YOURSELF ANOTHER DAY IN THE PAIN ROOM BEFORE I LET YOU DIE.
I ASSURE YOU THE BUMS DOWN ON SUNSET WILL BE WEARING ALL YOUR "STUFF" BY SUNRISE TOMORROW.
EXPLODING ARROW OR TEN.
KEY-FOB JOBBY.
SUCK IT, SUPER-BITCH.
NO--

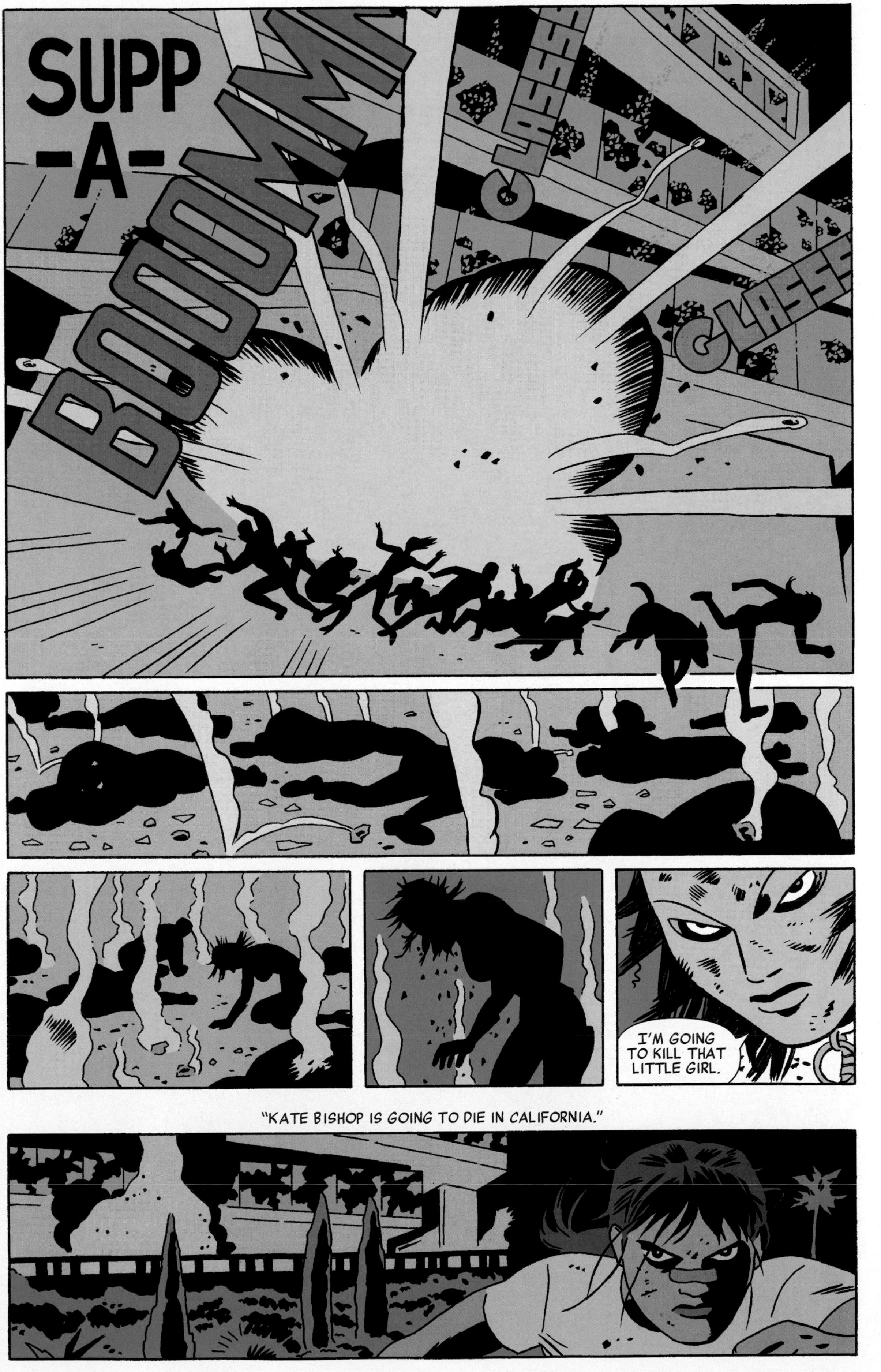
SUPP
-A-
BOOOM!
GLASSES
GLASSES
I'M GOING TO KILL THAT LITTLE GIRL.
"KATE BISHOP IS GOING TO DIE IN CALIFORNIA."

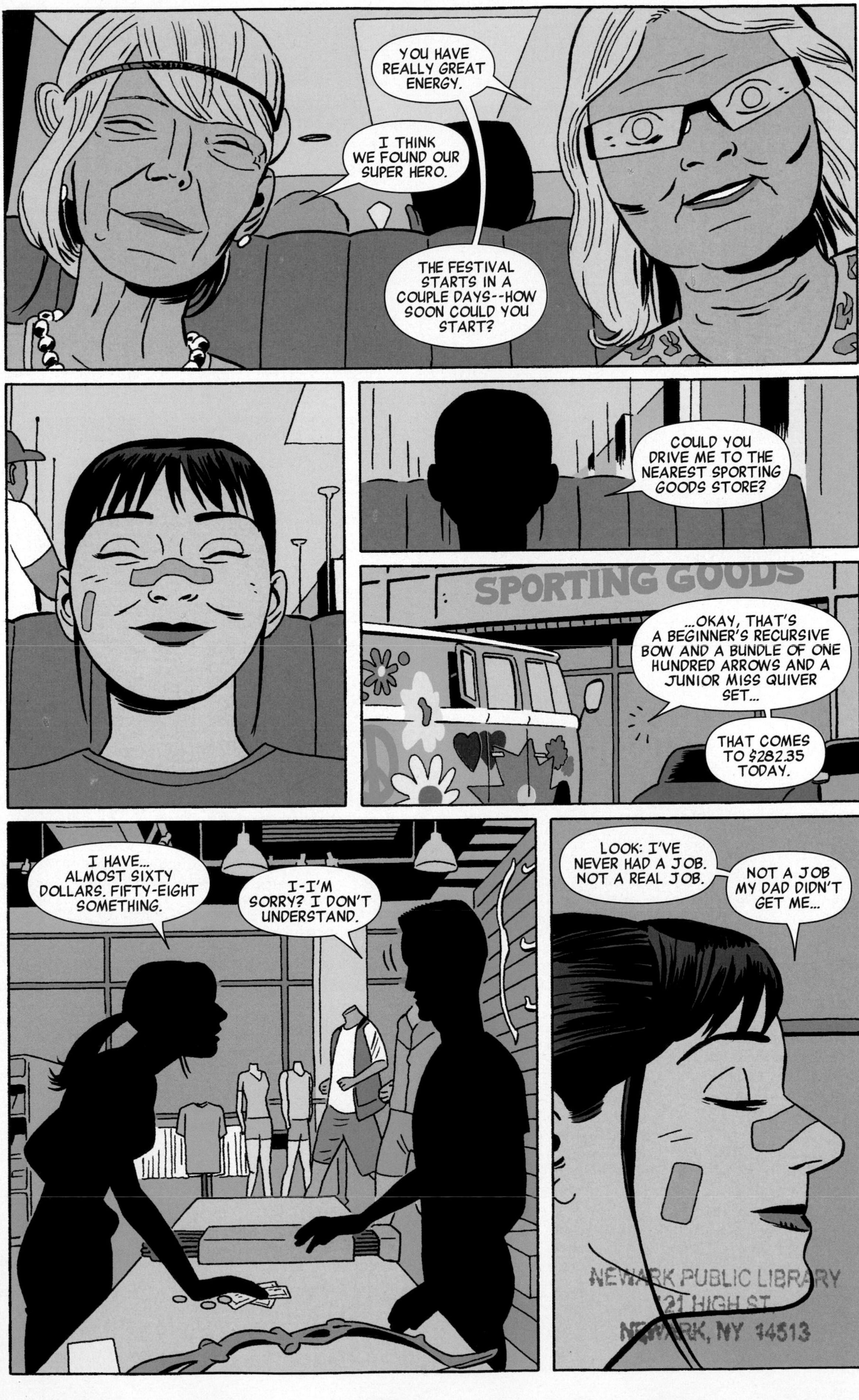
YOU HAVE REALLY GREAT ENERGY.
I THINK WE FOUND OUR SUPER HERO.
THE FESTIVAL STARTS IN A COUPLE DAYS--HOW SOON COULD YOU START?
COULD YOU DRIVE ME TO THE NEAREST SPORTING GOODS STORE?
SPORTING GOODS
...OKAY, THAT'S A BEGINNER'S RECURSIVE BOW AND A BUNDLE OF ONE HUNDRED ARROWS AND A JUNIOR MISS QUIVER SET...
THAT COMES TO $282.35 TODAY.
I HAVE... ALMOST SIXTY DOLLARS. FIFTY-EIGHT SOMETHING.
I-I'M SORRY? I DON'T UNDERSTAND.
LOOK: I'VE NEVER HAD A JOB. NOT A REAL JOB.
NOT A JOB MY DAD DIDN'T GET ME...

--But I've worked. I've worked hard for things.

Harder than you'd ever believe.

But I never needed a job because I never needed money until now.

Look, we're all adults here; we've all seen the 'Welcome to the Jungle' video.

I cowboyed out to Los Angeles and in the span of forty-eight hours got taken for everything I had. It's an old story, and maybe I should've known better.

Rookie mistake, right?

But I am telling you now: I might be young, but I am good. I work hard, and I'm a good person.

I know what's right. I know what's wrong. And if you give me this chance--

If you just give me one shot to show you how good I can be, how hard I work, how much I believe in doing the right thing--

--I won't let you down.

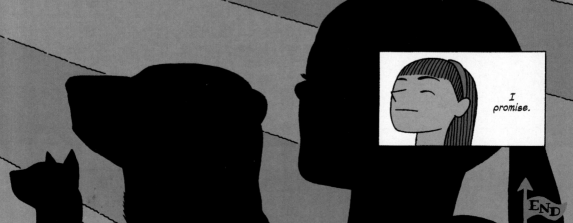

I promise.

END

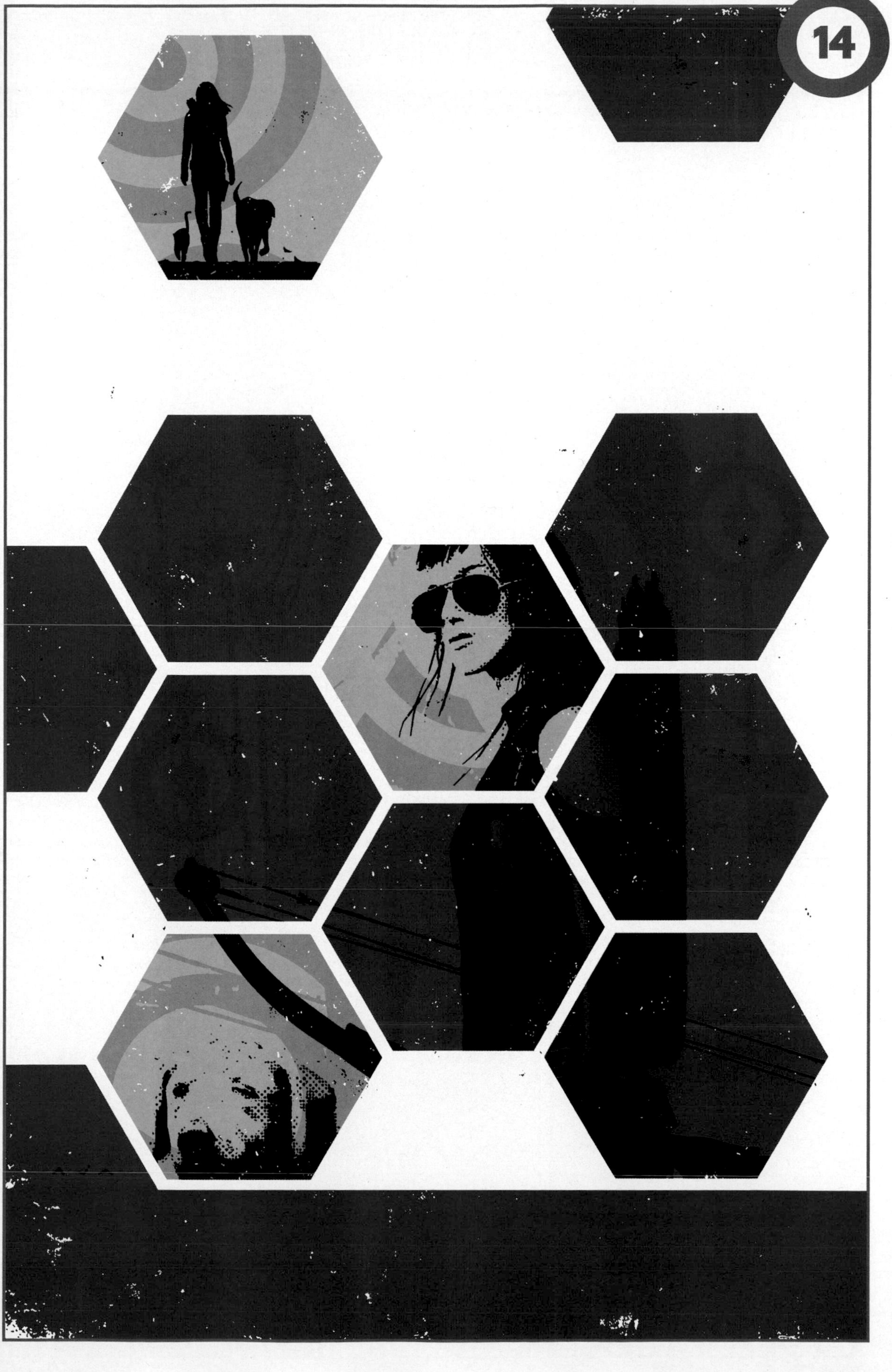
14

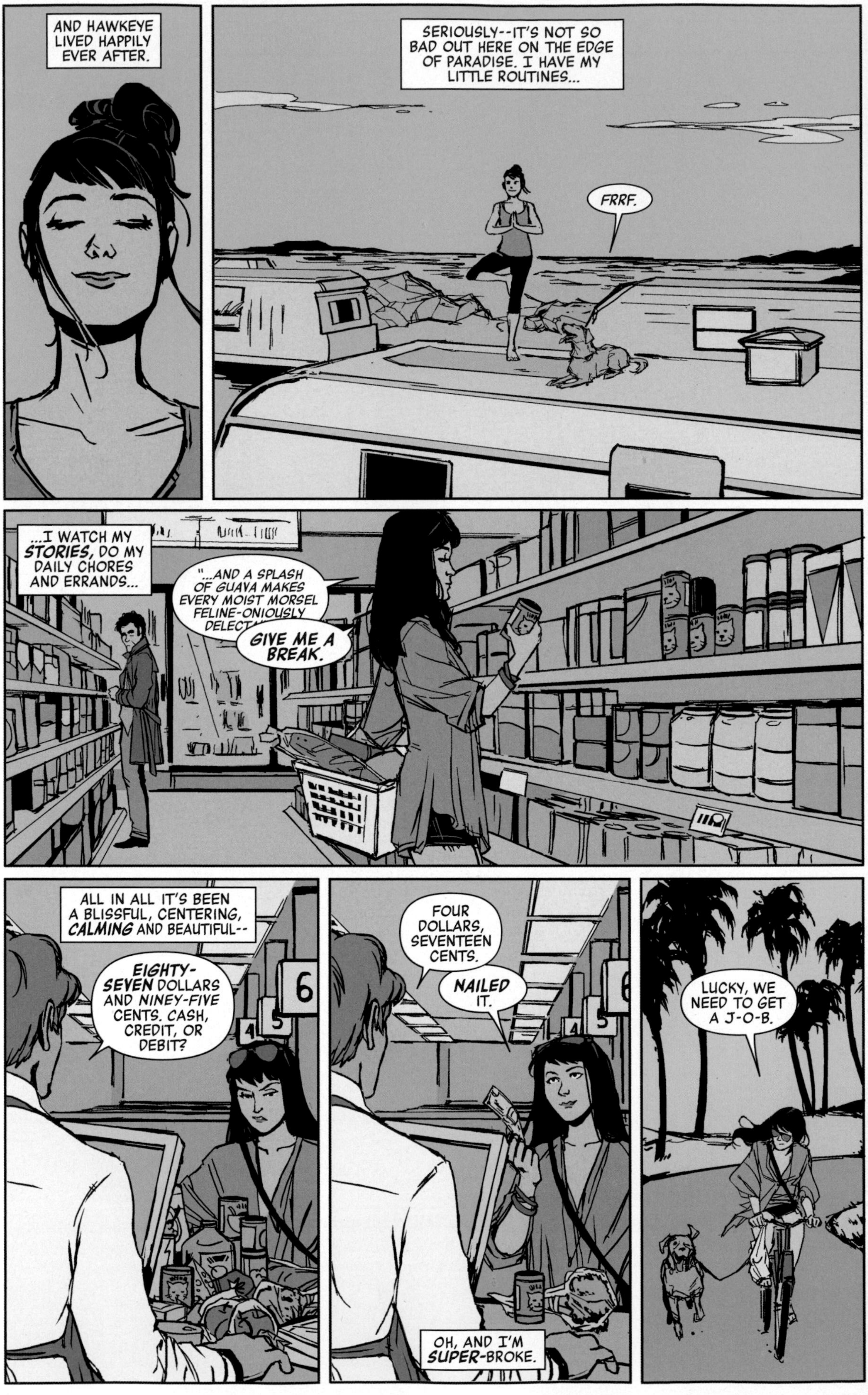
AND HAWKEYE LIVED HAPPILY EVER AFTER.
SERIOUSLY--IT'S NOT SO BAD OUT HERE ON THE EDGE OF PARADISE. I HAVE MY LITTLE ROUTINES...
FRRF.
...I WATCH MY STORIES, DO MY DAILY CHORES AND ERRANDS...
"...AND A SPLASH OF GUAVA MAKES EVERY MOIST MORSEL FELINE-ONIOUSLY DELECTA
GIVE ME A BREAK.
ALL IN ALL IT'S BEEN A BLISSFUL, CENTERING, CALMING AND BEAUTIFUL--
EIGHTY-SEVEN DOLLARS AND NINEY-FIVE CENTS. CASH, CREDIT, OR DEBIT?
FOUR DOLLARS, SEVENTEEN CENTS.
NAILED IT.
OH, AND I'M SUPER-BROKE.
LUCKY, WE NEED TO GET A J-O-B.

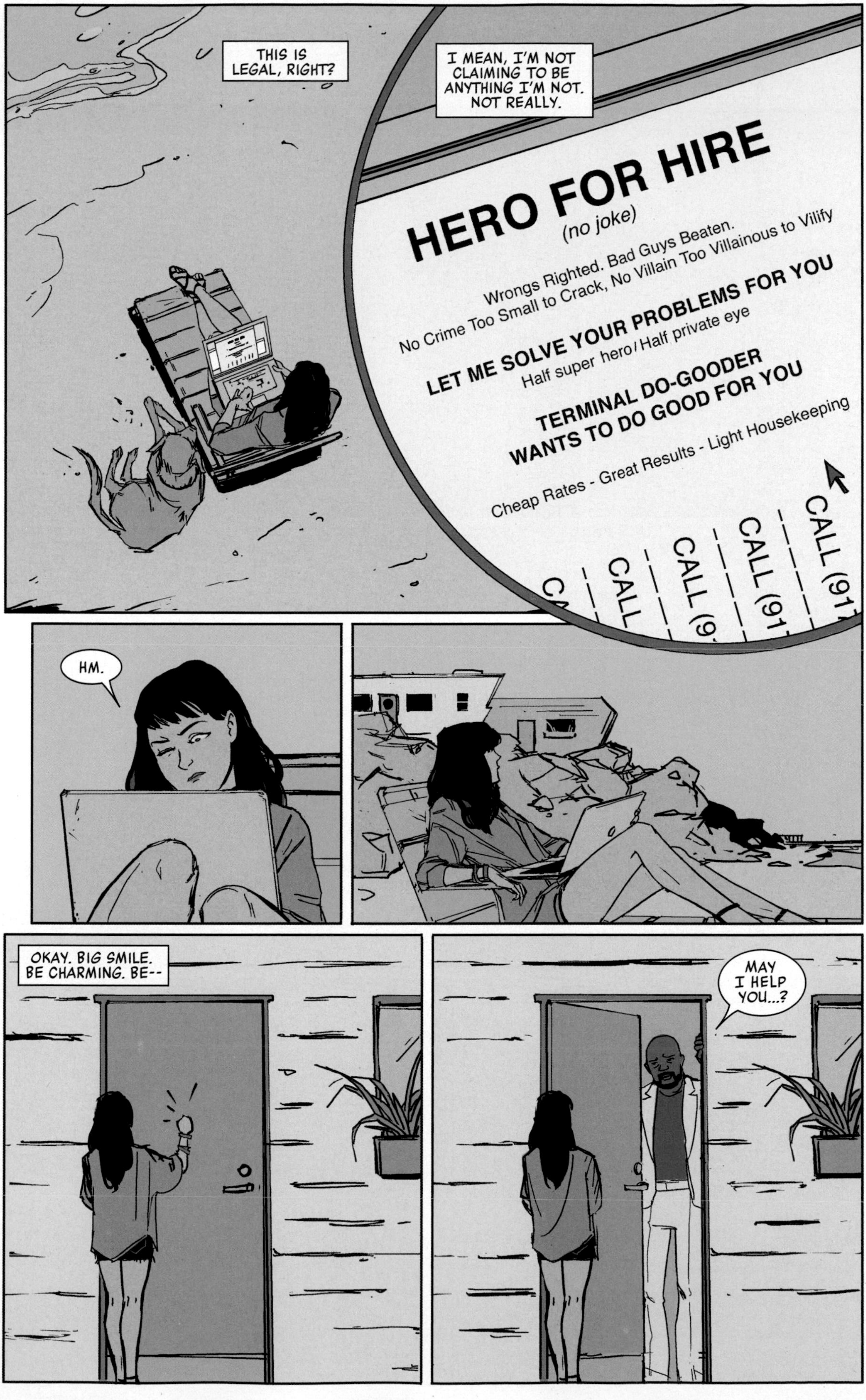
THIS IS LEGAL, RIGHT?
I MEAN, I'M NOT CLAIMING TO BE ANYTHING I'M NOT. NOT REALLY.
HERO FOR HIRE
(no joke)
Wrongs Righted. Bad Guys Beaten.
No Crime Too Small to Crack, No Villain Too Villainous to Vilify
LET ME SOLVE YOUR PROBLEMS FOR YOU
Half super hero/Half private eye
TERMINAL DO-GOODER
WANTS TO DO GOOD FOR YOU
Cheap Rates - Great Results - Light Housekeeping
HM.
OKAY. BIG SMILE. BE CHARMING. BE--
MAY I HELP YOU...?

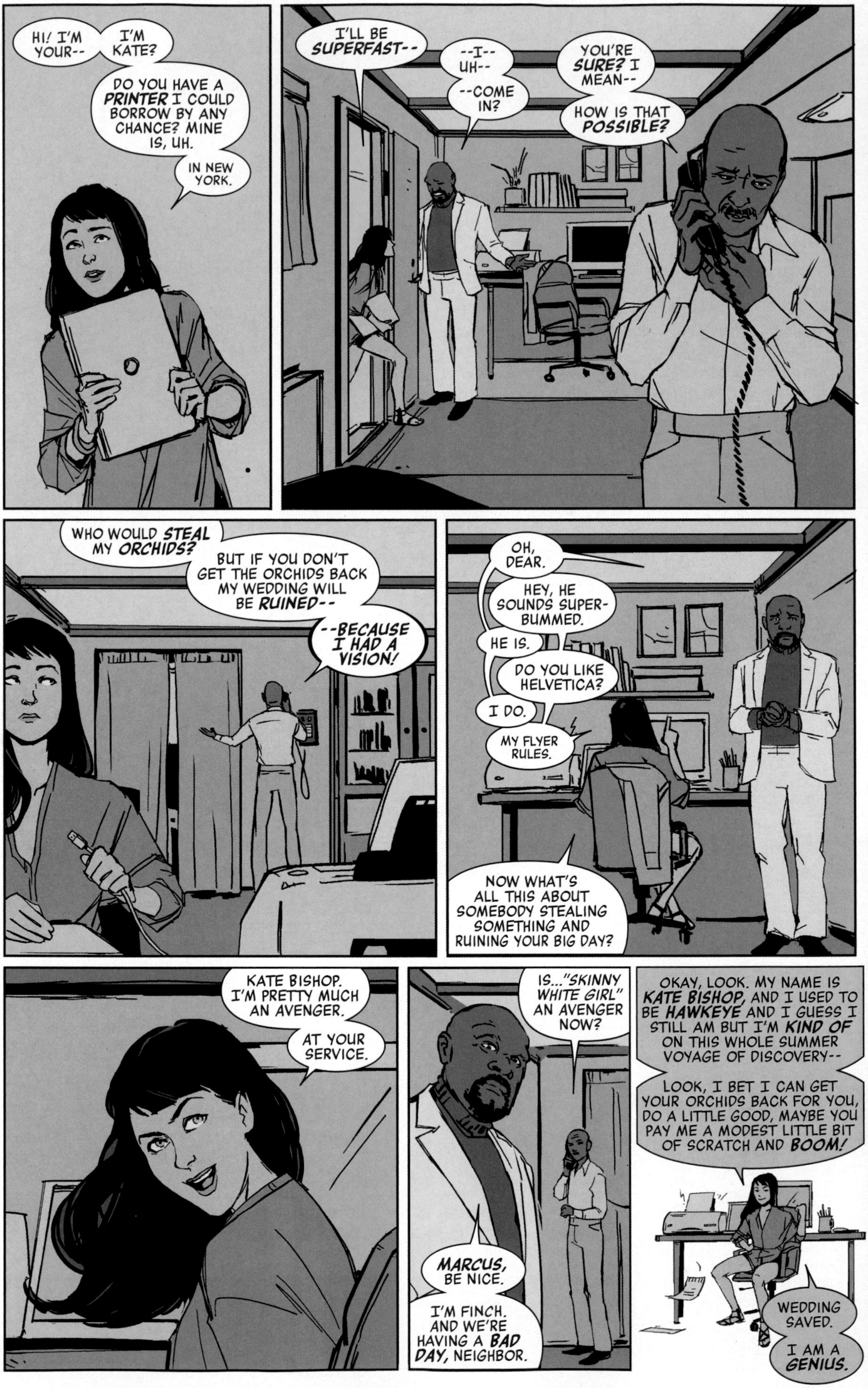
HI! I'M YOUR--
I'M KATE?
DO YOU HAVE A PRINTER I COULD BORROW BY ANY CHANCE? MINE IS, UH.
IN NEW YORK.
I'LL BE SUPERFAST--
--I-- UH--
--COME IN?
YOU'RE SURE? I MEAN--
HOW IS THAT POSSIBLE?
WHO WOULD STEAL MY ORCHIDS?
BUT IF YOU DON'T GET THE ORCHIDS BACK MY WEDDING WILL BE RUINED--
--BECAUSE I HAD A VISION!
OH, DEAR.
HEY, HE SOUNDS SUPER-BUMMED.
HE IS.
DO YOU LIKE HELVETICA?
I DO.
MY FLYER RULES.
NOW WHAT'S ALL THIS ABOUT SOMEBODY STEALING SOMETHING AND RUINING YOUR BIG DAY?
KATE BISHOP. I'M PRETTY MUCH AN AVENGER.
AT YOUR SERVICE.
IS..."SKINNY WHITE GIRL" AN AVENGER NOW?
MARCUS, BE NICE.
I'M FINCH. AND WE'RE HAVING A BAD DAY, NEIGHBOR.
OKAY, LOOK. MY NAME IS KATE BISHOP, AND I USED TO BE HAWKEYE AND I GUESS I STILL AM BUT I'M KIND OF ON THIS WHOLE SUMMER VOYAGE OF DISCOVERY--
LOOK, I BET I CAN GET YOUR ORCHIDS BACK FOR YOU, DO A LITTLE GOOD, MAYBE YOU PAY ME A MODEST LITTLE BIT OF SCRATCH AND BOOM!
WEDDING SAVED.
I AM A GENIUS.

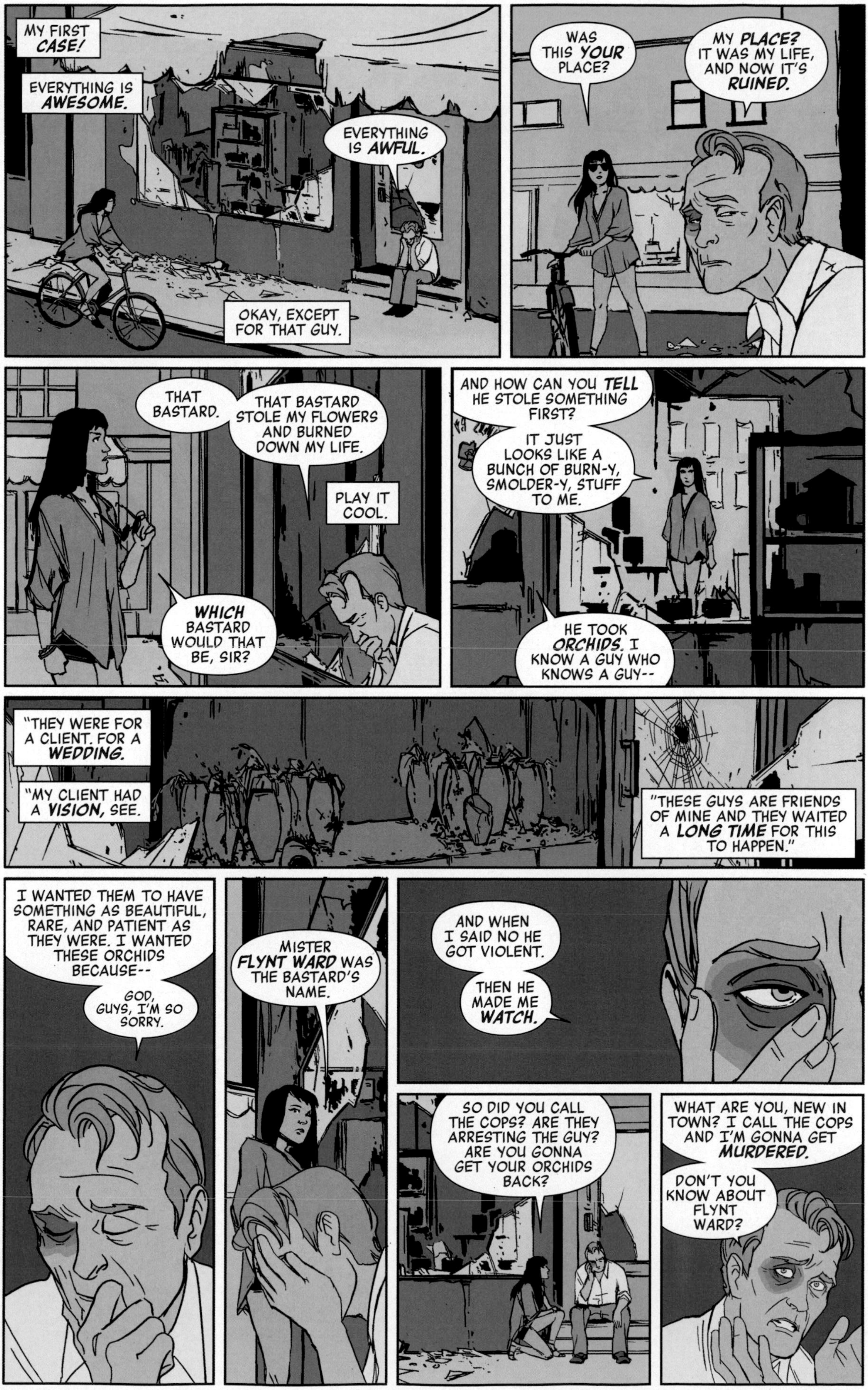
MY FIRST CASE!
EVERYTHING IS AWESOME.
EVERYTHING IS AWFUL.
OKAY, EXCEPT FOR THAT GUY.
WAS THIS YOUR PLACE?
MY PLACE? IT WAS MY LIFE, AND NOW IT'S RUINED.
THAT BASTARD.
THAT BASTARD STOLE MY FLOWERS AND BURNED DOWN MY LIFE.
PLAY IT COOL.
WHICH BASTARD WOULD THAT BE, SIR?
AND HOW CAN YOU TELL HE STOLE SOMETHING FIRST?
IT JUST LOOKS LIKE A BUNCH OF BURN-Y, SMOLDER-Y, STUFF TO ME.
HE TOOK ORCHIDS. I KNOW A GUY WHO KNOWS A GUY--
"THEY WERE FOR A CLIENT. FOR A WEDDING.
"MY CLIENT HAD A VISION, SEE.
"THESE GUYS ARE FRIENDS OF MINE AND THEY WAITED A LONG TIME FOR THIS TO HAPPEN."
I WANTED THEM TO HAVE SOMETHING AS BEAUTIFUL, RARE, AND PATIENT AS THEY WERE. I WANTED THESE ORCHIDS BECAUSE--
GOD, GUYS, I'M SO SORRY.
MISTER FLYNT WARD WAS THE BASTARD'S NAME.
AND WHEN I SAID NO HE GOT VIOLENT.
THEN HE MADE ME WATCH.
SO DID YOU CALL THE COPS? ARE THEY ARRESTING THE GUY? ARE YOU GONNA GET YOUR ORCHIDS BACK?
WHAT ARE YOU, NEW IN TOWN? I CALL THE COPS AND I'M GONNA GET MURDERED.
DON'T YOU KNOW ABOUT FLYNT WARD?

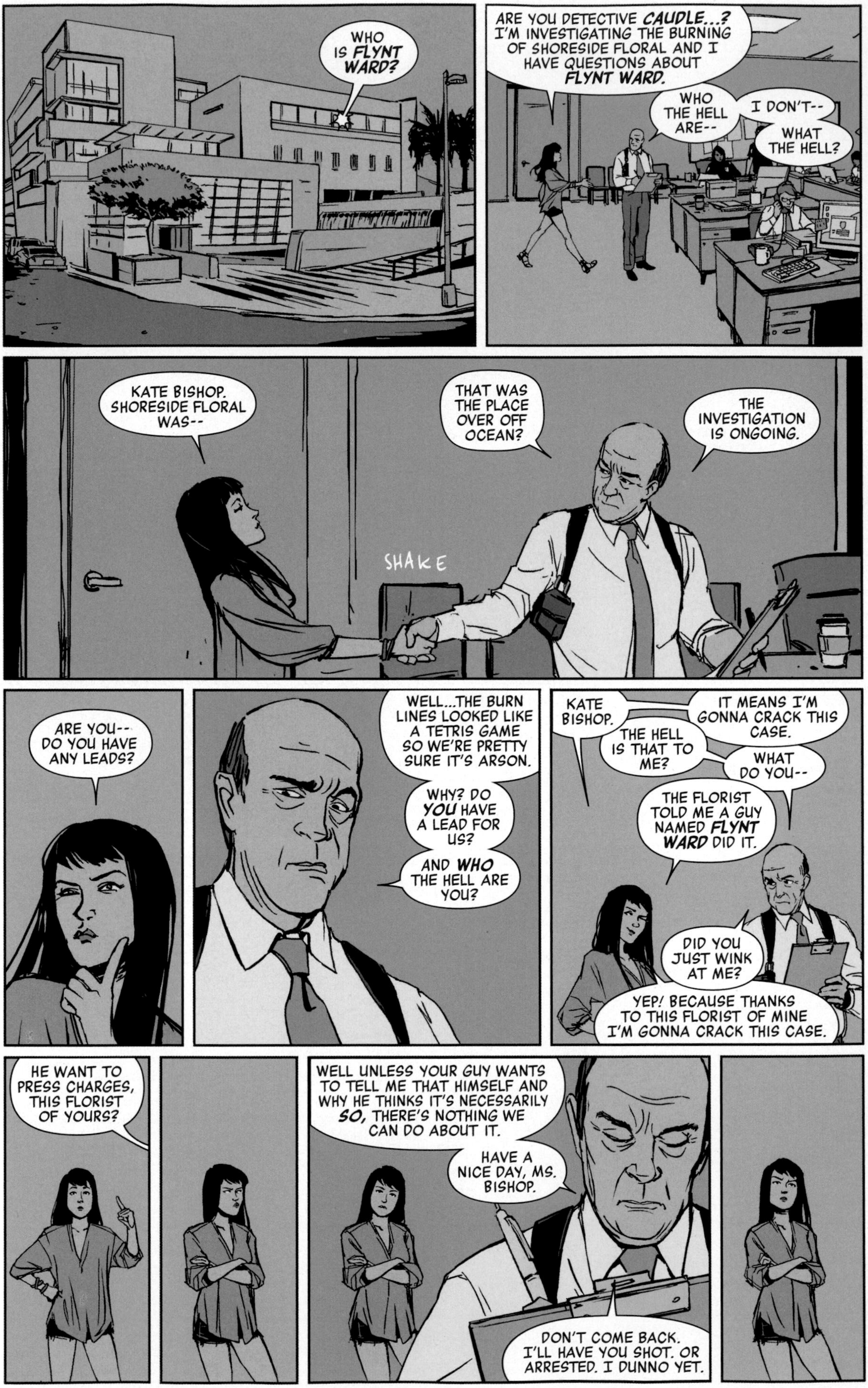
WHO IS FLYNT WARD?
ARE YOU DETECTIVE CAUDLE...? I'M INVESTIGATING THE BURNING OF SHORESIDE FLORAL AND I HAVE QUESTIONS ABOUT FLYNT WARD.
WHO THE HELL ARE--
I DON'T--
WHAT THE HELL?
KATE BISHOP. SHORESIDE FLORAL WAS--
THAT WAS THE PLACE OVER OFF OCEAN?
THE INVESTIGATION IS ONGOING.
SHAKE
ARE YOU-- DO YOU HAVE ANY LEADS?
WELL...THE BURN LINES LOOKED LIKE A TETRIS GAME SO WE'RE PRETTY SURE IT'S ARSON.
WHY? DO YOU HAVE A LEAD FOR US?
AND WHO THE HELL ARE YOU?
KATE BISHOP.
THE HELL IS THAT TO ME?
IT MEANS I'M GONNA CRACK THIS CASE.
WHAT DO YOU--
THE FLORIST TOLD ME A GUY NAMED FLYNT WARD DID IT.
DID YOU JUST WINK AT ME?
YEP! BECAUSE THANKS TO THIS FLORIST OF MINE I'M GONNA CRACK THIS CASE.
HE WANT TO PRESS CHARGES, THIS FLORIST OF YOURS?
WELL UNLESS YOUR GUY WANTS TO TELL ME THAT HIMSELF AND WHY HE THINKS IT'S NECESSARILY SO, THERE'S NOTHING WE CAN DO ABOUT IT.
HAVE A NICE DAY, MS. BISHOP.
DON'T COME BACK. I'LL HAVE YOU SHOT. OR ARRESTED. I DUNNO YET.

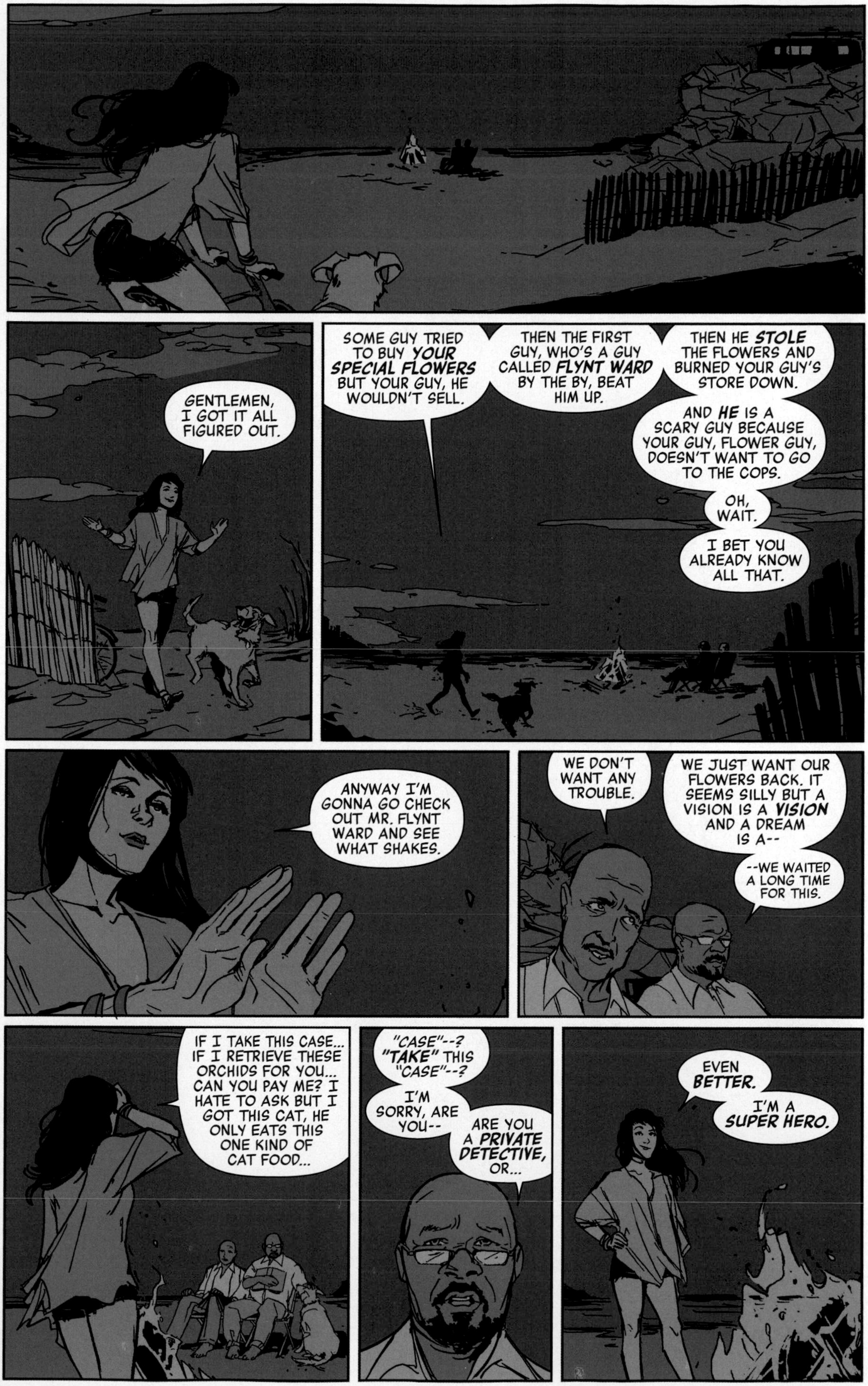
GENTLEMEN, I GOT IT ALL FIGURED OUT.
SOME GUY TRIED TO BUY YOUR SPECIAL FLOWERS BUT YOUR GUY, HE WOULDN'T SELL.
THEN THE FIRST GUY, WHO'S A GUY CALLED FLYNT WARD BY THE BY, BEAT HIM UP.
THEN HE STOLE THE FLOWERS AND BURNED YOUR GUY'S STORE DOWN.
AND HE IS A SCARY GUY BECAUSE YOUR GUY, FLOWER GUY, DOESN'T WANT TO GO TO THE COPS.
OH, WAIT.
I BET YOU ALREADY KNOW ALL THAT.
ANYWAY I'M GONNA GO CHECK OUT MR. FLYNT WARD AND SEE WHAT SHAKES.
WE DON'T WANT ANY TROUBLE.
WE JUST WANT OUR FLOWERS BACK. IT SEEMS SILLY BUT A VISION IS A VISION AND A DREAM IS A--
--WE WAITED A LONG TIME FOR THIS.
IF I TAKE THIS CASE... IF I RETRIEVE THESE ORCHIDS FOR YOU... CAN YOU PAY ME? I HATE TO ASK BUT I GOT THIS CAT, HE ONLY EATS THIS ONE KIND OF CAT FOOD...
"CASE"--? "TAKE" THIS "CASE"--?
I'M SORRY, ARE YOU--
ARE YOU A PRIVATE DETECTIVE, OR...
EVEN BETTER.
I'M A SUPER HERO.

criminal   arson

evidence

private detective

vestigator california   arson law

fornia arso   ow to be a private detective in california

aljdf:lkjlkj

HEY!

YOU!

UH--
OFFICER!

COP!

DETECTIVE
COP MAN!

"CAUDLE."

YES! THAT.
YES.

NICE
WORKING WITH
YOU TODAY.

WHO
ARE YOU
AGAIN?

ARSON CASE.
ANNOYING GIRL.
FLYNT WARD.

HOW CAN I
GET YOU TO
ARREST FLYNT
WARD? WHY AREN'T
YOU DOING
ANYTH--

YOU ARE MEDDLING IN AN
ONGOING INVESTIGATION,
KID! DON'T YOU GET IT?

THERE ARE REAL PEOPLE--
ACTUAL PROFESSIONAL ADULTS--
TRAINED IN THE LAW AND HOW
TO ENFORCE THOSE LAWS.

WE'RE THE GOOD
GUYS AND IF YOU REALLY
CARE ABOUT GETTING
THE BAD GUYS HERE--

YOU'LL
KNOCK IT
OFF, MISS
BISHOP.

OR I
WILL
ARREST
YOU.

NOT IF I
ARREST
YOU FIRST.

ZING.

NO, WAIT,
THAT ZING
SUCKED.

AND I DON'T
LIKE STUFF
THAT SUCKS.

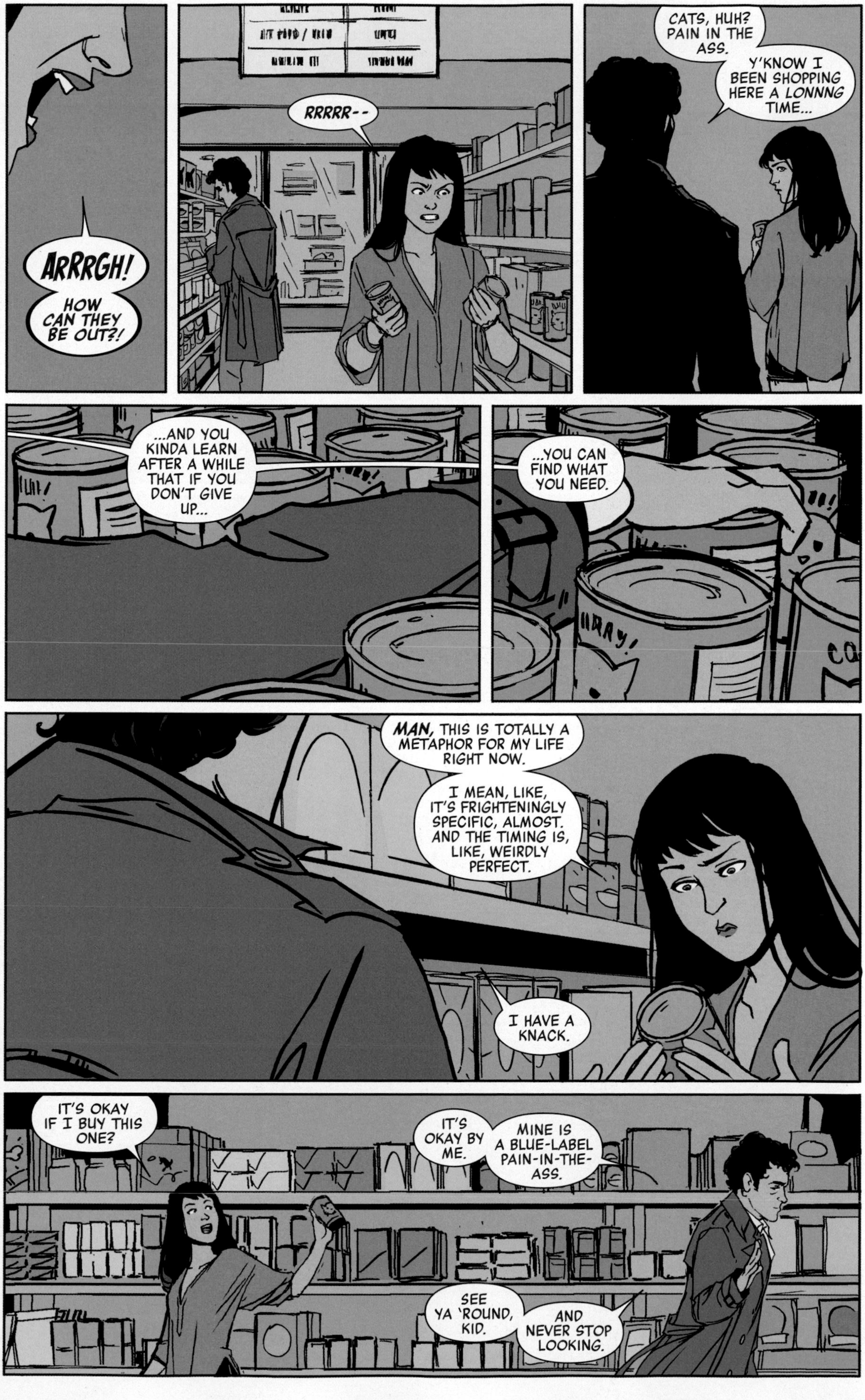
ARRRGH!
HOW CAN THEY BE OUT?!
RRRRR--
CATS, HUH? PAIN IN THE ASS.
Y'KNOW I BEEN SHOPPING HERE A LONNNG TIME...
...AND YOU KINDA LEARN AFTER A WHILE THAT IF YOU DON'T GIVE UP...
...YOU CAN FIND WHAT YOU NEED.
MAN, THIS IS TOTALLY A METAPHOR FOR MY LIFE RIGHT NOW.
I MEAN, LIKE, IT'S FRIGHTENINGLY SPECIFIC, ALMOST. AND THE TIMING IS, LIKE, WEIRDLY PERFECT.
I HAVE A KNACK.
IT'S OKAY IF I BUY THIS ONE?
IT'S OKAY BY ME.
MINE IS A BLUE-LABEL PAIN-IN-THE-ASS.
SEE YA 'ROUND, KID.
AND NEVER STOP LOOKING.

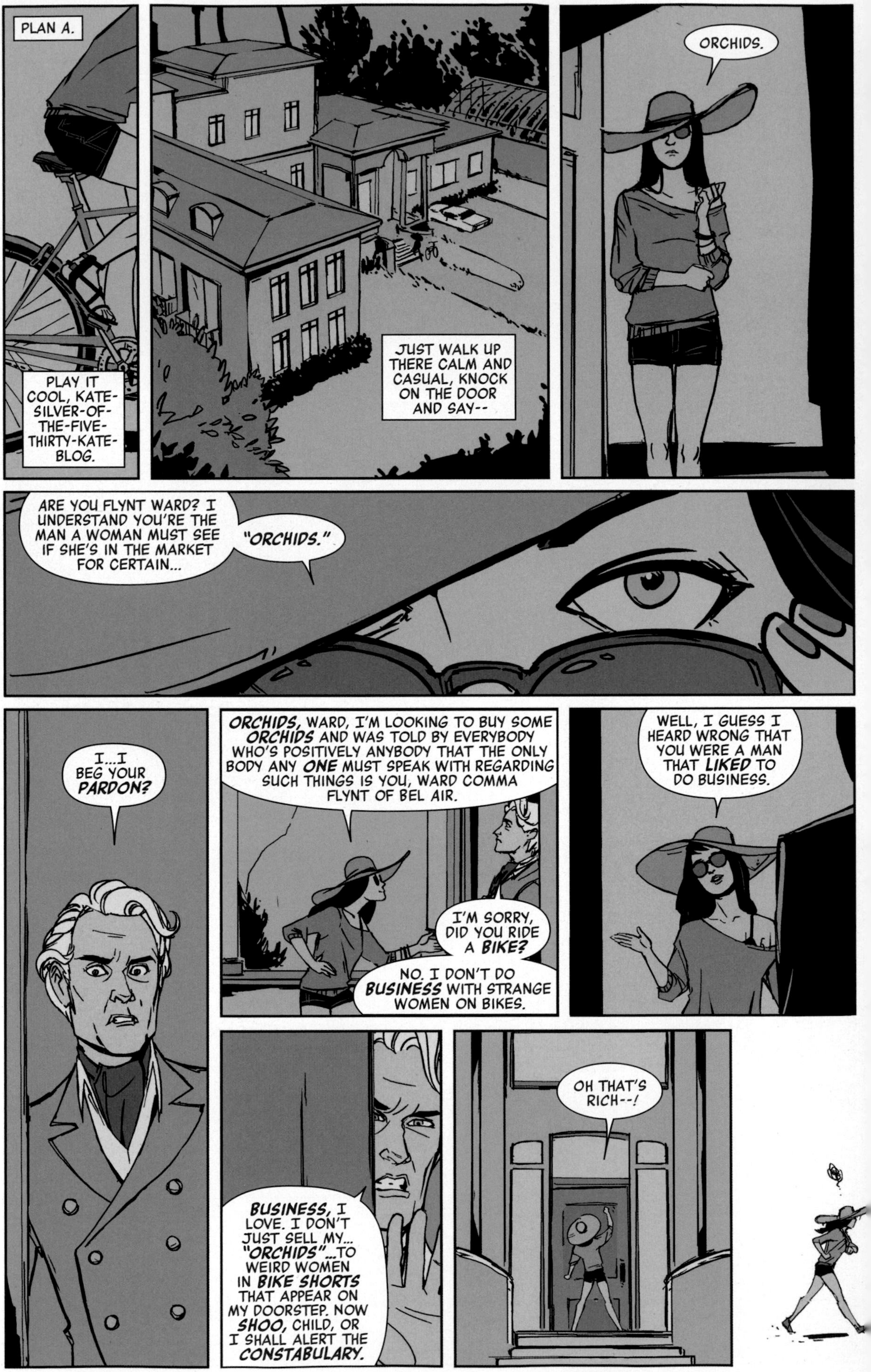
PLAN A.
PLAY IT COOL, KATE-SILVER-OF-THE-FIVE-THIRTY-KATE-BLOG.
JUST WALK UP THERE CALM AND CASUAL, KNOCK ON THE DOOR AND SAY--
ORCHIDS.
ARE YOU FLYNT WARD? I UNDERSTAND YOU'RE THE MAN A WOMAN MUST SEE IF SHE'S IN THE MARKET FOR CERTAIN...
"ORCHIDS."
I...I BEG YOUR PARDON?
ORCHIDS, WARD, I'M LOOKING TO BUY SOME ORCHIDS AND WAS TOLD BY EVERYBODY WHO'S POSITIVELY ANYBODY THAT THE ONLY BODY ANY ONE MUST SPEAK WITH REGARDING SUCH THINGS IS YOU, WARD COMMA FLYNT OF BEL AIR.
I'M SORRY, DID YOU RIDE A BIKE?
NO. I DON'T DO BUSINESS WITH STRANGE WOMEN ON BIKES.
WELL, I GUESS I HEARD WRONG THAT YOU WERE A MAN THAT LIKED TO DO BUSINESS.
BUSINESS, I LOVE. I DON'T JUST SELL MY... "ORCHIDS"...TO WEIRD WOMEN IN BIKE SHORTS THAT APPEAR ON MY DOORSTEP. NOW SHOO, CHILD, OR I SHALL ALERT THE CONSTABULARY.
OH THAT'S RICH--!

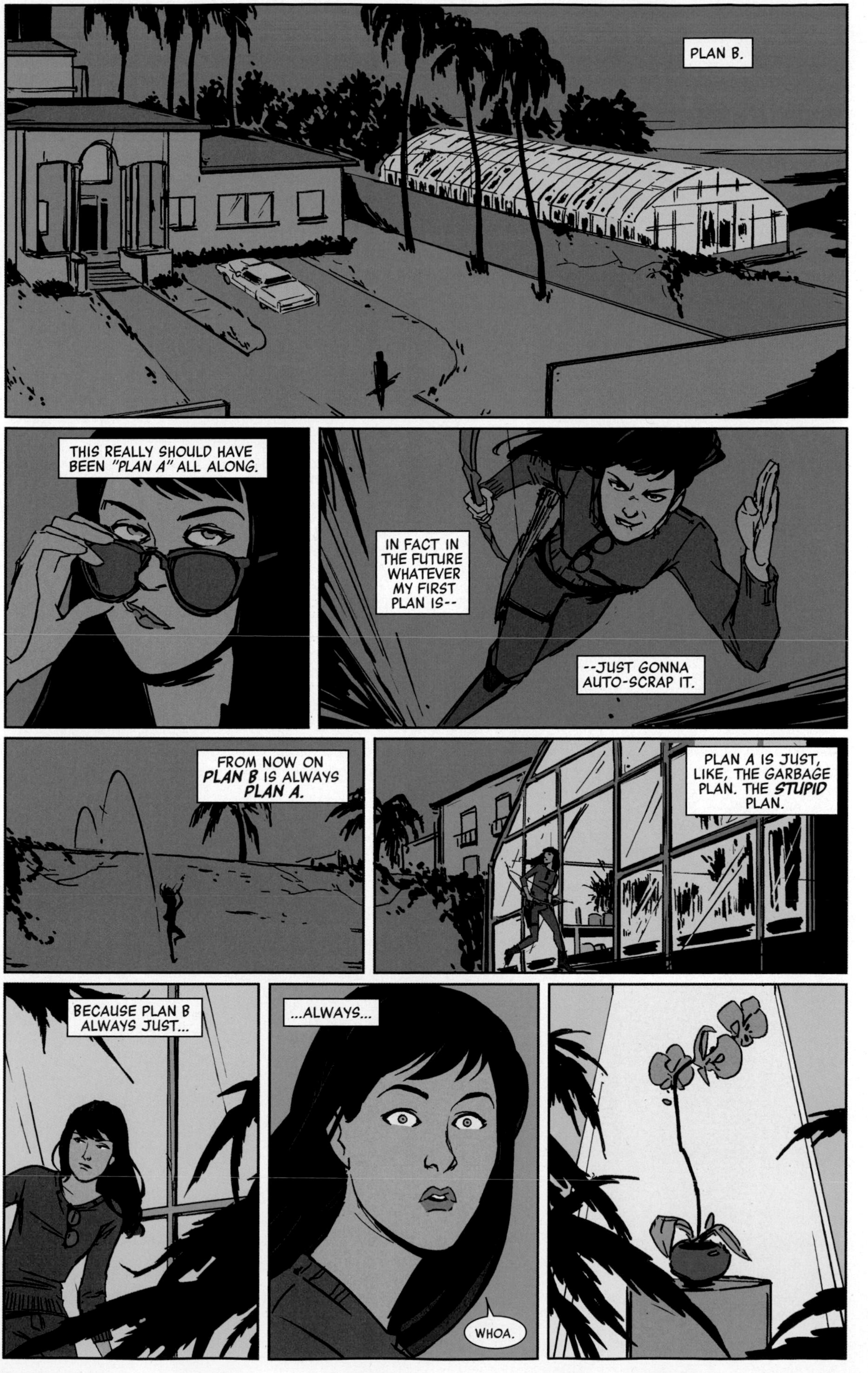
PLAN B.
THIS REALLY SHOULD HAVE BEEN "PLAN A" ALL ALONG.
IN FACT IN THE FUTURE WHATEVER MY FIRST PLAN IS--
--JUST GONNA AUTO-SCRAP IT.
FROM NOW ON PLAN B IS ALWAYS PLAN A.
PLAN A IS JUST, LIKE, THE GARBAGE PLAN. THE STUPID PLAN.
BECAUSE PLAN B ALWAYS JUST...
...ALWAYS...
WHOA.

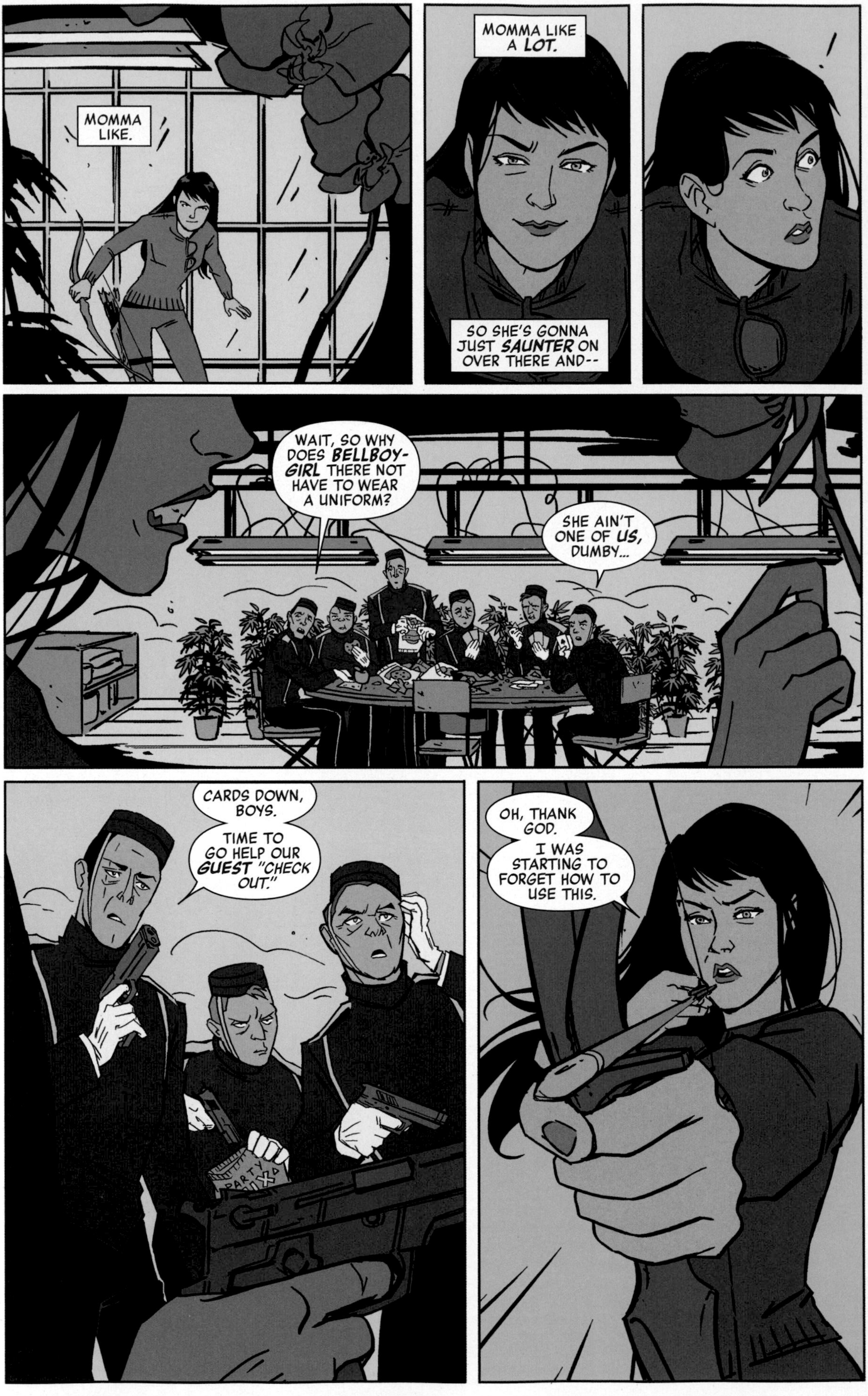
MOMMA LIKE.
MOMMA LIKE A LOT.
SO SHE'S GONNA JUST SAUNTER ON OVER THERE AND--
!
WAIT, SO WHY DOES BELLBOY-GIRL THERE NOT HAVE TO WEAR A UNIFORM?
SHE AIN'T ONE OF US, DUMBY...
CARDS DOWN, BOYS.
TIME TO GO HELP OUR GUEST "CHECK OUT."
OH, THANK GOD.
I WAS STARTING TO FORGET HOW TO USE THIS.

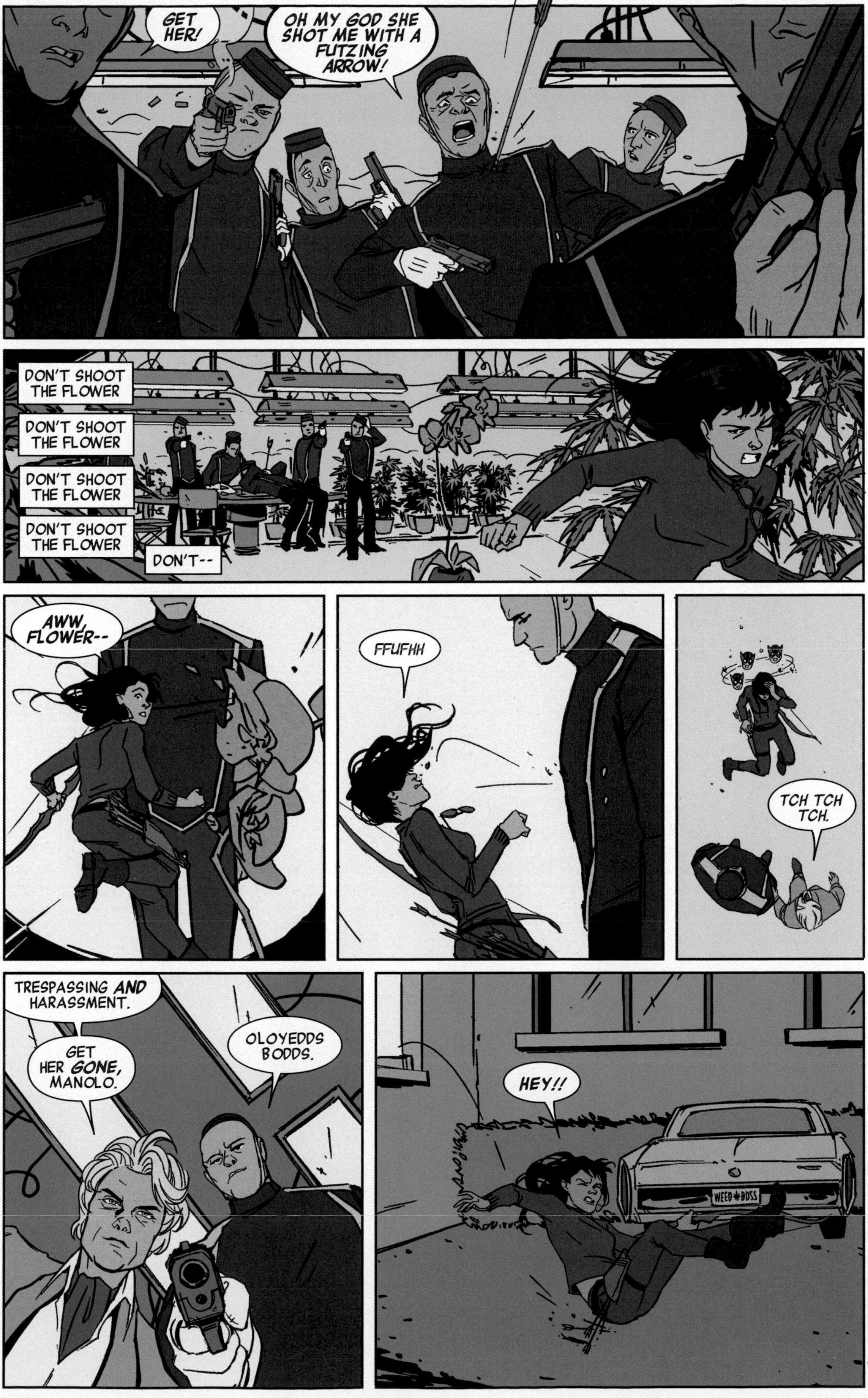
GET HER!
OH MY GOD SHE SHOT ME WITH A FUTZING ARROW!
DON'T SHOOT THE FLOWER
DON'T SHOOT THE FLOWER
DON'T SHOOT THE FLOWER
DON'T SHOOT THE FLOWER
DON'T--
AWW, FLOWER--
FFUFHH
TCH TCH TCH.
TRESPASSING AND HARASSMENT.
GET HER GONE, MANOLO.
OLOYEDDS BODDS.
HEY!!
WEED BOSS

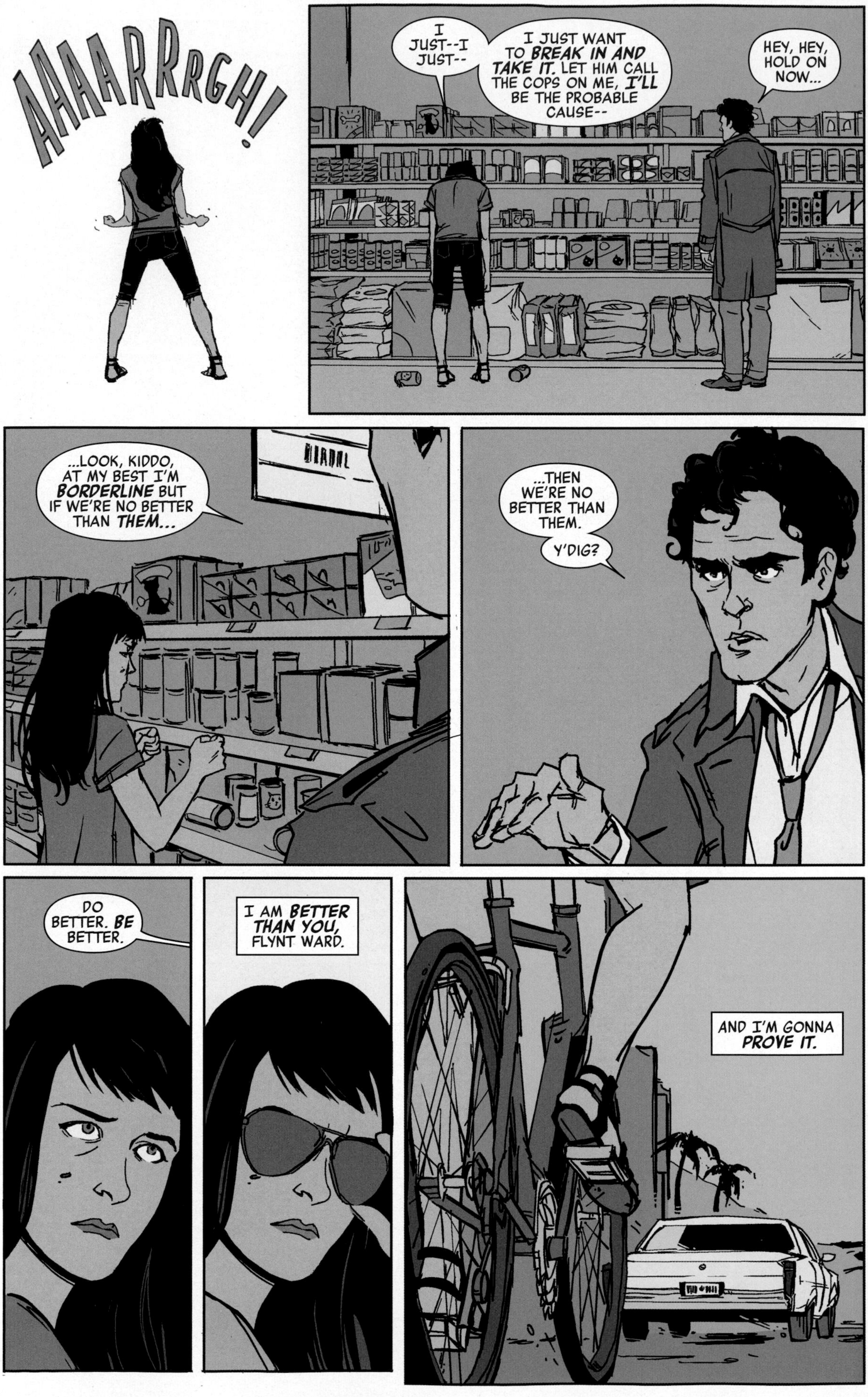
AAAARRRGH!
I JUST--I JUST--
I JUST WANT TO BREAK IN AND TAKE IT. LET HIM CALL THE COPS ON ME, I'LL BE THE PROBABLE CAUSE--
HEY, HEY, HOLD ON NOW...
...LOOK, KIDDO, AT MY BEST I'M BORDERLINE BUT IF WE'RE NO BETTER THAN THEM...
...THEN WE'RE NO BETTER THAN THEM.
Y'DIG?
DO BETTER. BE BETTER.
I AM BETTER THAN YOU, FLYNT WARD.
AND I'M GONNA PROVE IT.

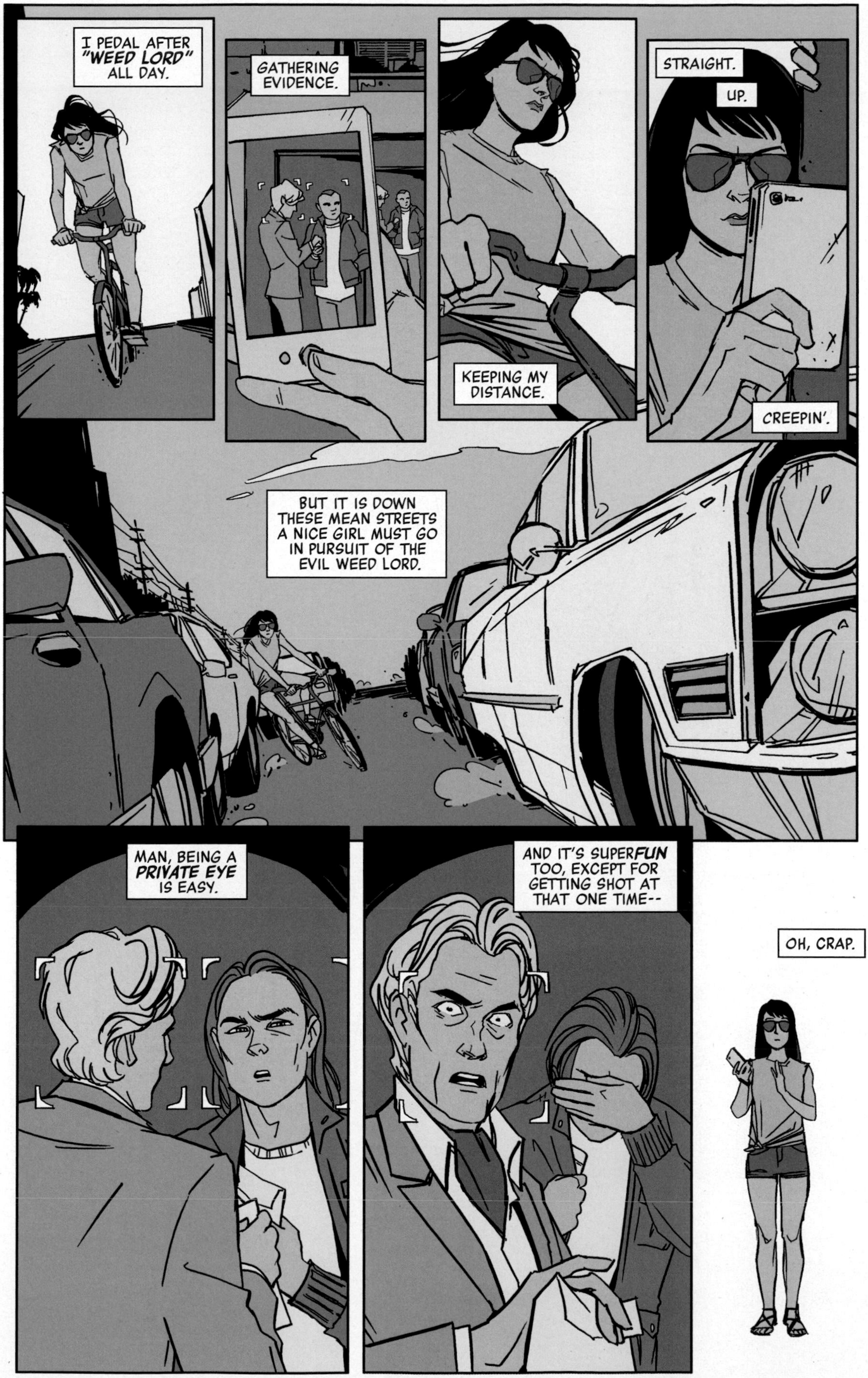
I PEDAL AFTER "WEED LORD" ALL DAY.
GATHERING EVIDENCE.
KEEPING MY DISTANCE.
STRAIGHT.
UP.
CREEPIN'.
BUT IT IS DOWN THESE MEAN STREETS A NICE GIRL MUST GO IN PURSUIT OF THE EVIL WEED LORD.
MAN, BEING A PRIVATE EYE IS EASY.
AND IT'S SUPERFUN TOO, EXCEPT FOR GETTING SHOT AT THAT ONE TIME--
OH, CRAP.

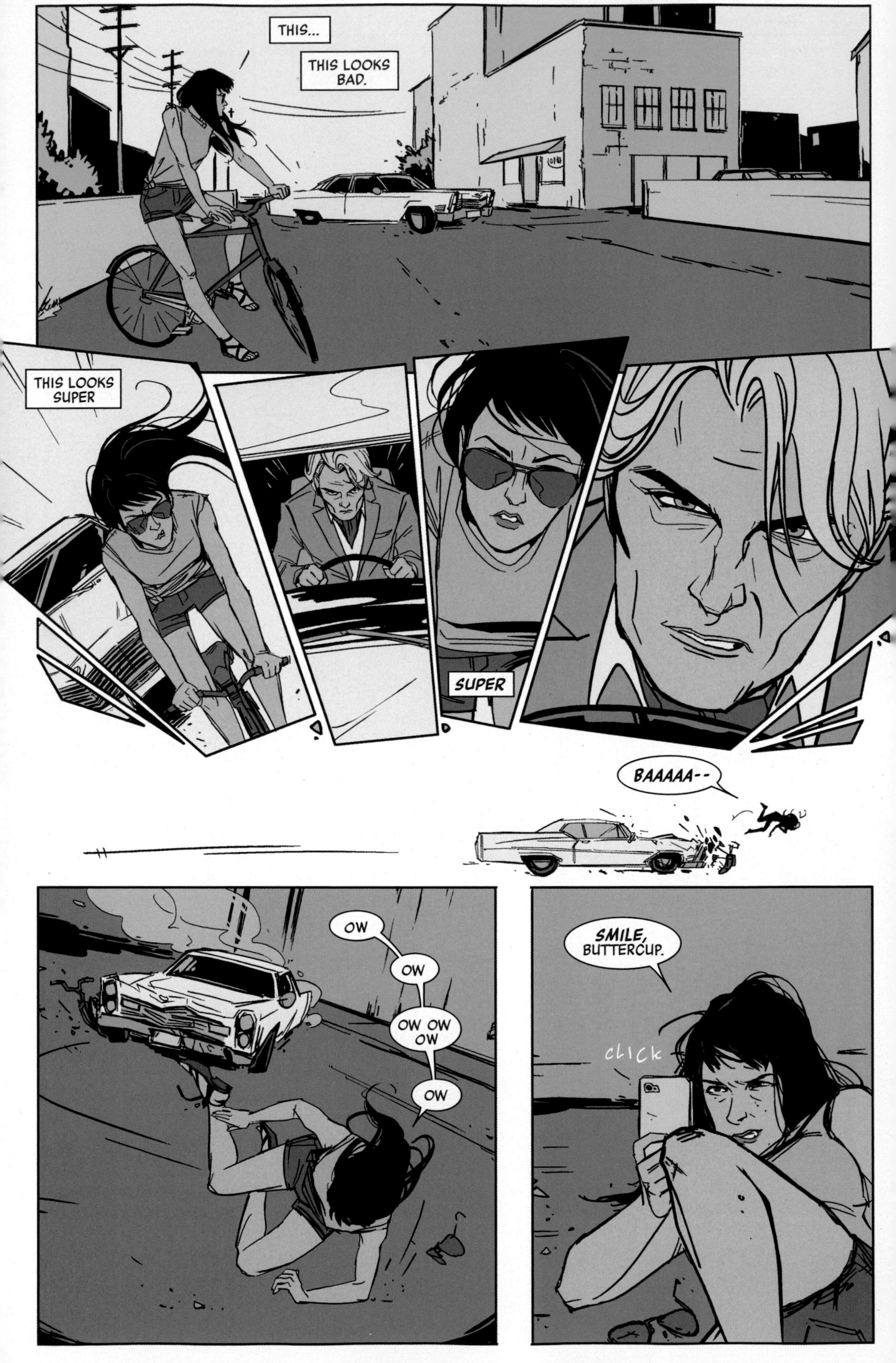
THIS...
THIS LOOKS BAD.
THIS LOOKS SUPER
SUPER
BAAAAA--
OW
OW
OW OW OW
OW
SMILE, BUTTERCUP.
CLICK

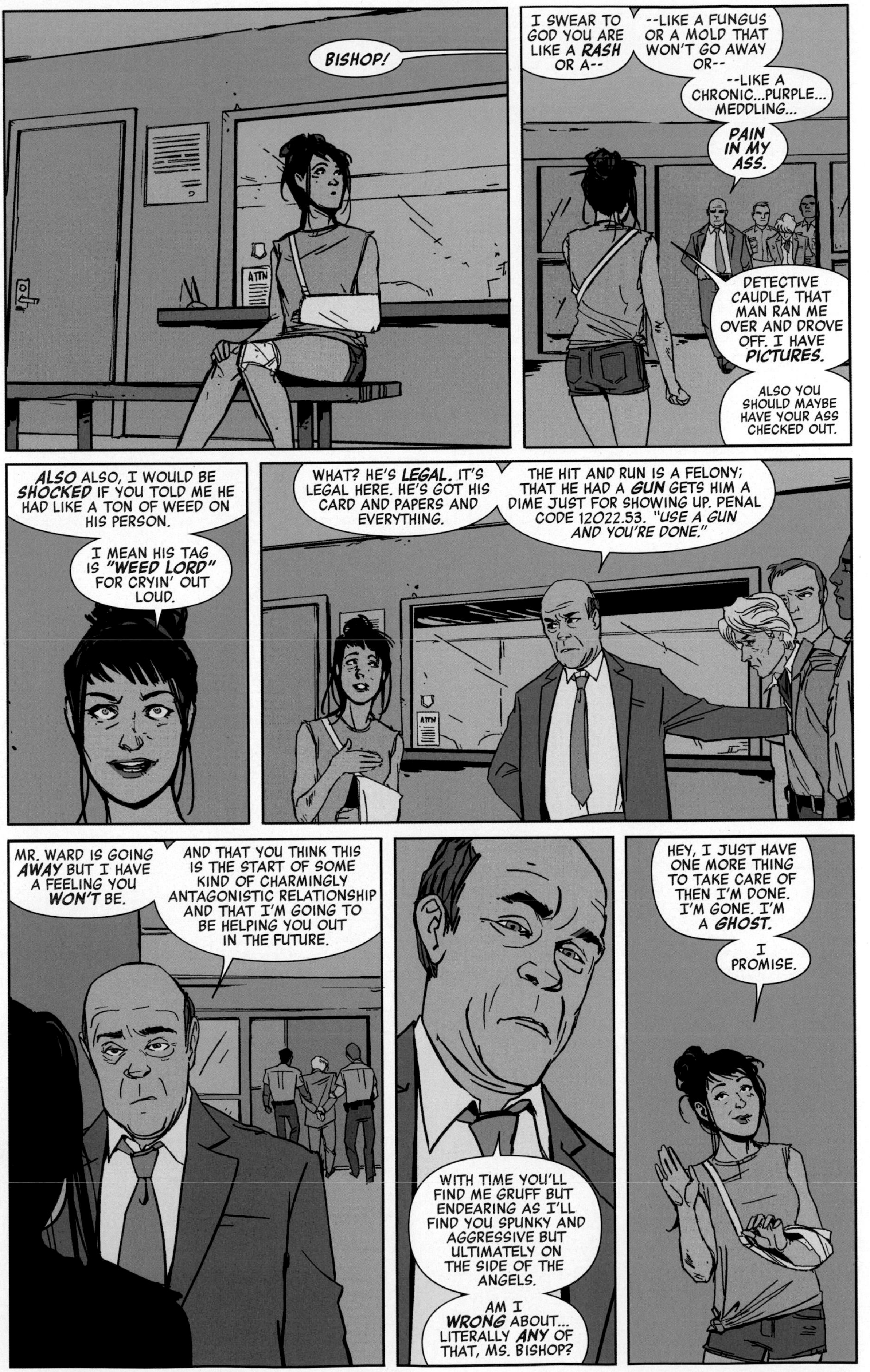
BISHOP!
I SWEAR TO GOD YOU ARE LIKE A RASH OR A--
--LIKE A FUNGUS OR A MOLD THAT WON'T GO AWAY OR--
--LIKE A CHRONIC...PURPLE... MEDDLING...
PAIN IN MY ASS.
DETECTIVE CAUDLE, THAT MAN RAN ME OVER AND DROVE OFF. I HAVE PICTURES.
ALSO YOU SHOULD MAYBE HAVE YOUR ASS CHECKED OUT.
ALSO ALSO, I WOULD BE SHOCKED IF YOU TOLD ME HE HAD LIKE A TON OF WEED ON HIS PERSON.
I MEAN HIS TAG IS "WEED LORD" FOR CRYIN' OUT LOUD.
WHAT? HE'S LEGAL. IT'S LEGAL HERE. HE'S GOT HIS CARD AND PAPERS AND EVERYTHING.
THE HIT AND RUN IS A FELONY; THAT HE HAD A GUN GETS HIM A DIME JUST FOR SHOWING UP. PENAL CODE 12022.53. "USE A GUN AND YOU'RE DONE."
MR. WARD IS GOING AWAY BUT I HAVE A FEELING YOU WON'T BE.
AND THAT YOU THINK THIS IS THE START OF SOME KIND OF CHARMINGLY ANTAGONISTIC RELATIONSHIP AND THAT I'M GOING TO BE HELPING YOU OUT IN THE FUTURE.
WITH TIME YOU'LL FIND ME GRUFF BUT ENDEARING AS I'LL FIND YOU SPUNKY AND AGGRESSIVE BUT ULTIMATELY ON THE SIDE OF THE ANGELS.
AM I WRONG ABOUT... LITERALLY ANY OF THAT, MS. BISHOP?
HEY, I JUST HAVE ONE MORE THING TO TAKE CARE OF THEN I'M DONE. I'M GONE. I'M A GHOST.
I PROMISE.

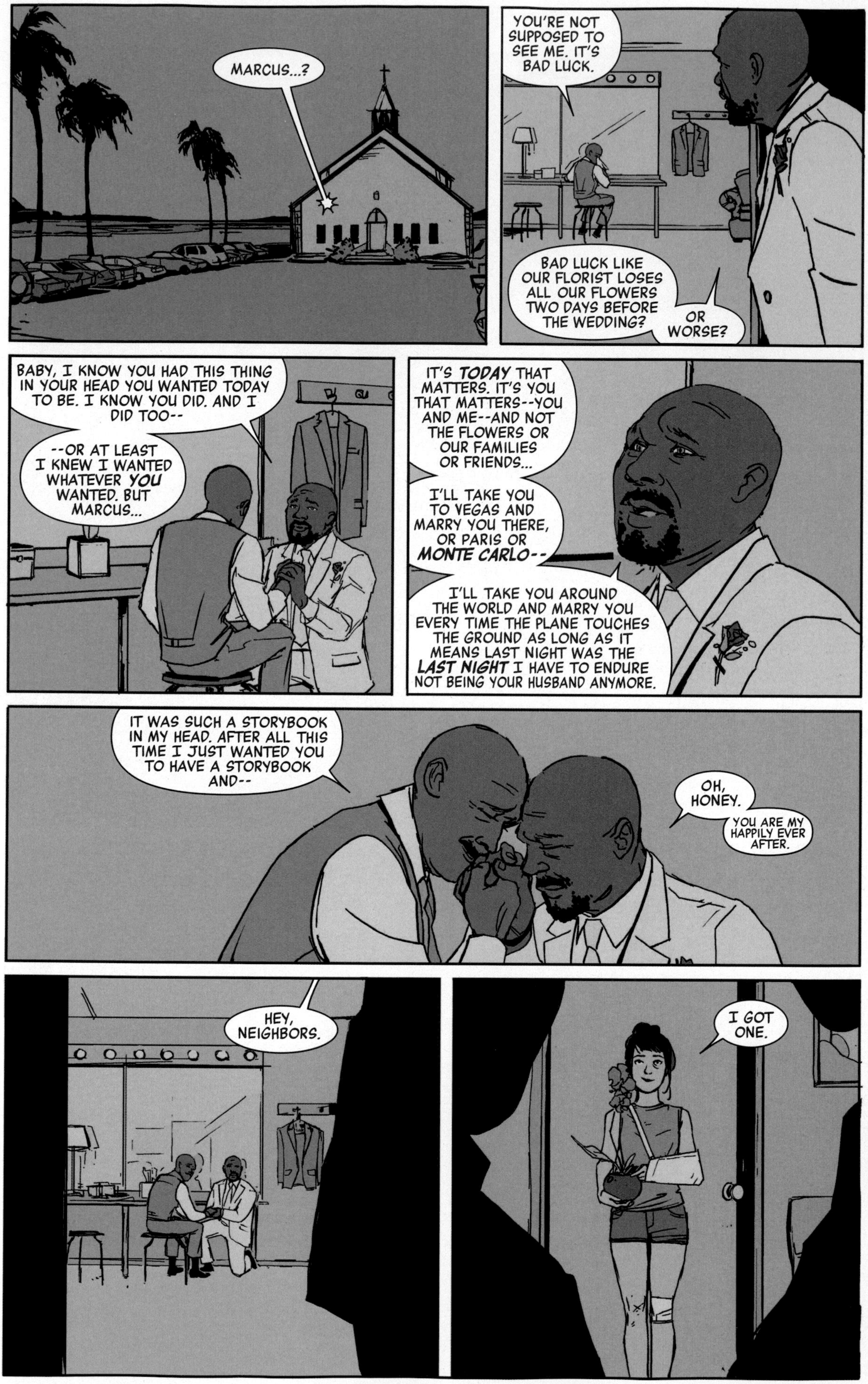
MARCUS...?
YOU'RE NOT SUPPOSED TO SEE ME. IT'S BAD LUCK.
BAD LUCK LIKE OUR FLORIST LOSES ALL OUR FLOWERS TWO DAYS BEFORE THE WEDDING?
OR WORSE?
BABY, I KNOW YOU HAD THIS THING IN YOUR HEAD YOU WANTED TODAY TO BE. I KNOW YOU DID. AND I DID TOO--
--OR AT LEAST I KNEW I WANTED WHATEVER YOU WANTED. BUT MARCUS...
IT'S TODAY THAT MATTERS. IT'S YOU THAT MATTERS--YOU AND ME--AND NOT THE FLOWERS OR OUR FAMILIES OR FRIENDS...
I'LL TAKE YOU TO VEGAS AND MARRY YOU THERE, OR PARIS OR MONTE CARLO--
I'LL TAKE YOU AROUND THE WORLD AND MARRY YOU EVERY TIME THE PLANE TOUCHES THE GROUND AS LONG AS IT MEANS LAST NIGHT WAS THE LAST NIGHT I HAVE TO ENDURE NOT BEING YOUR HUSBAND ANYMORE.
IT WAS SUCH A STORYBOOK IN MY HEAD. AFTER ALL THIS TIME I JUST WANTED YOU TO HAVE A STORYBOOK AND--
OH, HONEY.
YOU ARE MY HAPPILY EVER AFTER.
HEY, NEIGHBORS.
I GOT ONE.

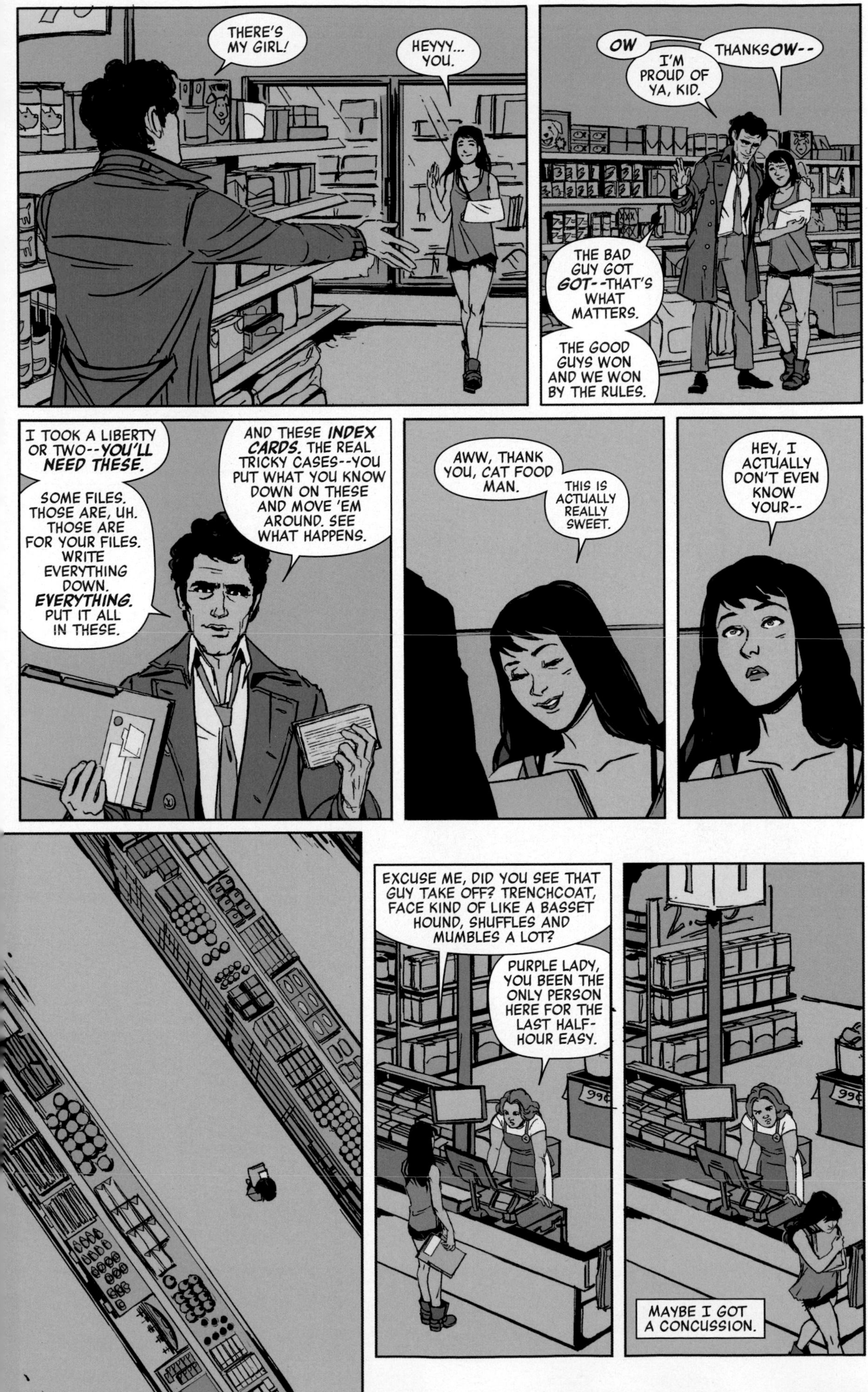
THERE'S MY GIRL!
HEYYY... YOU.
OW
I'M PROUD OF YA, KID.
THANKSOW--
THE BAD GUY GOT GOT--THAT'S WHAT MATTERS.
THE GOOD GUYS WON AND WE WON BY THE RULES.
I TOOK A LIBERTY OR TWO--YOU'LL NEED THESE.
SOME FILES. THOSE ARE, UH. THOSE ARE FOR YOUR FILES. WRITE EVERYTHING DOWN. EVERYTHING. PUT IT ALL IN THESE.
AND THESE INDEX CARDS. THE REAL TRICKY CASES--YOU PUT WHAT YOU KNOW DOWN ON THESE AND MOVE 'EM AROUND. SEE WHAT HAPPENS.
AWW, THANK YOU, CAT FOOD MAN.
THIS IS ACTUALLY REALLY SWEET.
HEY, I ACTUALLY DON'T EVEN KNOW YOUR--
EXCUSE ME, DID YOU SEE THAT GUY TAKE OFF? TRENCHCOAT, FACE KIND OF LIKE A BASSET HOUND, SHUFFLES AND MUMBLES A LOT?
PURPLE LADY, YOU BEEN THE ONLY PERSON HERE FOR THE LAST HALF-HOUR EASY.
99¢
MAYBE I GOT A CONCUSSION.

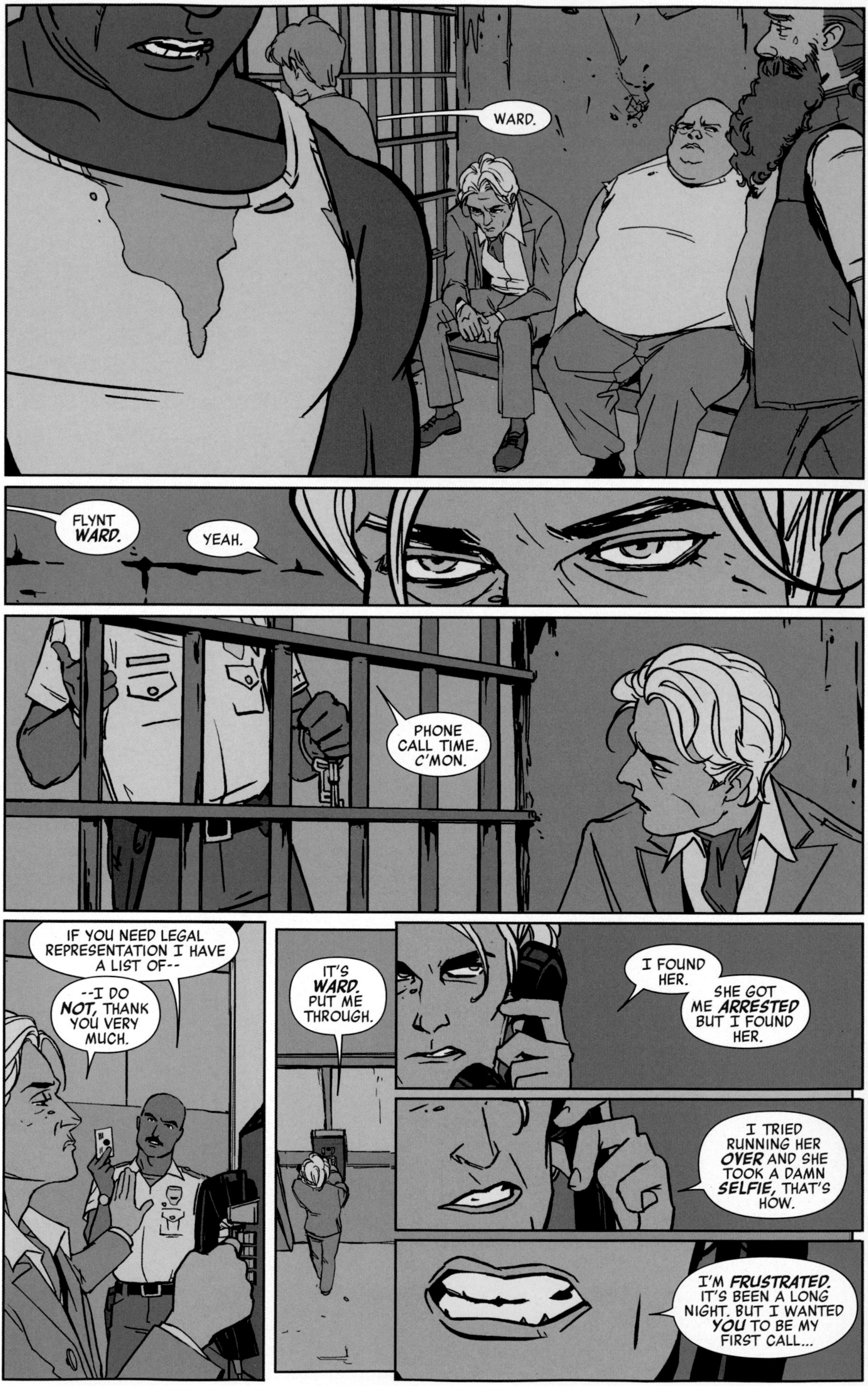
WARD.
FLYNT WARD.
YEAH.
PHONE CALL TIME. C'MON.
IF YOU NEED LEGAL REPRESENTATION I HAVE A LIST OF--
--I DO NOT, THANK YOU VERY MUCH.
IT'S WARD. PUT ME THROUGH.
I FOUND HER.
SHE GOT ME ARRESTED BUT I FOUND HER.
I TRIED RUNNING HER OVER AND SHE TOOK A DAMN SELFIE, THAT'S HOW.
I'M FRUSTRATED. IT'S BEEN A LONG NIGHT. BUT I WANTED YOU TO BE MY FIRST CALL...

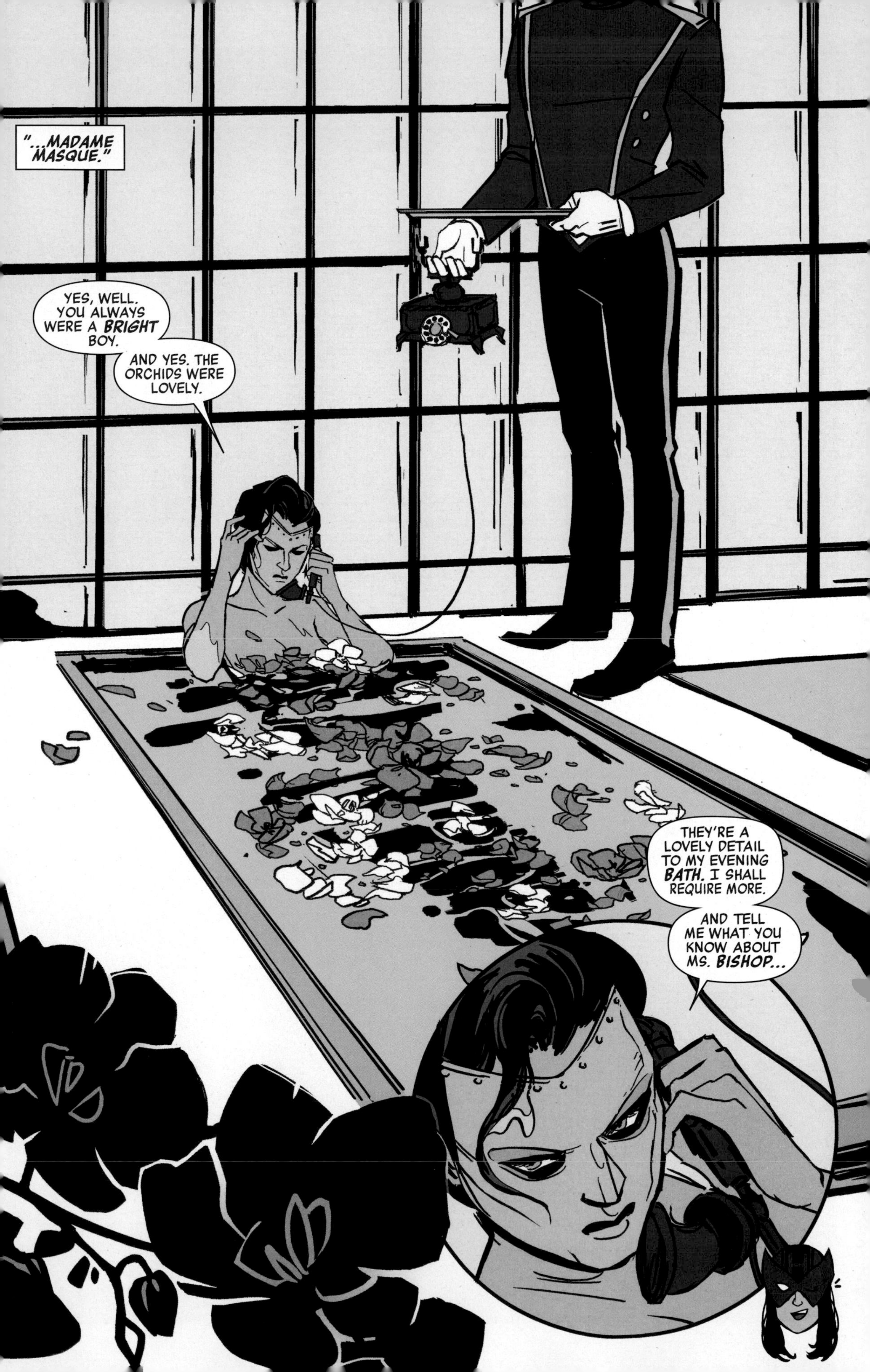
"...MADAME MASQUE."
YES, WELL. YOU ALWAYS WERE A BRIGHT BOY.
AND YES. THE ORCHIDS WERE LOVELY.
THEY'RE A LOVELY DETAIL TO MY EVENING BATH. I SHALL REQUIRE MORE.
AND TELL ME WHAT YOU KNOW ABOUT MS. BISHOP...

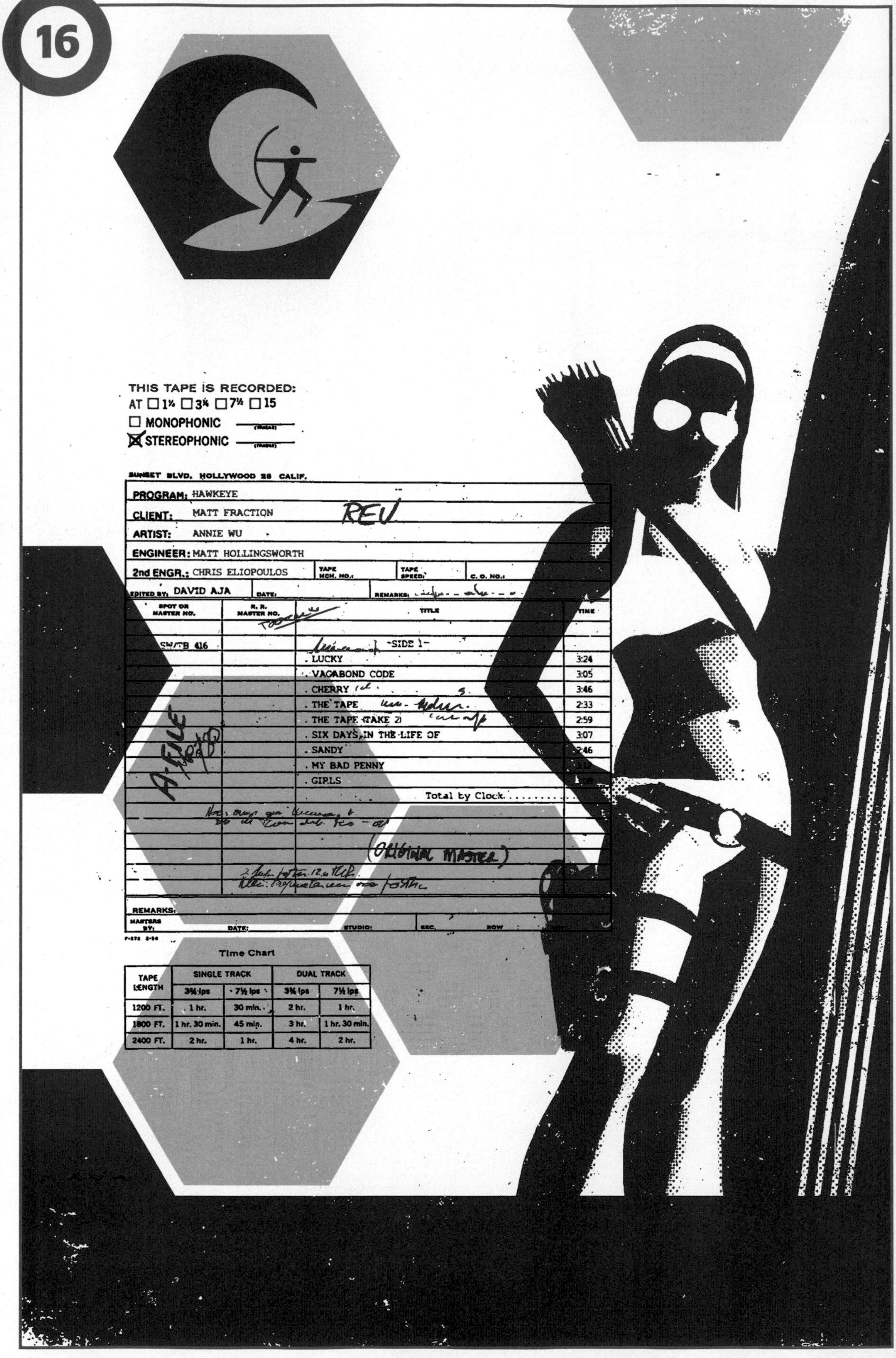
16
THIS TAPE IS RECORDED:
AT 1⅞ 3¾ 7½ 15
MONOPHONIC
STEREOPHONIC
SUNSET BLVD. HOLLYWOOD 28 CALIF.
PROGRAM: HAWKEYE
CLIENT: MATT FRACTION
REV
ARTIST: ANNIE WU
ENGINEER: MATT HOLLINGSWORTH
2nd ENGR.: CHRIS ELIOPOULOS
TAPE MCH. NO.:
TAPE SPEED:
C. O. NO.:
EDITED BY: DAVID AJA
DATE:
REMARKS:
SPOT OR MASTER NO.
R. R. MASTER NO.
TITLE
TIME
SW/TB 416
-SIDE 1-
LUCKY 3:24
VAGABOND CODE 3:05
CHERRY 3:46
THE TAPE 2:33
THE TAPE (TAKE 2) 2:59
SIX DAYS IN THE LIFE OF 3:07
SANDY
MY BAD PENNY
GIRLS
Total by Clock
A-SIDE
(ORIGINAL MASTER)
REMARKS:
MASTERS BY:
DATE:
STUDIO:
SEC.
ROW
Time Chart
TAPE LENGTH
SINGLE TRACK
DUAL TRACK
3¾ ips
7½ ips
3¾ ips
7½ ips
1200 FT. 1 hr. 30 min. 2 hr. 1 hr.
1800 FT. 1 hr. 30 min. 45 min. 3 hr. 1 hr. 30 min.
2400 FT. 2 hr. 1 hr. 4 hr. 2 hr.

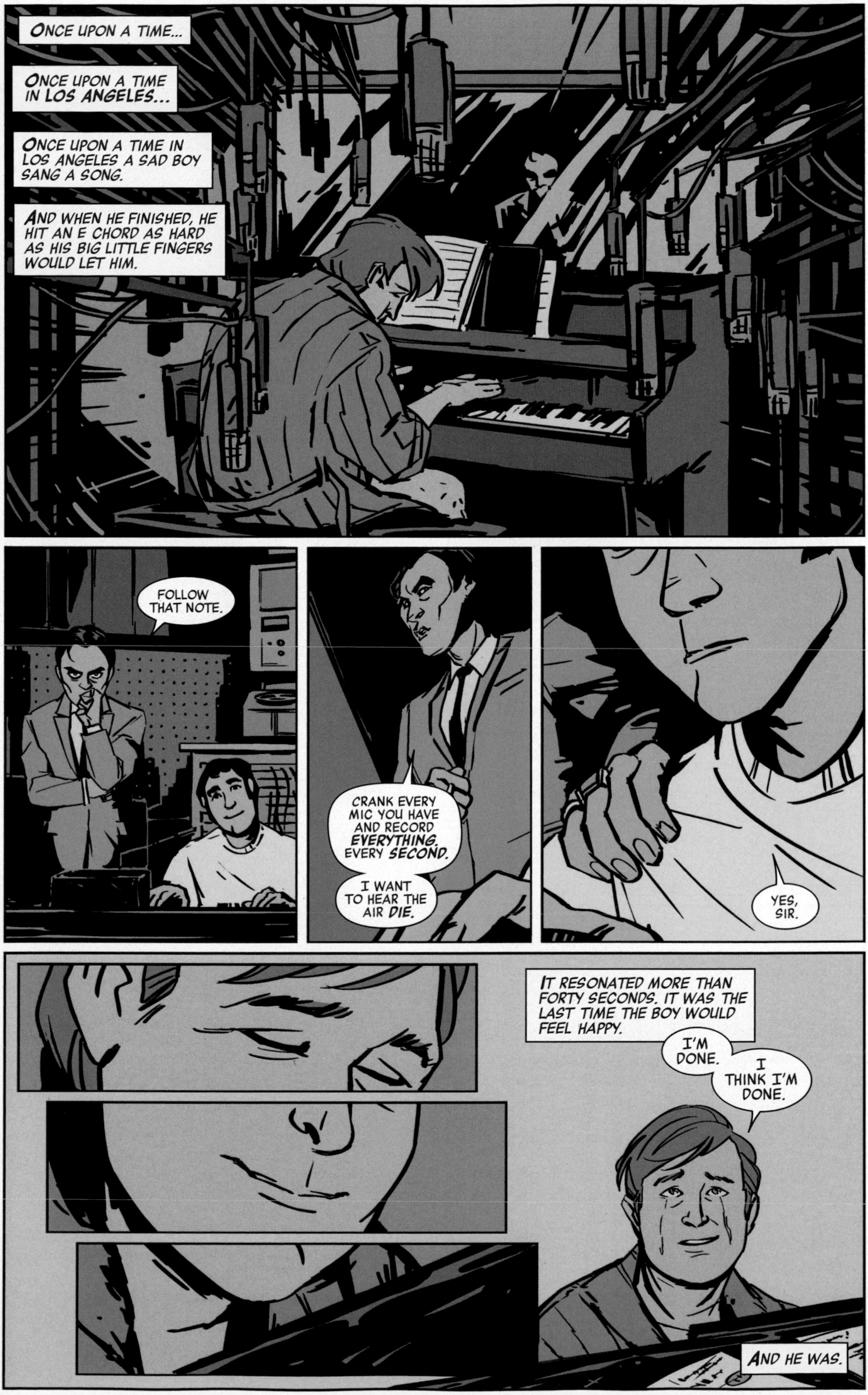
ONCE UPON A TIME...
ONCE UPON A TIME IN LOS ANGELES...
ONCE UPON A TIME IN LOS ANGELES A SAD BOY SANG A SONG.
AND WHEN HE FINISHED, HE HIT AN E CHORD AS HARD AS HIS BIG LITTLE FINGERS WOULD LET HIM.
FOLLOW THAT NOTE.
CRANK EVERY MIC YOU HAVE AND RECORD EVERYTHING. EVERY SECOND.
I WANT TO HEAR THE AIR DIE.
YES, SIR.
IT RESONATED MORE THAN FORTY SECONDS. IT WAS THE LAST TIME THE BOY WOULD FEEL HAPPY.
I'M DONE.
I THINK I'M DONE.
AND HE WAS.

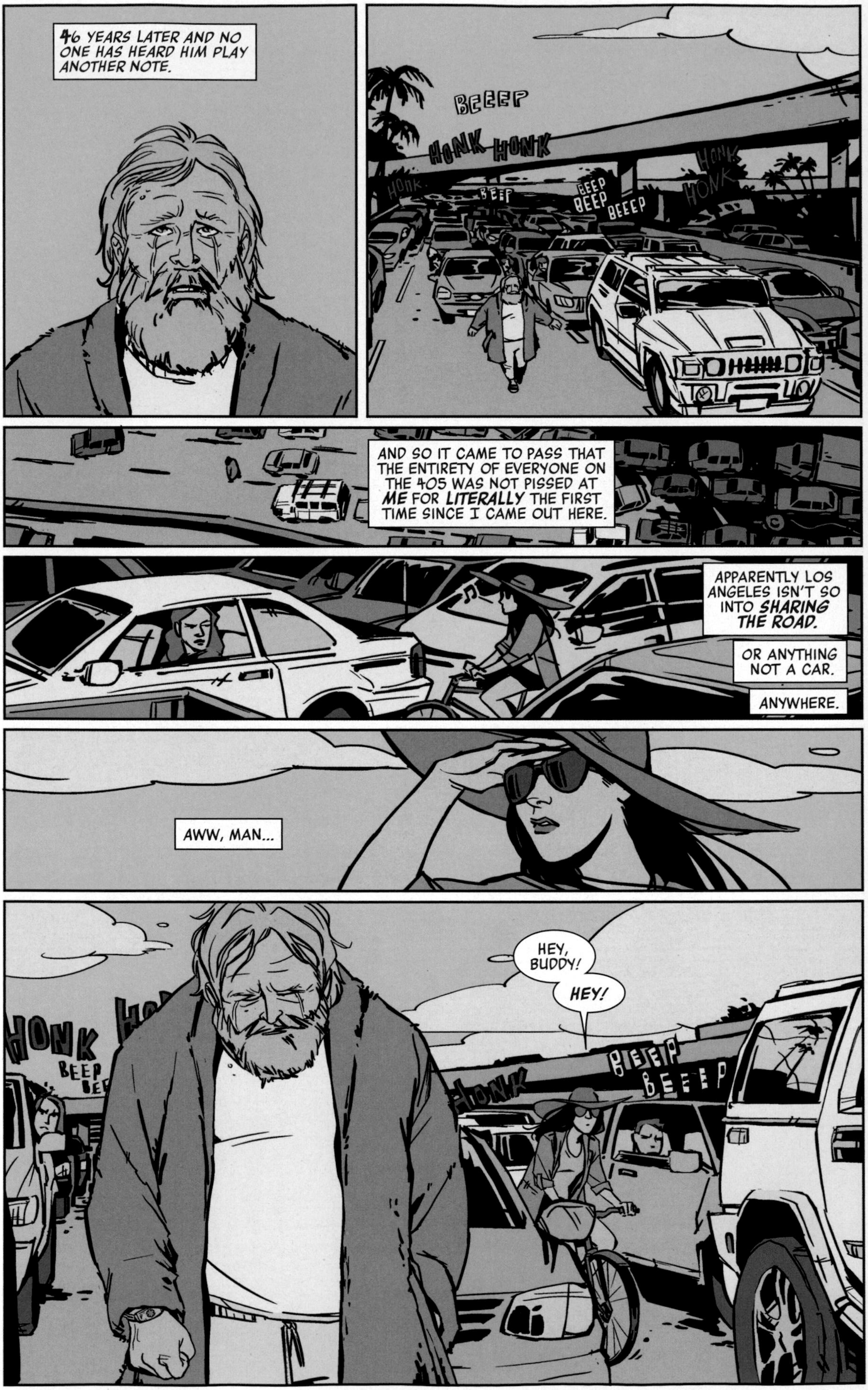
46 YEARS LATER AND NO ONE HAS HEARD HIM PLAY ANOTHER NOTE.
BEEEP
HONK HONK
HONK
BEEP
BEEP BEEP
BEEEP
HONK HONK
AND SO IT CAME TO PASS THAT THE ENTIRETY OF EVERYONE ON THE 405 WAS NOT PISSED AT ME FOR LITERALLY THE FIRST TIME SINCE I CAME OUT HERE.
APPARENTLY LOS ANGELES ISN'T SO INTO SHARING THE ROAD.
OR ANYTHING NOT A CAR.
ANYWHERE.
AWW, MAN...
HEY, BUDDY!
HEY!
HONK
BEEP
HONK
BEEP
BEEEP

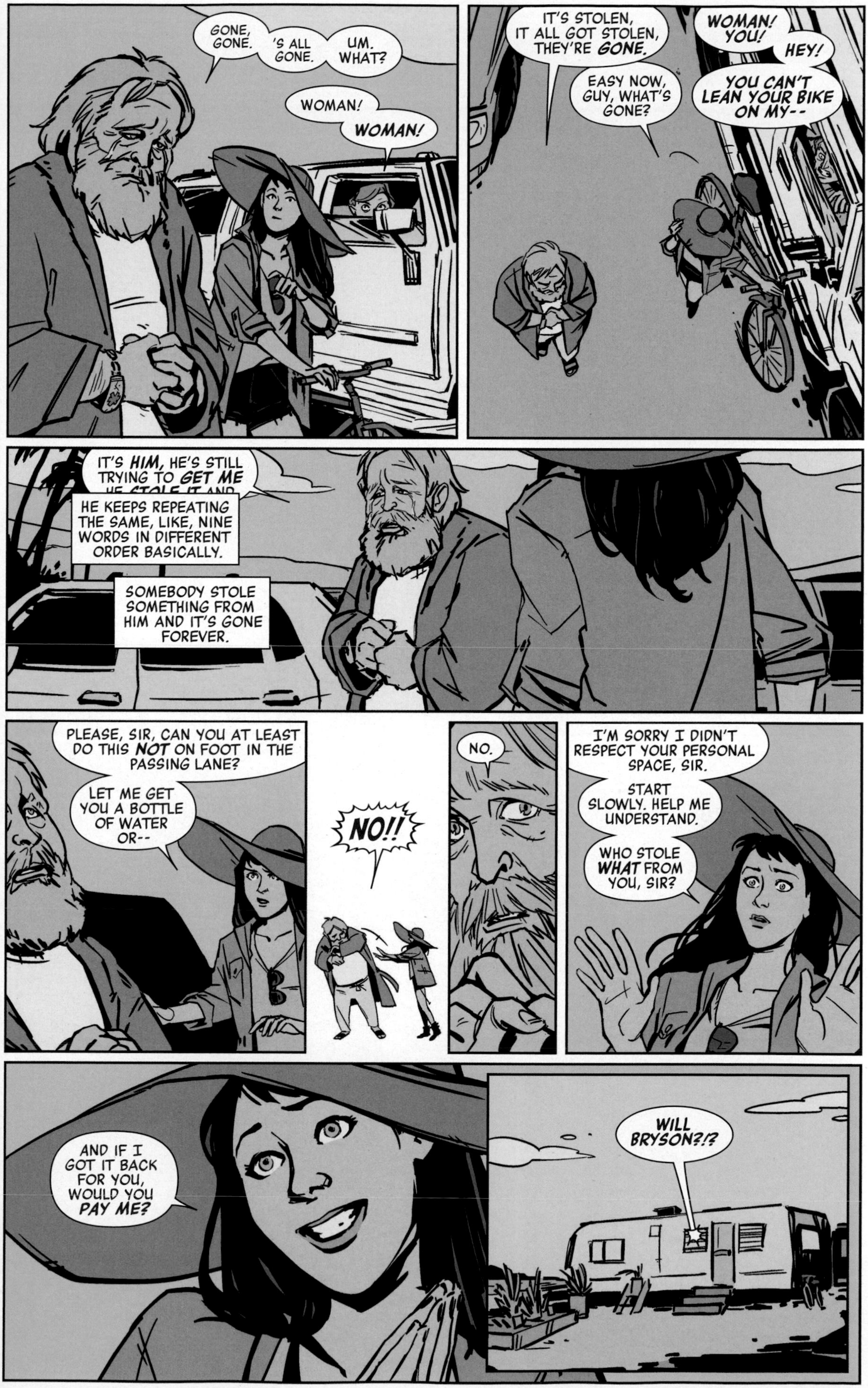
GONE, GONE.
'S ALL GONE.
UM. WHAT?
WOMAN!
WOMAN!
IT'S STOLEN, IT ALL GOT STOLEN, THEY'RE GONE.
EASY NOW, GUY, WHAT'S GONE?
WOMAN! YOU!
HEY!
YOU CAN'T LEAN YOUR BIKE ON MY--
IT'S HIM, HE'S STILL TRYING TO GET ME
HE KEEPS REPEATING THE SAME, LIKE, NINE WORDS IN DIFFERENT ORDER BASICALLY.
SOMEBODY STOLE SOMETHING FROM HIM AND IT'S GONE FOREVER.
PLEASE, SIR, CAN YOU AT LEAST DO THIS NOT ON FOOT IN THE PASSING LANE?
LET ME GET YOU A BOTTLE OF WATER OR--
NO!!
NO.
I'M SORRY I DIDN'T RESPECT YOUR PERSONAL SPACE, SIR.
START SLOWLY. HELP ME UNDERSTAND.
WHO STOLE WHAT FROM YOU, SIR?
AND IF I GOT IT BACK FOR YOU, WOULD YOU PAY ME?
WILL BRYSON?!?

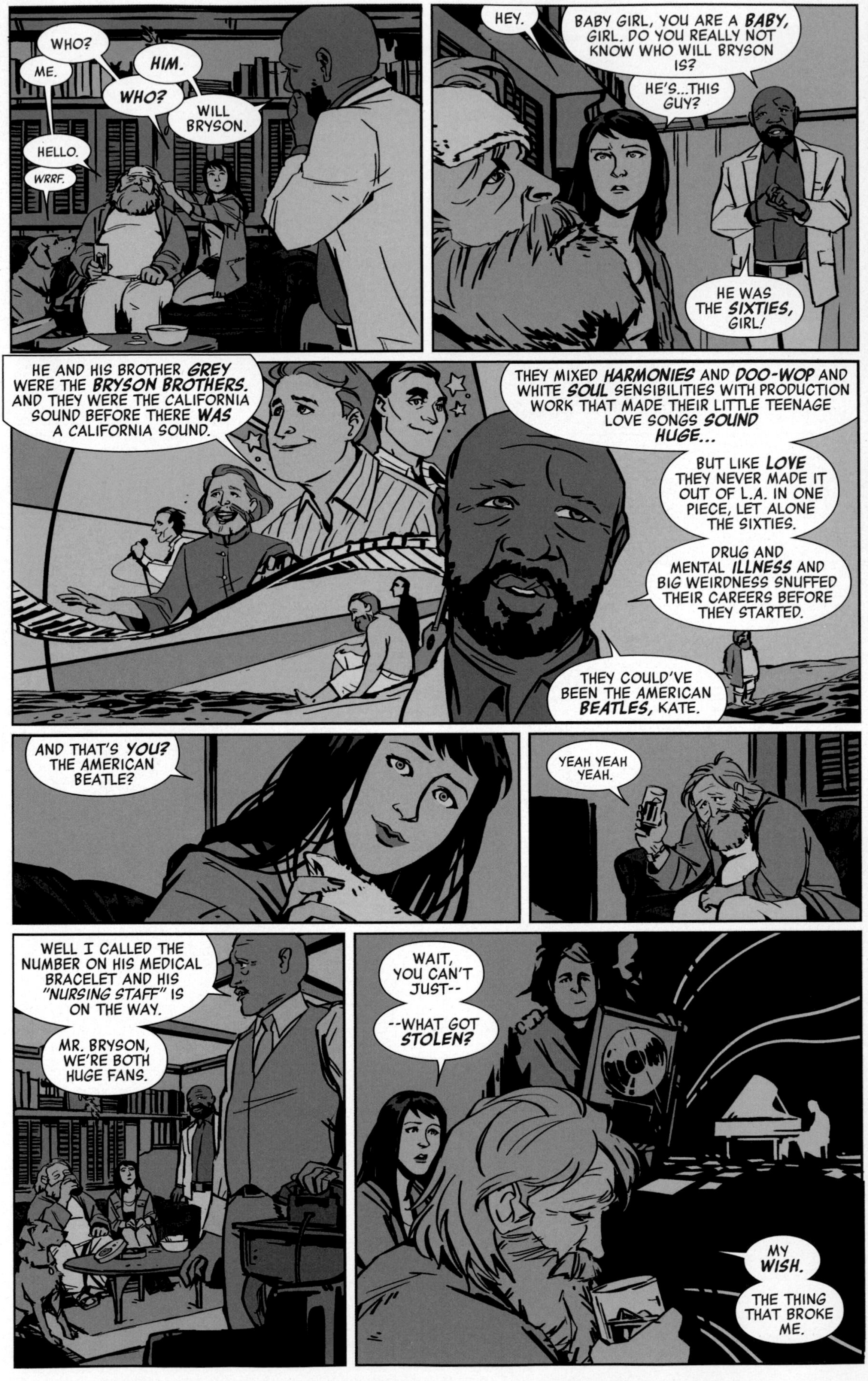
WHO?
ME.
HIM.
WHO?
WILL BRYSON.
HELLO.
WRRF.
HEY.
BABY GIRL, YOU ARE A BABY, GIRL. DO YOU REALLY NOT KNOW WHO WILL BRYSON IS?
HE'S...THIS GUY?
HE WAS THE SIXTIES, GIRL!
HE AND HIS BROTHER GREY WERE THE BRYSON BROTHERS. AND THEY WERE THE CALIFORNIA SOUND BEFORE THERE WAS A CALIFORNIA SOUND.
THEY MIXED HARMONIES AND DOO-WOP AND WHITE SOUL SENSIBILITIES WITH PRODUCTION WORK THAT MADE THEIR LITTLE TEENAGE LOVE SONGS SOUND HUGE...
BUT LIKE LOVE THEY NEVER MADE IT OUT OF L.A. IN ONE PIECE, LET ALONE THE SIXTIES.
DRUG AND MENTAL ILLNESS AND BIG WEIRDNESS SNUFFED THEIR CAREERS BEFORE THEY STARTED.
THEY COULD'VE BEEN THE AMERICAN BEATLES, KATE.
AND THAT'S YOU? THE AMERICAN BEATLE?
YEAH YEAH YEAH.
WELL I CALLED THE NUMBER ON HIS MEDICAL BRACELET AND HIS "NURSING STAFF" IS ON THE WAY.
MR. BRYSON, WE'RE BOTH HUGE FANS.
WAIT, YOU CAN'T JUST--
--WHAT GOT STOLEN?
MY WISH.
THE THING THAT BROKE ME.

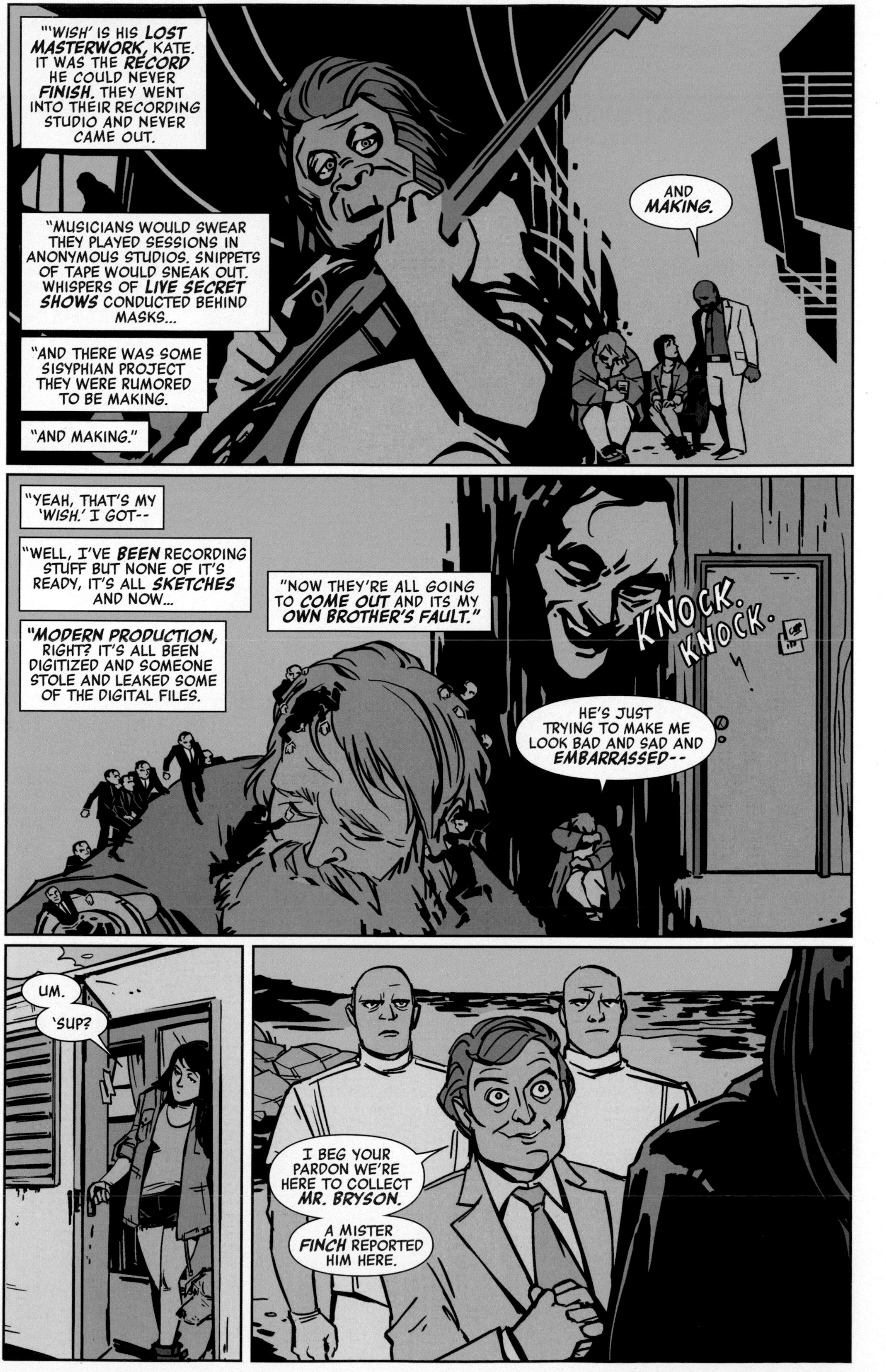
"'WISH' IS HIS LOST MASTERWORK, KATE. IT WAS THE RECORD HE COULD NEVER FINISH. THEY WENT INTO THEIR RECORDING STUDIO AND NEVER CAME OUT.
"MUSICIANS WOULD SWEAR THEY PLAYED SESSIONS IN ANONYMOUS STUDIOS. SNIPPETS OF TAPE WOULD SNEAK OUT. WHISPERS OF LIVE SECRET SHOWS CONDUCTED BEHIND MASKS...
"AND THERE WAS SOME SISYPHIAN PROJECT THEY WERE RUMORED TO BE MAKING.
"AND MAKING."
AND MAKING.
"YEAH, THAT'S MY 'WISH.' I GOT--
"WELL, I'VE BEEN RECORDING STUFF BUT NONE OF IT'S READY, IT'S ALL SKETCHES AND NOW...
"MODERN PRODUCTION, RIGHT? IT'S ALL BEEN DIGITIZED AND SOMEONE STOLE AND LEAKED SOME OF THE DIGITAL FILES.
"NOW THEY'RE ALL GOING TO COME OUT AND ITS MY OWN BROTHER'S FAULT."
KNOCK. KNOCK.
HE'S JUST TRYING TO MAKE ME LOOK BAD AND SAD AND EMBARRASSED--
UM.
'SUP?
I BEG YOUR PARDON WE'RE HERE TO COLLECT MR. BRYSON.
A MISTER FINCH REPORTED HIM HERE.

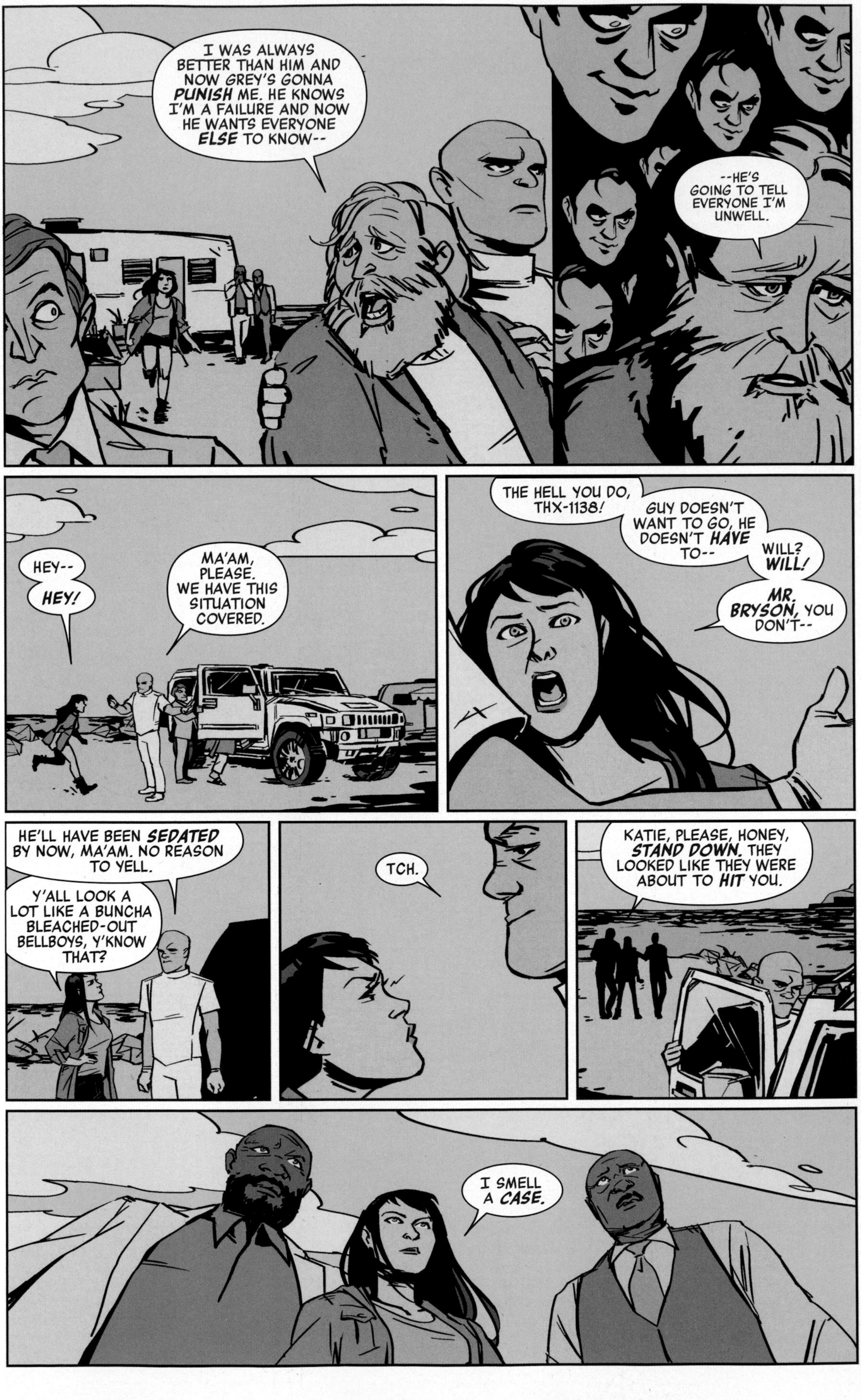
I WAS ALWAYS BETTER THAN HIM AND NOW GREY'S GONNA PUNISH ME. HE KNOWS I'M A FAILURE AND NOW HE WANTS EVERYONE ELSE TO KNOW--
--HE'S GOING TO TELL EVERYONE I'M UNWELL.
HEY--
HEY!
MA'AM, PLEASE. WE HAVE THIS SITUATION COVERED.
THE HELL YOU DO, THX-1138!
GUY DOESN'T WANT TO GO, HE DOESN'T HAVE TO--
WILL? WILL!
MR. BRYSON, YOU DON'T--
HE'LL HAVE BEEN SEDATED BY NOW, MA'AM. NO REASON TO YELL.
Y'ALL LOOK A LOT LIKE A BUNCHA BLEACHED-OUT BELLBOYS, Y'KNOW THAT?
TCH.
KATIE, PLEASE, HONEY, STAND DOWN. THEY LOOKED LIKE THEY WERE ABOUT TO HIT YOU.
I SMELL A CASE.

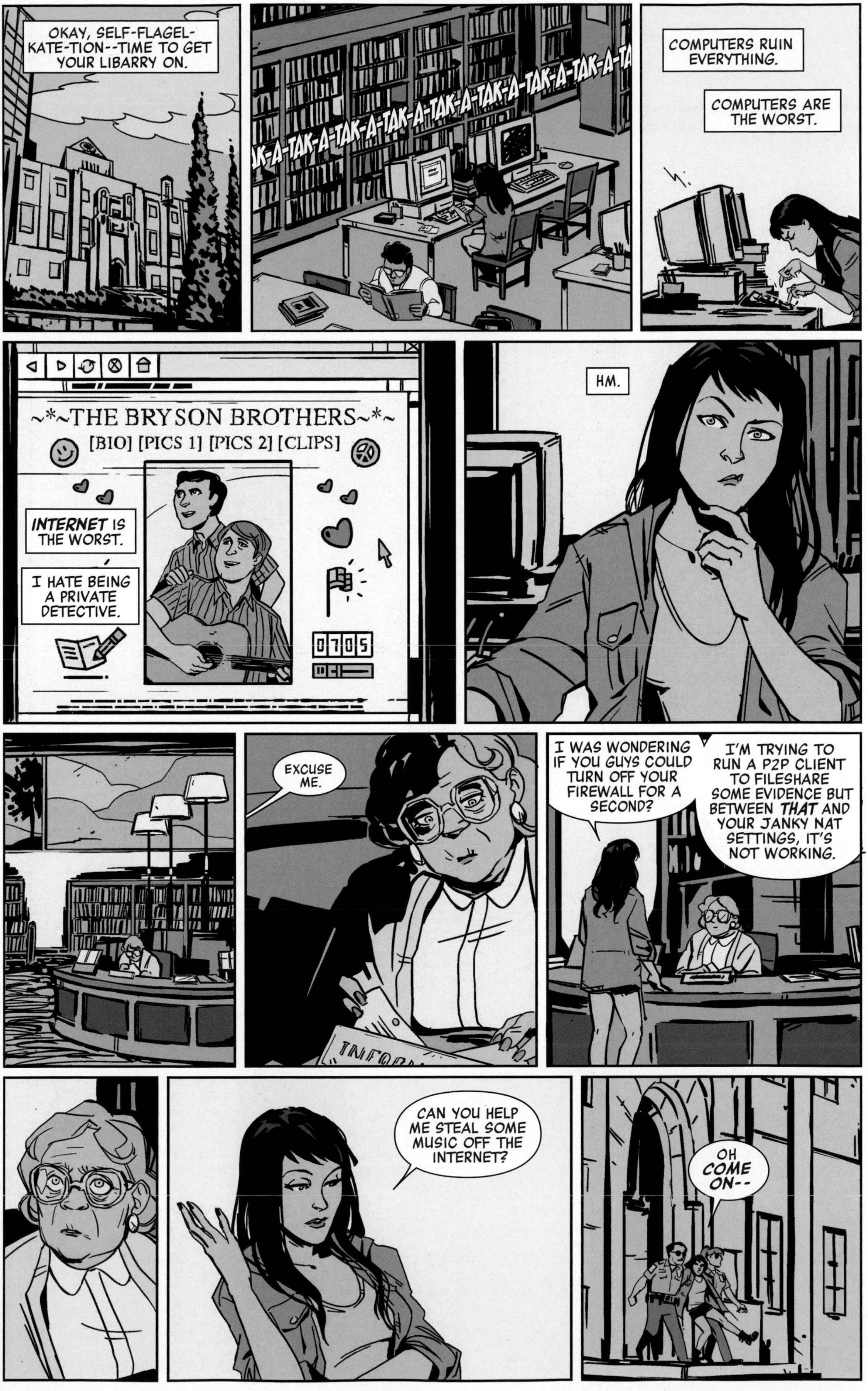
OKAY, SELF-FLAGEL-KATE-TION--TIME TO GET YOUR LIBARRY ON.
-AK-A-TAK-A-TAK-A-TAK-A-TAK-A-TAK-A-TAK-A-TAK-A-TAK-A-TA
COMPUTERS RUIN EVERYTHING.
COMPUTERS ARE THE WORST.
~*~THE BRYSON BROTHERS~*~
[BIO] [PICS 1] [PICS 2] [CLIPS]
INTERNET IS THE WORST.
I HATE BEING A PRIVATE DETECTIVE.
0705
HM.
EXCUSE ME.
I WAS WONDERING IF YOU GUYS COULD TURN OFF YOUR FIREWALL FOR A SECOND?
I'M TRYING TO RUN A P2P CLIENT TO FILESHARE SOME EVIDENCE BUT BETWEEN THAT AND YOUR JANKY NAT SETTINGS, IT'S NOT WORKING.
CAN YOU HELP ME STEAL SOME MUSIC OFF THE INTERNET?
OH COME ON--

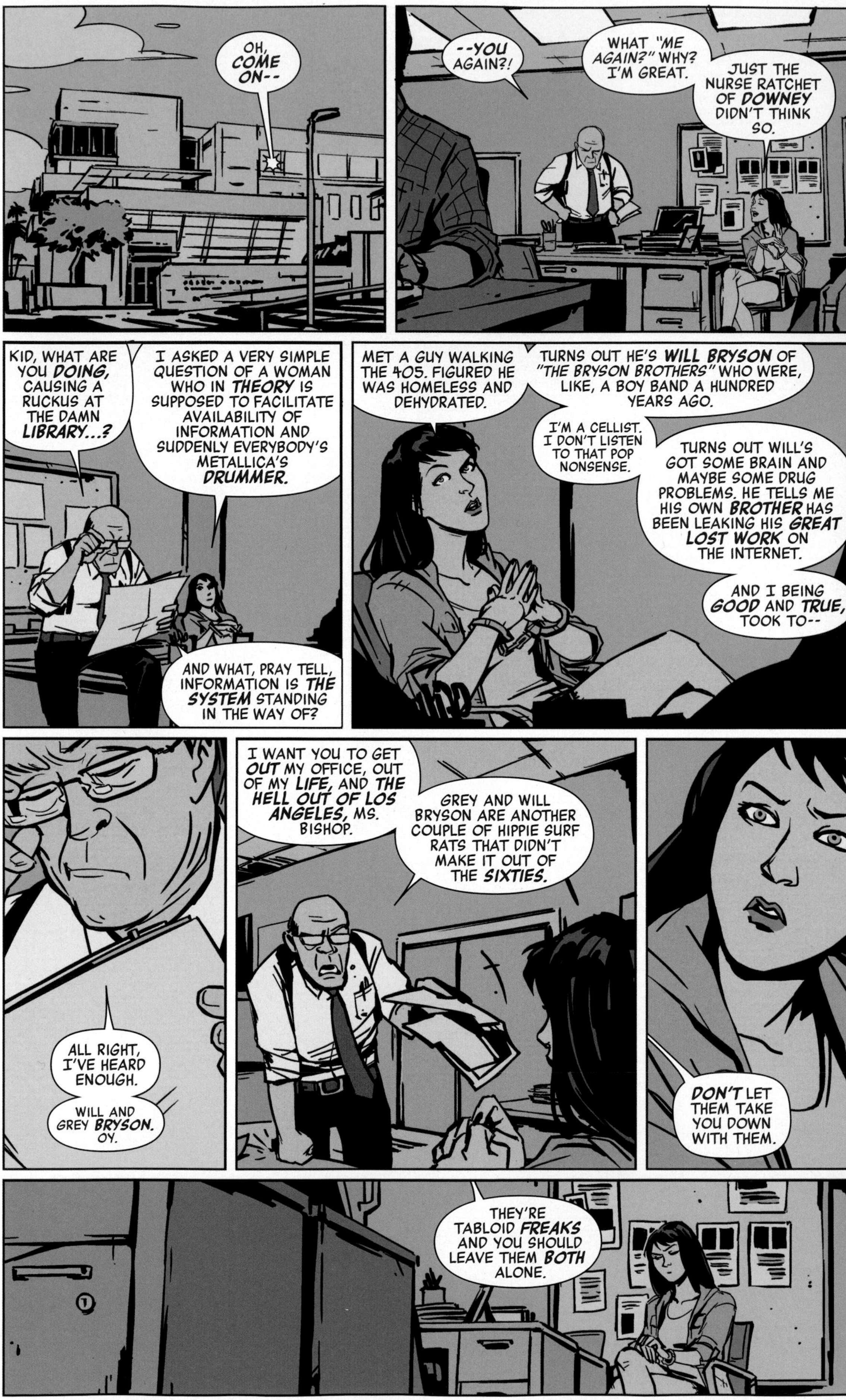
OH, COME ON--
--YOU AGAIN?!
WHAT "ME AGAIN?" WHY? I'M GREAT.
JUST THE NURSE RATCHET OF DOWNEY DIDN'T THINK SO.
KID, WHAT ARE YOU DOING, CAUSING A RUCKUS AT THE DAMN LIBRARY...?
I ASKED A VERY SIMPLE QUESTION OF A WOMAN WHO IN THEORY IS SUPPOSED TO FACILITATE AVAILABILITY OF INFORMATION AND SUDDENLY EVERYBODY'S METALLICA'S DRUMMER.
AND WHAT, PRAY TELL, INFORMATION IS THE SYSTEM STANDING IN THE WAY OF?
MET A GUY WALKING THE 405. FIGURED HE WAS HOMELESS AND DEHYDRATED.
TURNS OUT HE'S WILL BRYSON OF "THE BRYSON BROTHERS" WHO WERE, LIKE, A BOY BAND A HUNDRED YEARS AGO.
I'M A CELLIST. I DON'T LISTEN TO THAT POP NONSENSE.
TURNS OUT WILL'S GOT SOME BRAIN AND MAYBE SOME DRUG PROBLEMS. HE TELLS ME HIS OWN BROTHER HAS BEEN LEAKING HIS GREAT LOST WORK ON THE INTERNET.
AND I BEING GOOD AND TRUE, TOOK TO--
ALL RIGHT, I'VE HEARD ENOUGH.
WILL AND GREY BRYSON. OY.
I WANT YOU TO GET OUT MY OFFICE, OUT OF MY LIFE, AND THE HELL OUT OF LOS ANGELES, MS. BISHOP.
GREY AND WILL BRYSON ARE ANOTHER COUPLE OF HIPPIE SURF RATS THAT DIDN'T MAKE IT OUT OF THE SIXTIES.
DON'T LET THEM TAKE YOU DOWN WITH THEM.
THEY'RE TABLOID FREAKS AND YOU SHOULD LEAVE THEM BOTH ALONE.

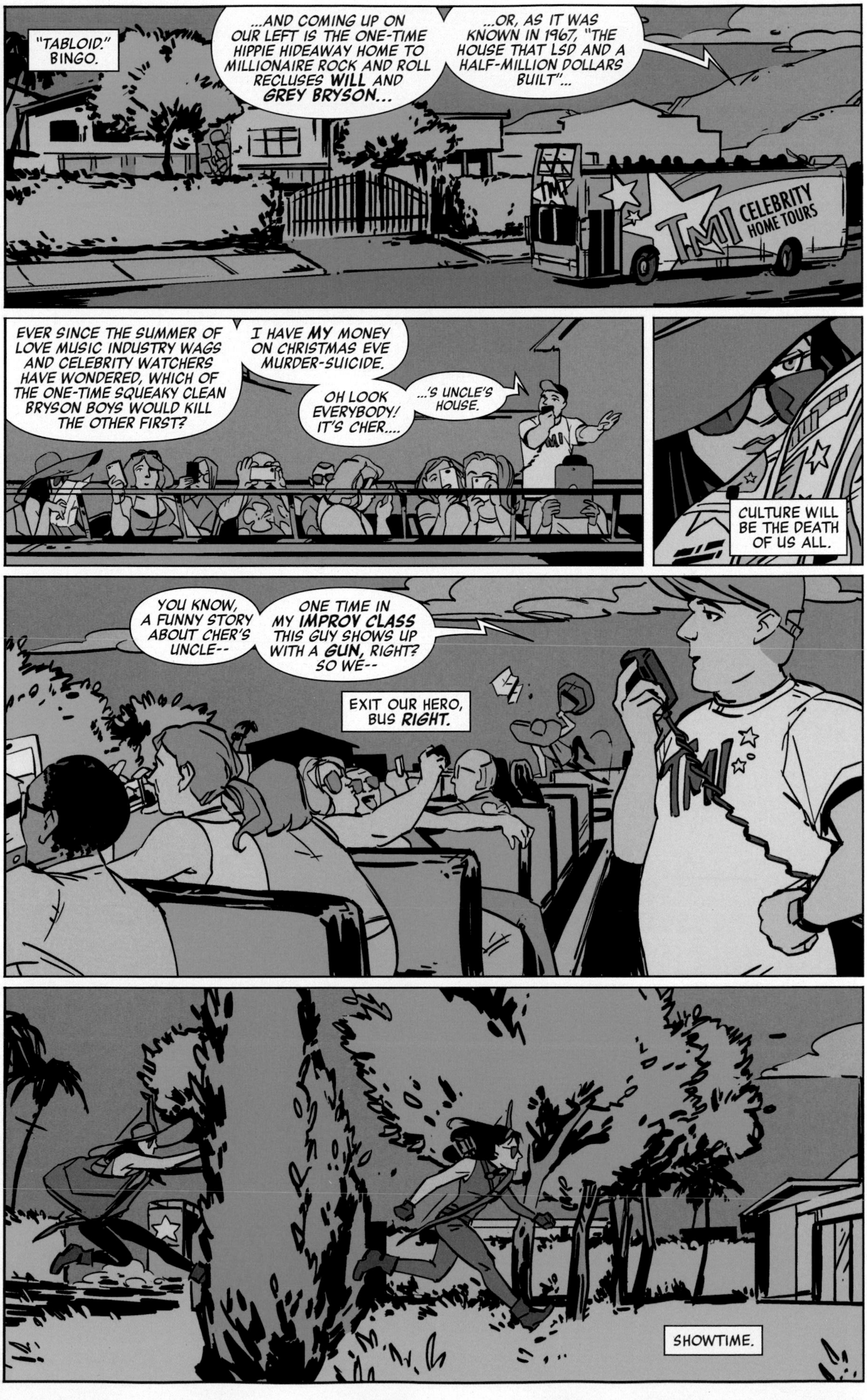
"TABLOID." BINGO.
...AND COMING UP ON OUR LEFT IS THE ONE-TIME HIPPIE HIDEAWAY HOME TO MILLIONAIRE ROCK AND ROLL RECLUSES WILL AND GREY BRYSON...
...OR, AS IT WAS KNOWN IN 1967, "THE HOUSE THAT LSD AND A HALF-MILLION DOLLARS BUILT"...
TMI CELEBRITY HOME TOURS
EVER SINCE THE SUMMER OF LOVE MUSIC INDUSTRY WAGS AND CELEBRITY WATCHERS HAVE WONDERED, WHICH OF THE ONE-TIME SQUEAKY CLEAN BRYSON BOYS WOULD KILL THE OTHER FIRST?
I HAVE MY MONEY ON CHRISTMAS EVE MURDER-SUICIDE.
OH LOOK EVERYBODY! IT'S CHER....
...'S UNCLE'S HOUSE.
CULTURE WILL BE THE DEATH OF US ALL.
YOU KNOW, A FUNNY STORY ABOUT CHER'S UNCLE--
ONE TIME IN MY IMPROV CLASS THIS GUY SHOWS UP WITH A GUN, RIGHT? SO WE--
EXIT OUR HERO, BUS RIGHT.
SHOWTIME.

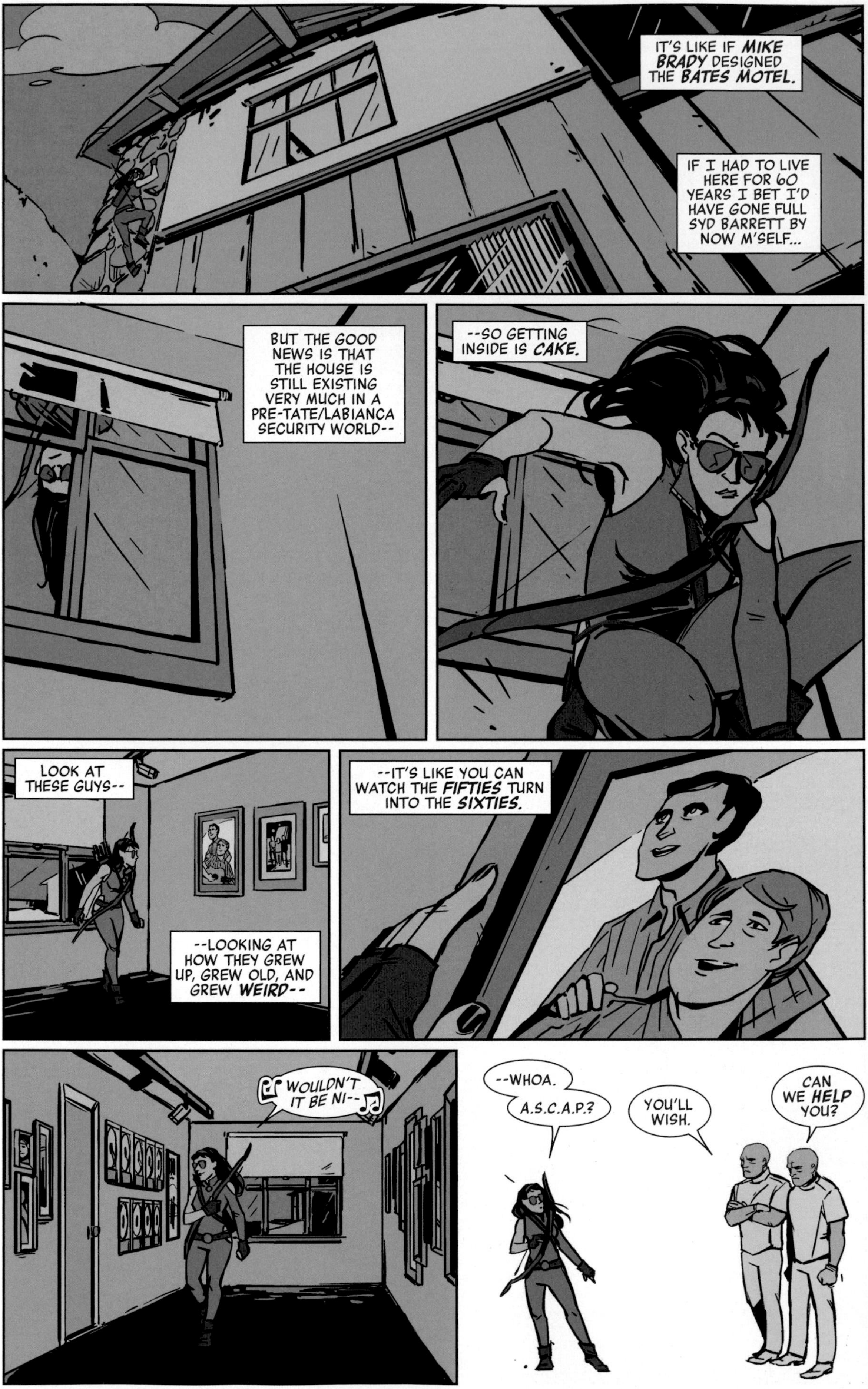
IT'S LIKE IF MIKE BRADY DESIGNED THE BATES MOTEL.
IF I HAD TO LIVE HERE FOR 60 YEARS I BET I'D HAVE GONE FULL SYD BARRETT BY NOW M'SELF...
BUT THE GOOD NEWS IS THAT THE HOUSE IS STILL EXISTING VERY MUCH IN A PRE-TATE/LABIANCA SECURITY WORLD--
--SO GETTING INSIDE IS CAKE.
LOOK AT THESE GUYS--
--LOOKING AT HOW THEY GREW UP, GREW OLD, AND GREW WEIRD--
--IT'S LIKE YOU CAN WATCH THE FIFTIES TURN INTO THE SIXTIES.
WOULDN'T IT BE NI--
--WHOA. A.S.C.A.P.?
YOU'LL WISH.
CAN WE HELP YOU?

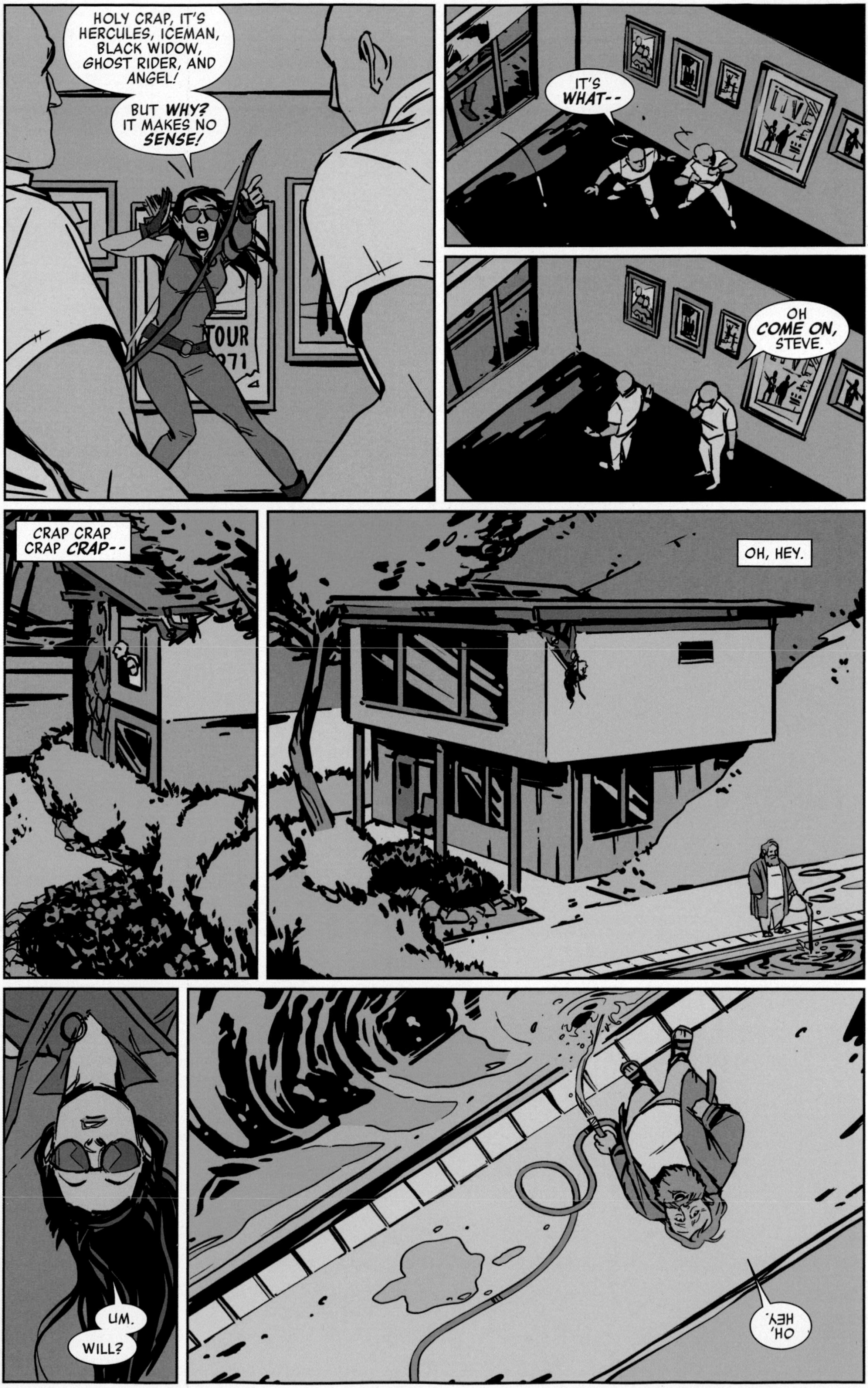

HOLY CRAP, IT'S HERCULES, ICEMAN, BLACK WIDOW, GHOST RIDER, AND ANGEL!
BUT WHY? IT MAKES NO SENSE!
TOUR
IT'S WHAT--
OH COME ON, STEVE.
CRAP CRAP CRAP CRAP--
OH, HEY.
UM.
WILL?
OH, HEY.

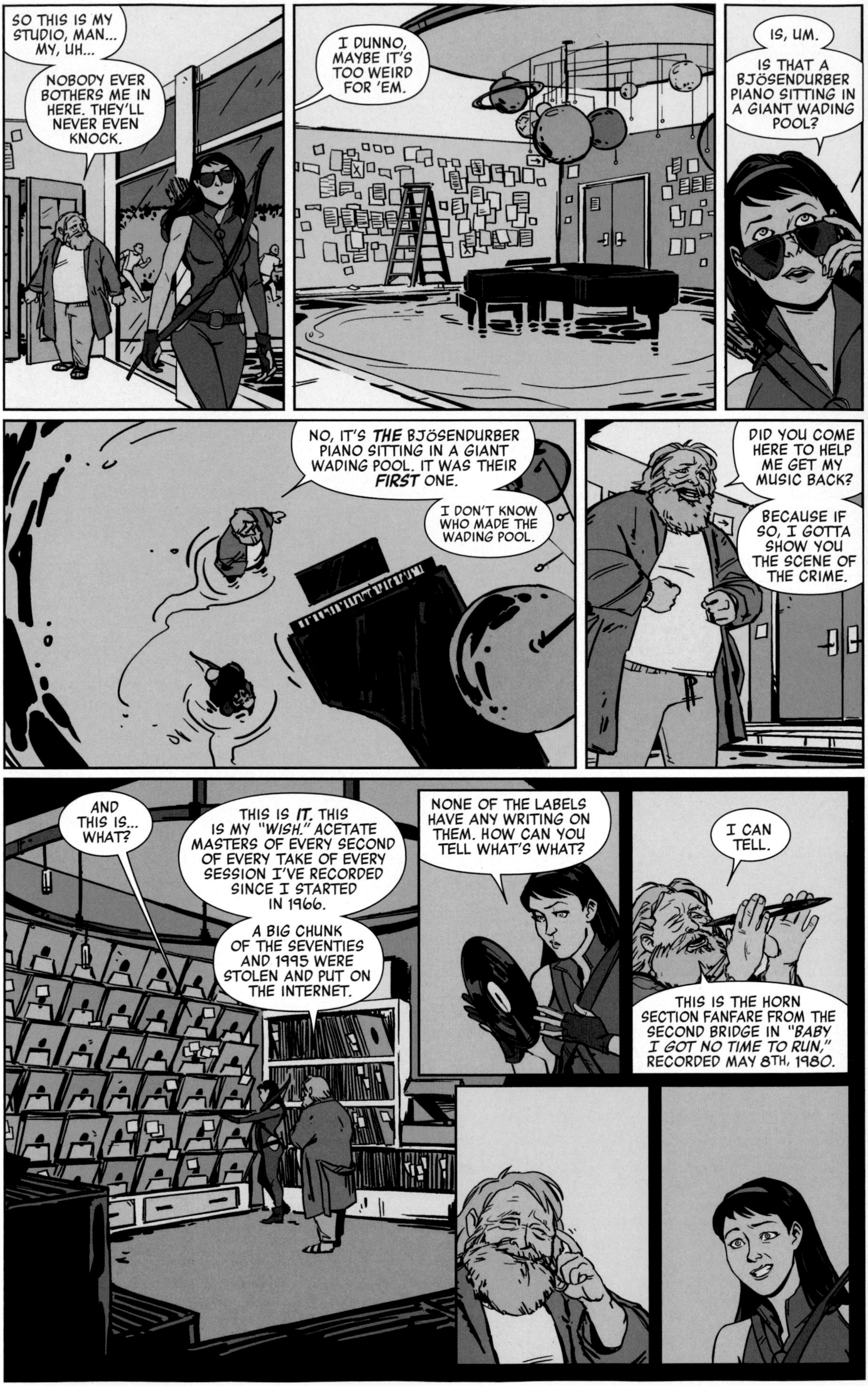
SO THIS IS MY STUDIO, MAN... MY, UH...
NOBODY EVER BOTHERS ME IN HERE. THEY'LL NEVER EVEN KNOCK.
I DUNNO, MAYBE IT'S TOO WEIRD FOR 'EM.
IS, UM.
IS THAT A BJÖSENDURBER PIANO SITTING IN A GIANT WADING POOL?
NO, IT'S *THE* BJÖSENDURBER PIANO SITTING IN A GIANT WADING POOL. IT WAS THEIR *FIRST* ONE.
I DON'T KNOW WHO MADE THE WADING POOL.
DID YOU COME HERE TO HELP ME GET MY MUSIC BACK?
BECAUSE IF SO, I GOTTA SHOW YOU THE SCENE OF THE CRIME.
AND THIS IS... WHAT?
THIS IS *IT.* THIS IS MY *"WISH."* ACETATE MASTERS OF EVERY SECOND OF EVERY TAKE OF EVERY SESSION I'VE RECORDED SINCE I STARTED IN 1966.
A BIG CHUNK OF THE SEVENTIES AND 1995 WERE STOLEN AND PUT ON THE INTERNET.
NONE OF THE LABELS HAVE ANY WRITING ON THEM. HOW CAN YOU TELL WHAT'S WHAT?
I CAN TELL.
THIS IS THE HORN SECTION FANFARE FROM THE SECOND BRIDGE IN *"BABY I GOT NO TIME TO RUN,"* RECORDED MAY 8TH, 1980.

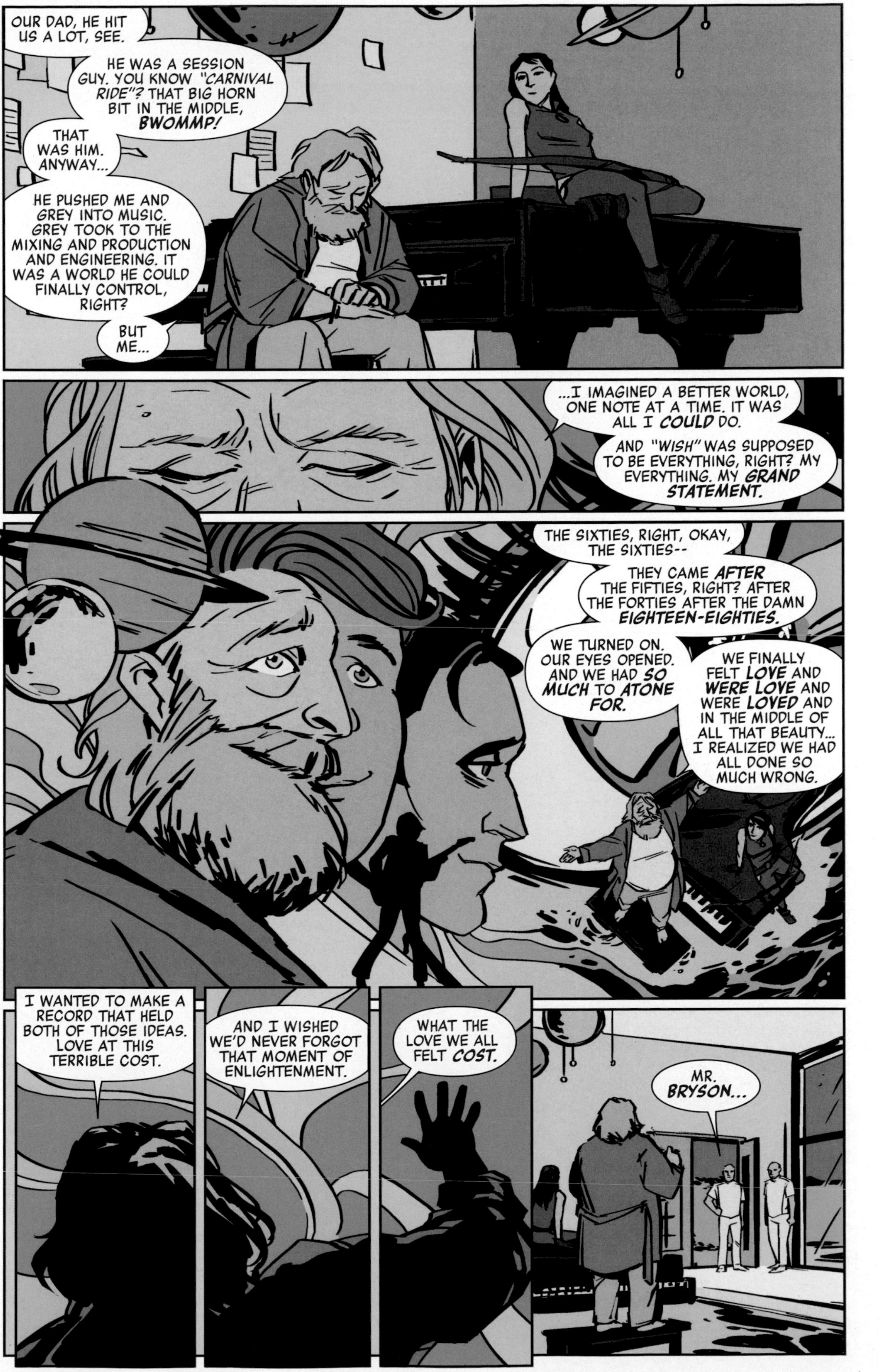

OUR DAD, HE HIT US A LOT, SEE.
HE WAS A SESSION GUY. YOU KNOW "CARNIVAL RIDE"? THAT BIG HORN BIT IN THE MIDDLE, BWOMMP!
THAT WAS HIM. ANYWAY...
HE PUSHED ME AND GREY INTO MUSIC. GREY TOOK TO THE MIXING AND PRODUCTION AND ENGINEERING. IT WAS A WORLD HE COULD FINALLY CONTROL, RIGHT?
BUT ME...
...I IMAGINED A BETTER WORLD, ONE NOTE AT A TIME. IT WAS ALL I COULD DO.
AND "WISH" WAS SUPPOSED TO BE EVERYTHING, RIGHT? MY EVERYTHING. MY GRAND STATEMENT.
THE SIXTIES, RIGHT, OKAY, THE SIXTIES--
THEY CAME AFTER THE FIFTIES, RIGHT? AFTER THE FORTIES AFTER THE DAMN EIGHTEEN-EIGHTIES.
WE TURNED ON. OUR EYES OPENED. AND WE HAD SO MUCH TO ATONE FOR.
WE FINALLY FELT LOVE AND WERE LOVE AND WERE LOVED AND IN THE MIDDLE OF ALL THAT BEAUTY... I REALIZED WE HAD ALL DONE SO MUCH WRONG.
I WANTED TO MAKE A RECORD THAT HELD BOTH OF THOSE IDEAS. LOVE AT THIS TERRIBLE COST.
AND I WISHED WE'D NEVER FORGOT THAT MOMENT OF ENLIGHTENMENT.
WHAT THE LOVE WE ALL FELT COST.
MR. BRYSON...

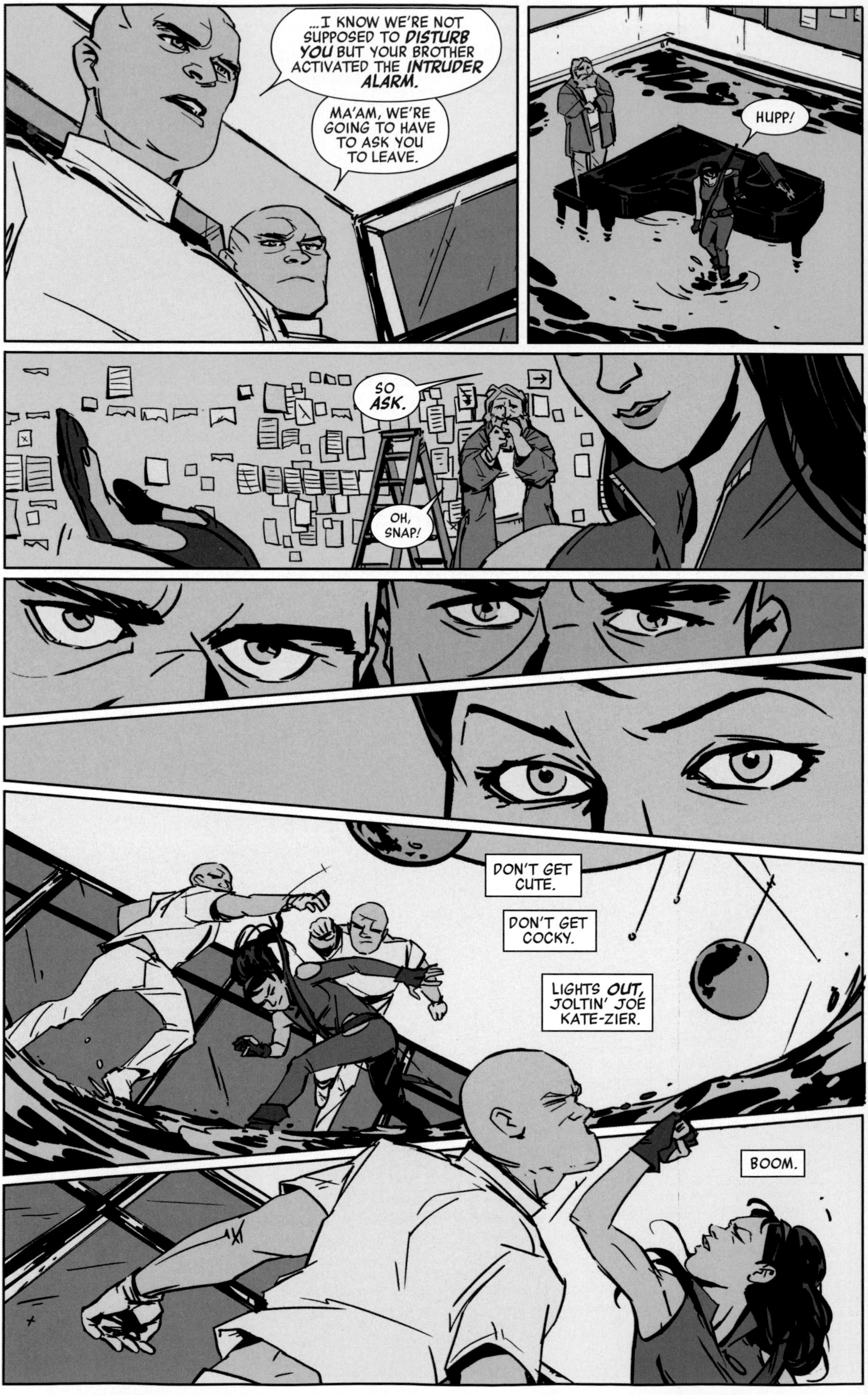
...I KNOW WE'RE NOT SUPPOSED TO DISTURB YOU BUT YOUR BROTHER ACTIVATED THE INTRUDER ALARM.
MA'AM, WE'RE GOING TO HAVE TO ASK YOU TO LEAVE.
HUPP!
SO ASK.
OH, SNAP!
DON'T GET CUTE.
DON'T GET COCKY.
LIGHTS OUT, JOLTIN' JOE KATE-ZIER.
BOOM.

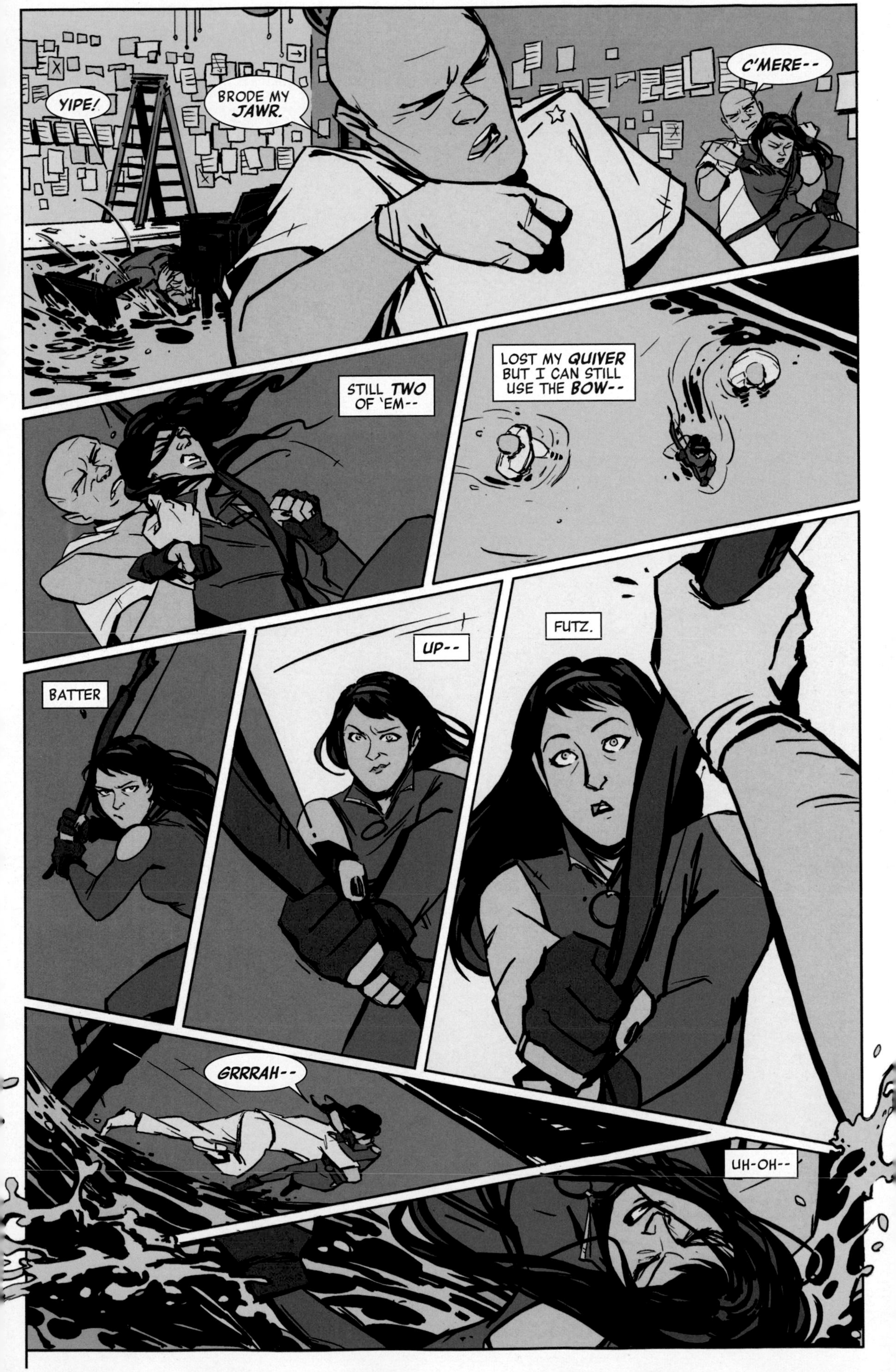

YIPE!
BRODE MY JAWR.
C'MERE--
STILL TWO OF 'EM--
LOST MY QUIVER BUT I CAN STILL USE THE BOW--
BATTER
UP--
FUTZ.
GRRRAH--
UH-OH--

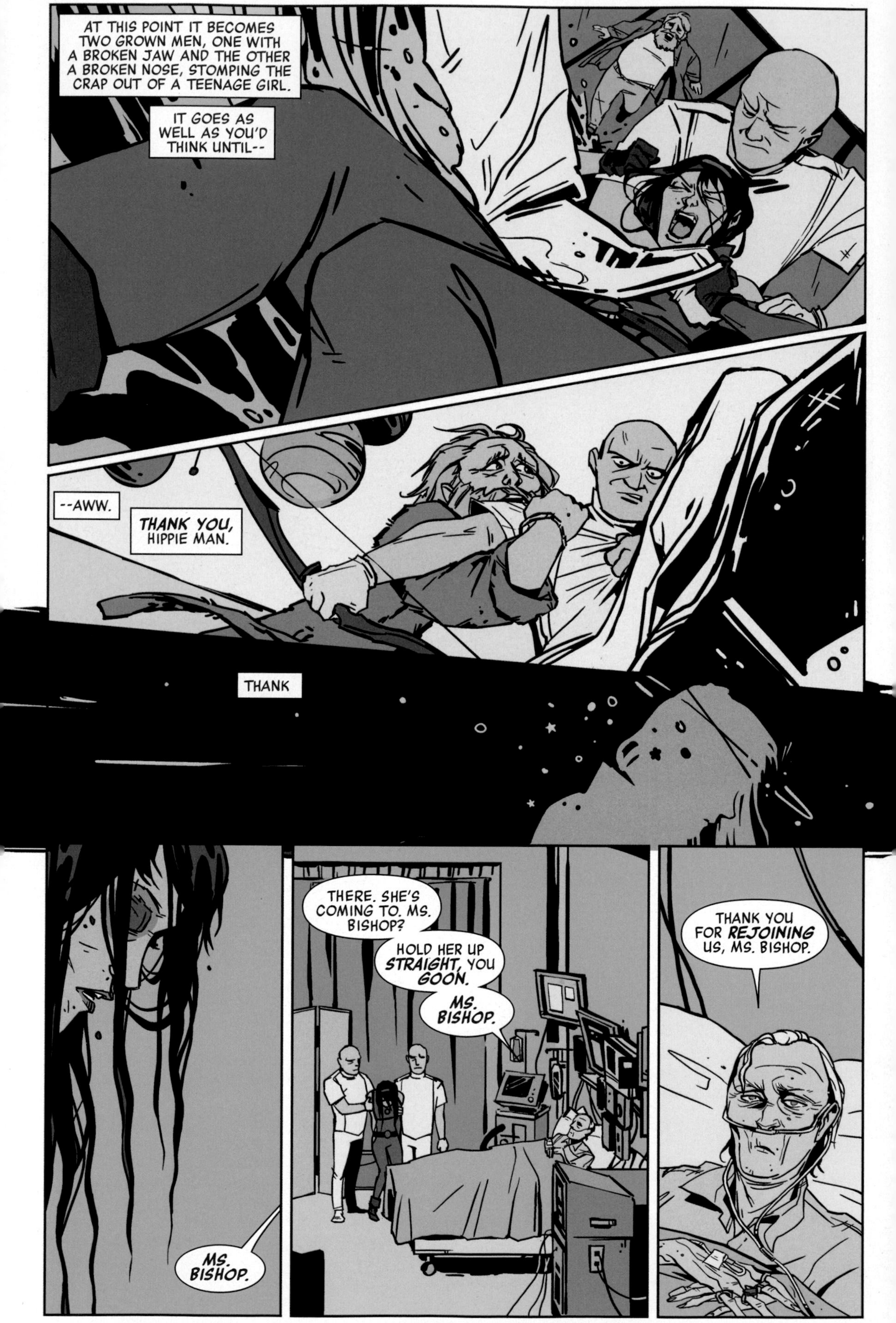
AT THIS POINT IT BECOMES TWO GROWN MEN, ONE WITH A BROKEN JAW AND THE OTHER A BROKEN NOSE, STOMPING THE CRAP OUT OF A TEENAGE GIRL.
IT GOES AS WELL AS YOU'D THINK UNTIL--
--AWW.
THANK YOU, HIPPIE MAN.
THANK
MS. BISHOP.
THERE. SHE'S COMING TO. MS. BISHOP?
HOLD HER UP STRAIGHT, YOU GOON.
MS. BISHOP.
THANK YOU FOR REJOINING US, MS. BISHOP.

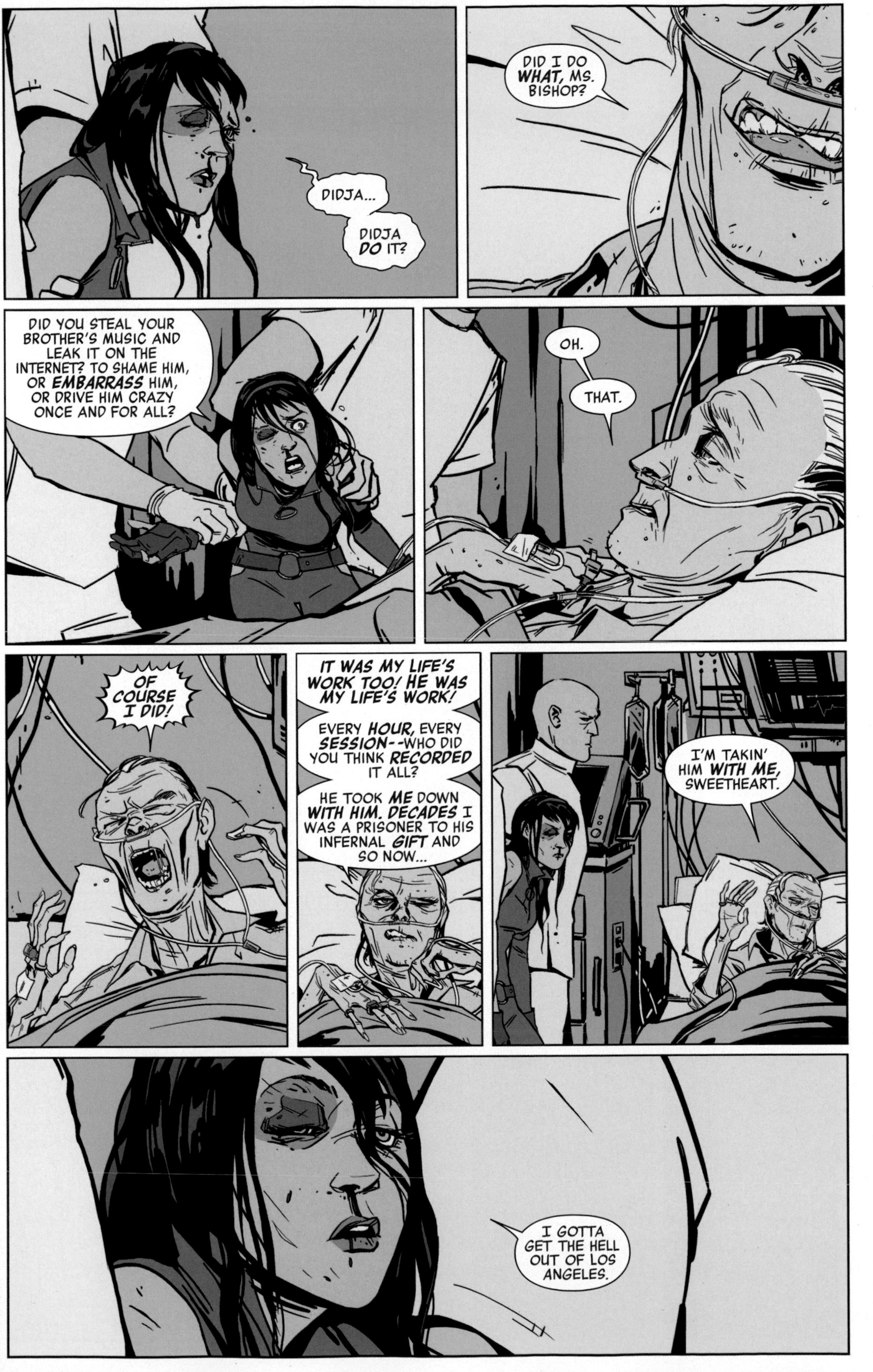
DIDJA...
DIDJA DO IT?
DID I DO WHAT, MS. BISHOP?
DID YOU STEAL YOUR BROTHER'S MUSIC AND LEAK IT ON THE INTERNET? TO SHAME HIM, OR EMBARRASS HIM, OR DRIVE HIM CRAZY ONCE AND FOR ALL?
OH.
THAT.
OF COURSE I DID!
IT WAS MY LIFE'S WORK TOO! HE WAS MY LIFE'S WORK!
EVERY HOUR, EVERY SESSION--WHO DID YOU THINK RECORDED IT ALL?
HE TOOK ME DOWN WITH HIM. DECADES I WAS A PRISONER TO HIS INFERNAL GIFT AND SO NOW...
I'M TAKIN' HIM WITH ME, SWEETHEART.
I GOTTA GET THE HELL OUT OF LOS ANGELES.

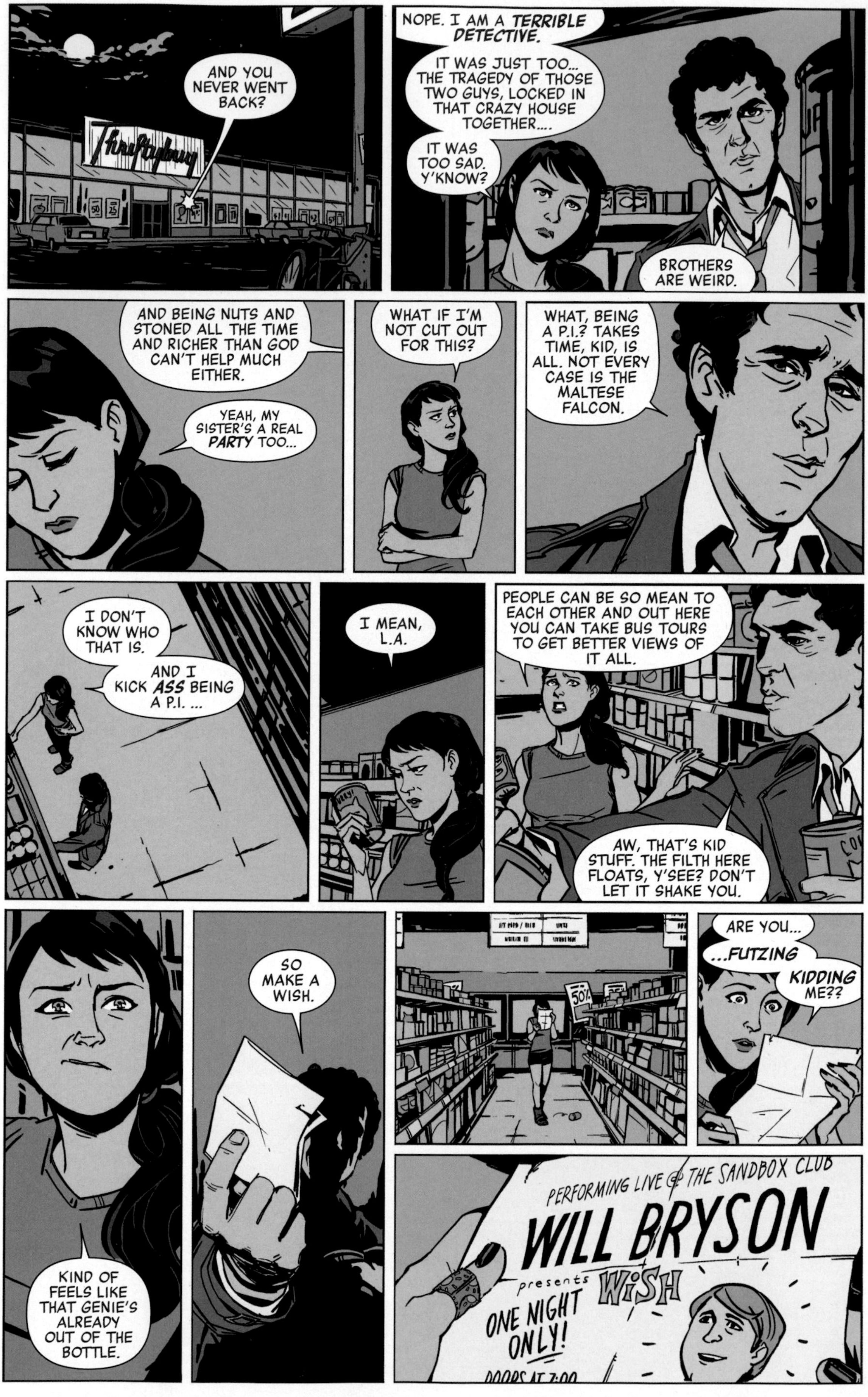
AND YOU NEVER WENT BACK?
NOPE. I AM A TERRIBLE DETECTIVE.
IT WAS JUST TOO... THE TRAGEDY OF THOSE TWO GUYS, LOCKED IN THAT CRAZY HOUSE TOGETHER....
IT WAS TOO SAD. Y'KNOW?
BROTHERS ARE WEIRD.
AND BEING NUTS AND STONED ALL THE TIME AND RICHER THAN GOD CAN'T HELP MUCH EITHER.
YEAH, MY SISTER'S A REAL PARTY TOO...
WHAT IF I'M NOT CUT OUT FOR THIS?
WHAT, BEING A P.I.? TAKES TIME, KID, IS ALL. NOT EVERY CASE IS THE MALTESE FALCON.
I DON'T KNOW WHO THAT IS.
AND I KICK ASS BEING A P.I. ...
I MEAN, L.A.
PEOPLE CAN BE SO MEAN TO EACH OTHER AND OUT HERE YOU CAN TAKE BUS TOURS TO GET BETTER VIEWS OF IT ALL.
AW, THAT'S KID STUFF. THE FILTH HERE FLOATS, Y'SEE? DON'T LET IT SHAKE YOU.
KIND OF FEELS LIKE THAT GENIE'S ALREADY OUT OF THE BOTTLE.
SO MAKE A WISH.
ARE YOU...
...FUTZING
KIDDING ME??
PERFORMING LIVE @ THE SANDBOX CLUB
WILL BRYSON
presents
WISH
ONE NIGHT ONLY!

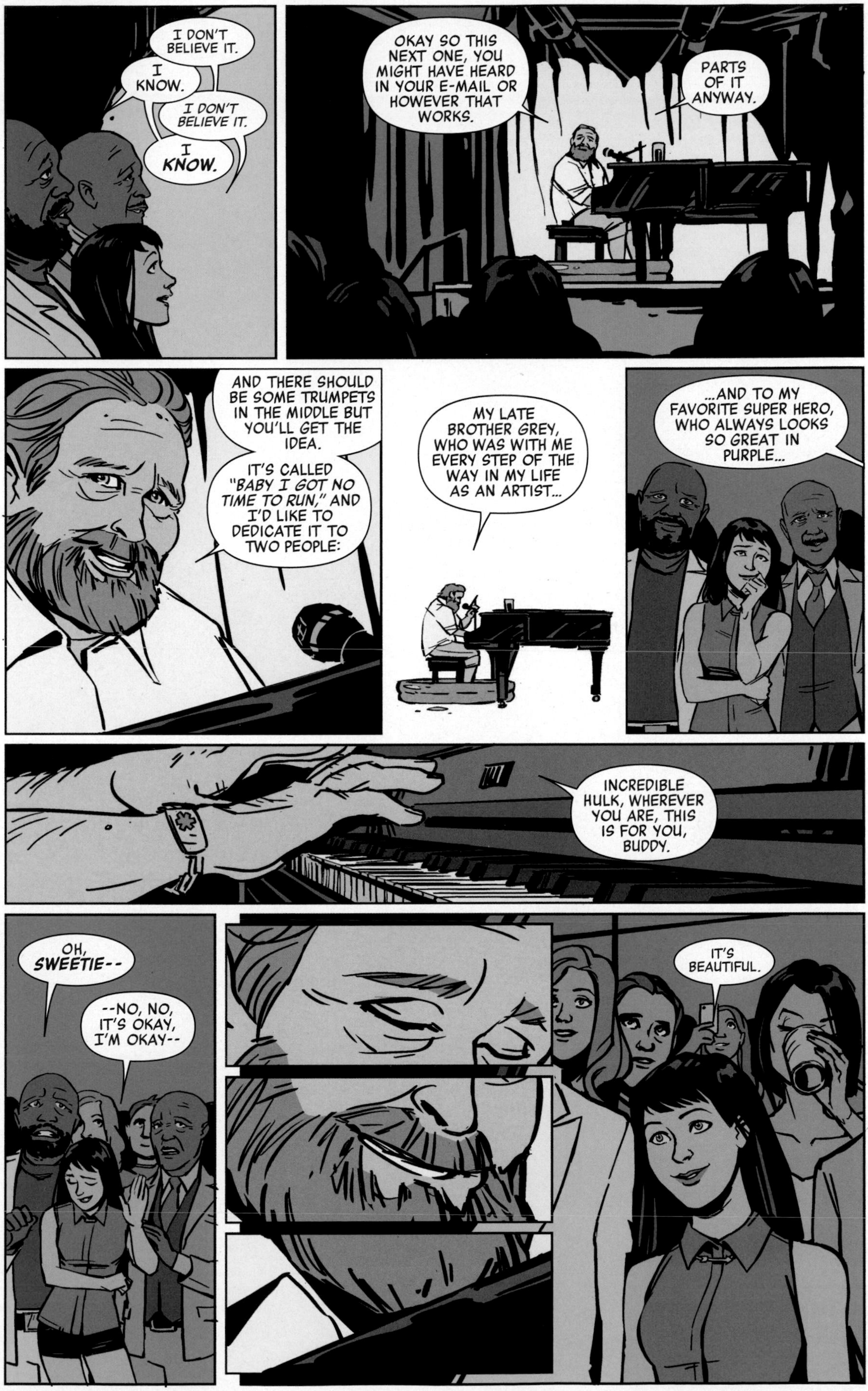
I DON'T BELIEVE IT.
I KNOW.
I DON'T BELIEVE IT.
I **KNOW.**
OKAY SO THIS NEXT ONE, YOU MIGHT HAVE HEARD IN YOUR E-MAIL OR HOWEVER THAT WORKS.
PARTS OF IT ANYWAY.
AND THERE SHOULD BE SOME TRUMPETS IN THE MIDDLE BUT YOU'LL GET THE IDEA.
IT'S CALLED "*BABY I GOT NO TIME TO RUN*," AND I'D LIKE TO DEDICATE IT TO TWO PEOPLE:
MY LATE BROTHER GREY, WHO WAS WITH ME EVERY STEP OF THE WAY IN MY LIFE AS AN ARTIST...
...AND TO MY FAVORITE SUPER HERO, WHO ALWAYS LOOKS SO GREAT IN PURPLE...
INCREDIBLE HULK, WHEREVER YOU ARE, THIS IS FOR YOU, BUDDY.
OH, **SWEETIE--**
--NO, NO, IT'S OKAY, I'M OKAY--
IT'S BEAUTIFUL.

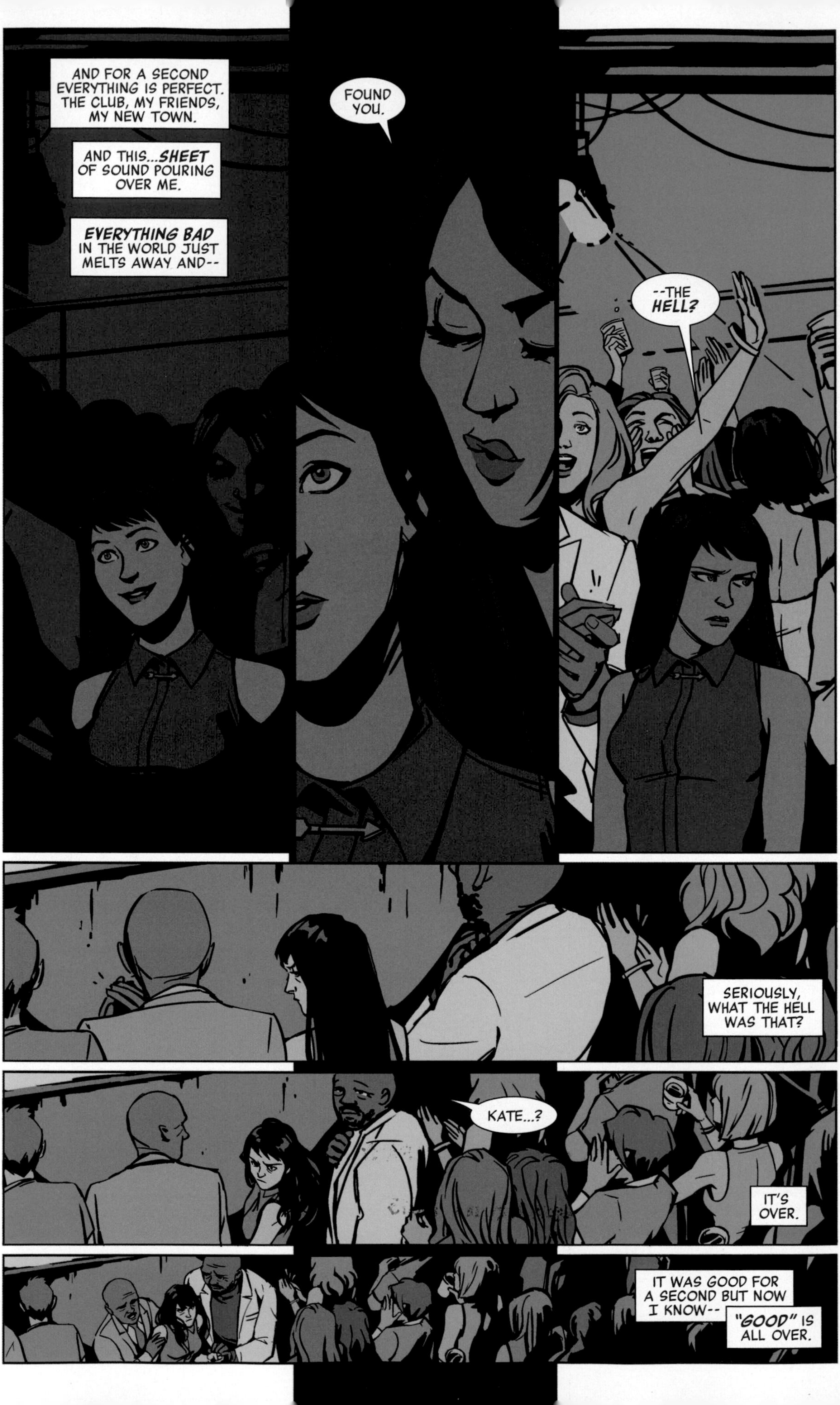

AND FOR A SECOND EVERYTHING IS PERFECT. THE CLUB, MY FRIENDS, MY NEW TOWN.
AND THIS...SHEET OF SOUND POURING OVER ME.
EVERYTHING BAD IN THE WORLD JUST MELTS AWAY AND--
FOUND YOU.
--THE HELL?
SERIOUSLY, WHAT THE HELL WAS THAT?
KATE...?
IT'S OVER.
IT WAS GOOD FOR A SECOND BUT NOW I KNOW--
"GOOD" IS ALL OVER.

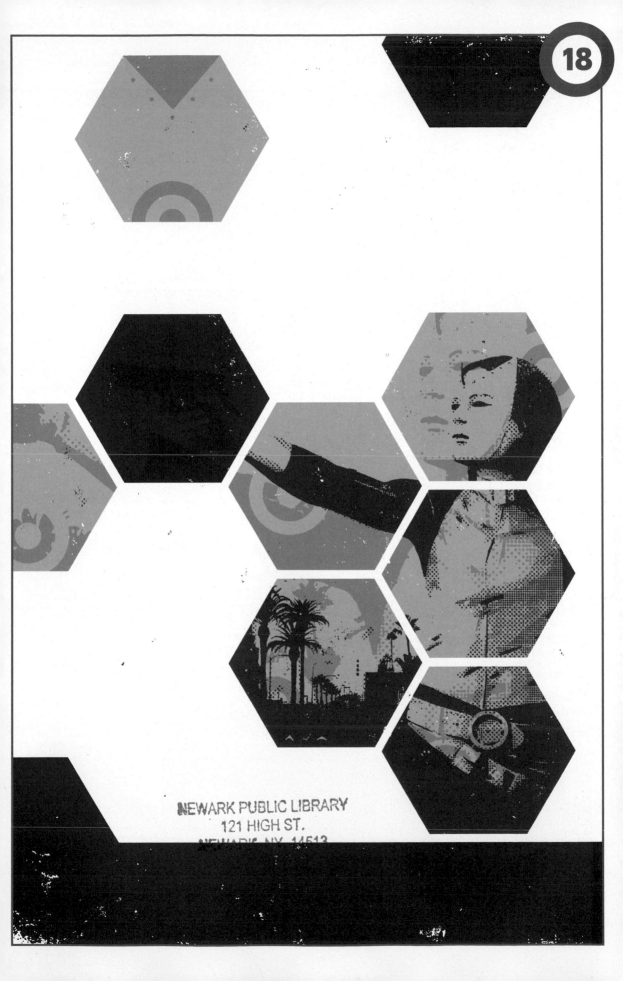

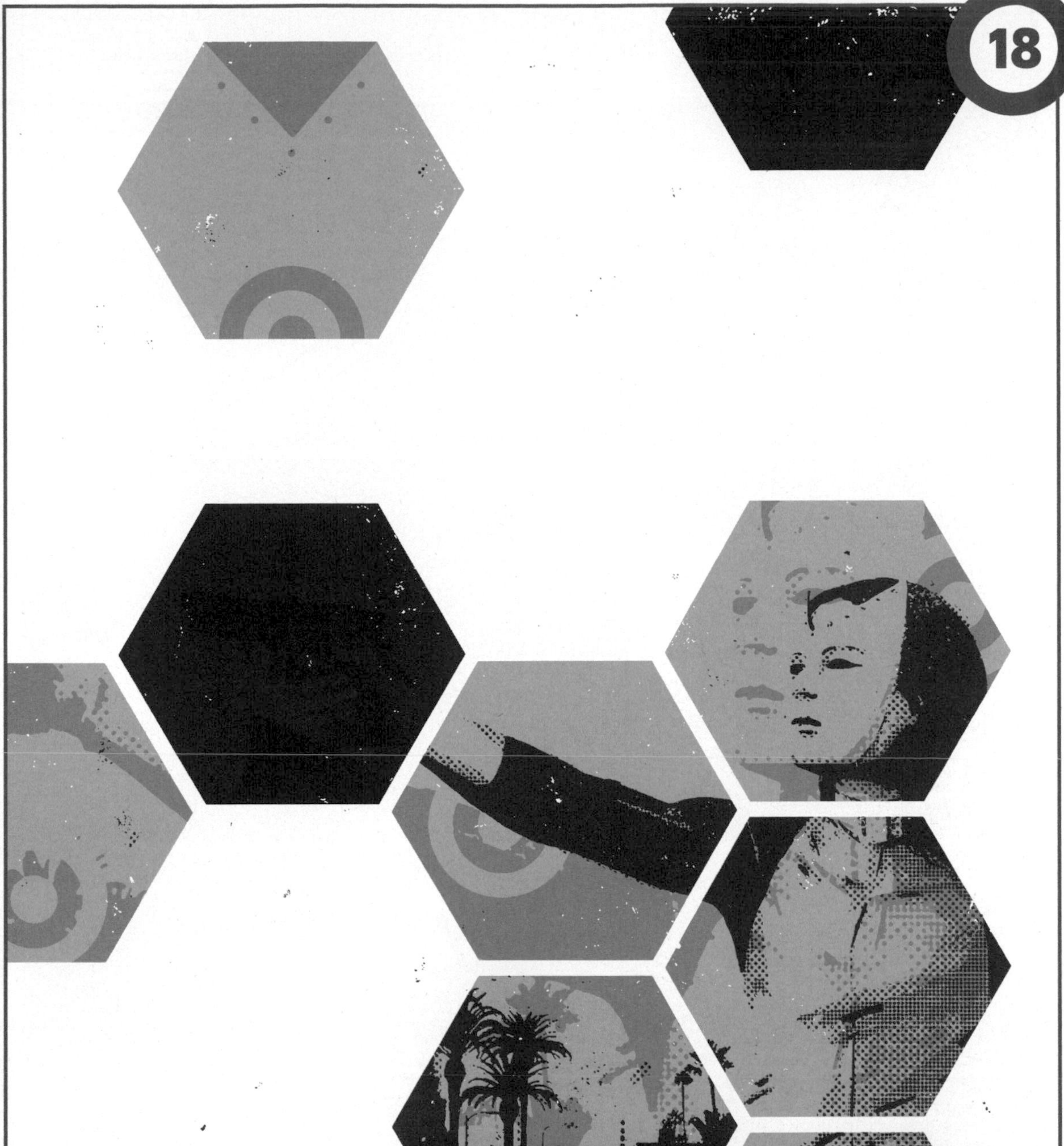
18

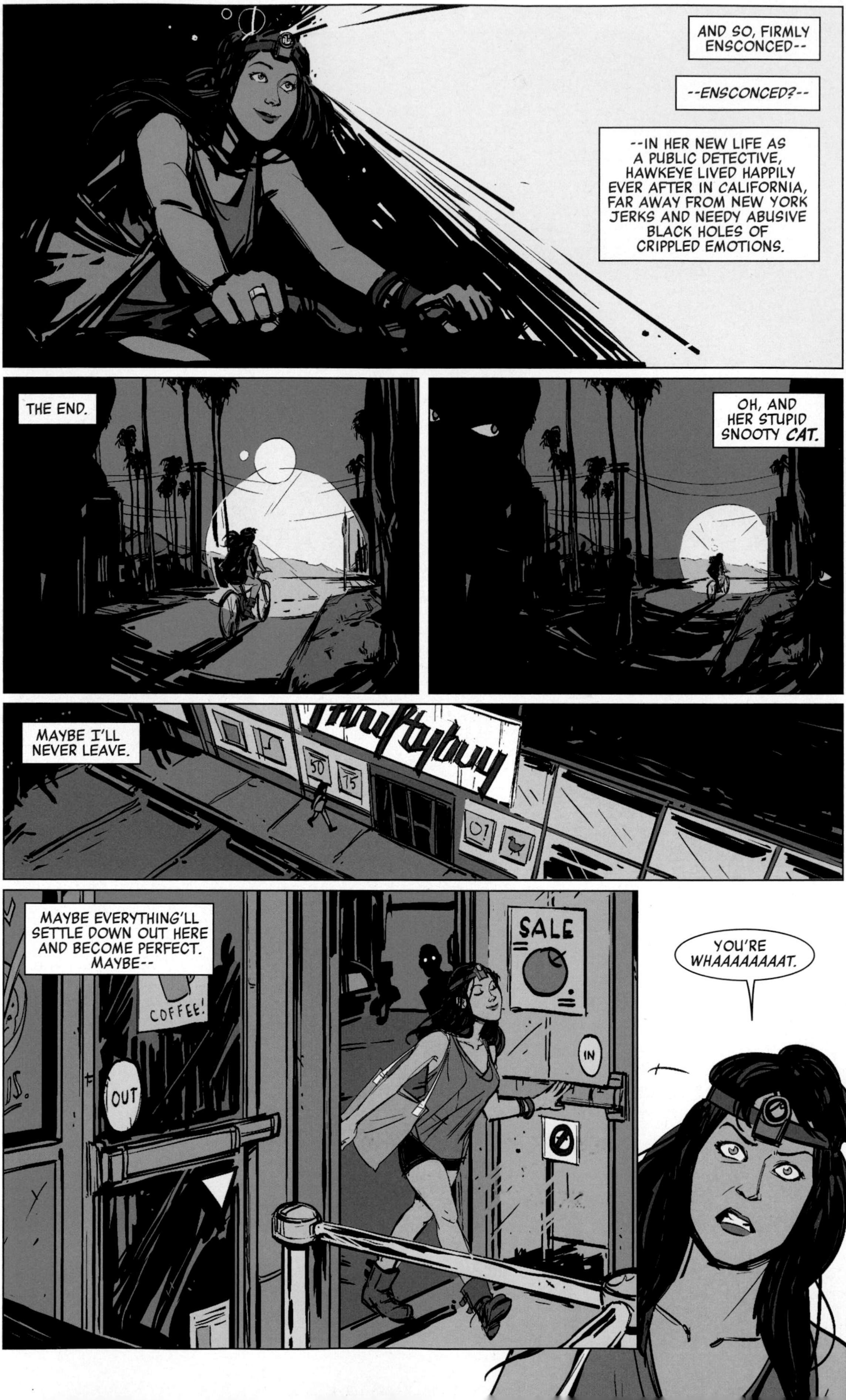
AND SO, FIRMLY ENSCONCED--
--ENSCONCED?--
--IN HER NEW LIFE AS A PUBLIC DETECTIVE, HAWKEYE LIVED HAPPILY EVER AFTER IN CALIFORNIA, FAR AWAY FROM NEW YORK JERKS AND NEEDY ABUSIVE BLACK HOLES OF CRIPPLED EMOTIONS.
THE END.
OH, AND HER STUPID SNOOTY CAT.
MAYBE I'LL NEVER LEAVE.
50
75
MAYBE EVERYTHING'LL SETTLE DOWN OUT HERE AND BECOME PERFECT. MAYBE--
SALE
COFFEE!
IN
OUT
YOU'RE WHAAAAAAAAT.

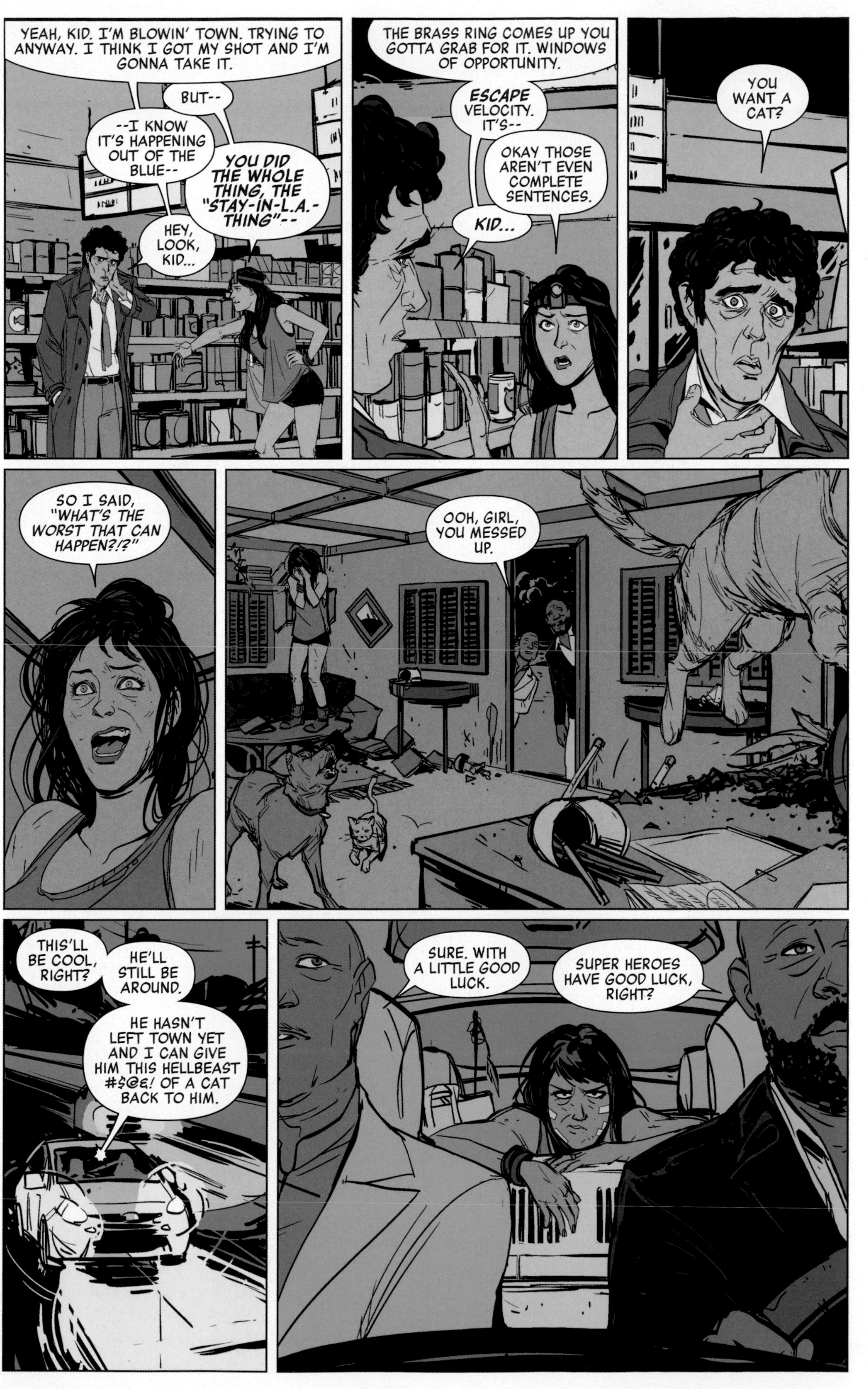
YEAH, KID. I'M BLOWIN' TOWN. TRYING TO ANYWAY. I THINK I GOT MY SHOT AND I'M GONNA TAKE IT.
BUT--
--I KNOW IT'S HAPPENING OUT OF THE BLUE--
YOU DID THE WHOLE THING, THE "STAY-IN-L.A.-THING"--
HEY, LOOK, KID...
THE BRASS RING COMES UP YOU GOTTA GRAB FOR IT. WINDOWS OF OPPORTUNITY.
ESCAPE VELOCITY. IT'S--
OKAY THOSE AREN'T EVEN COMPLETE SENTENCES.
KID...
YOU WANT A CAT?
SO I SAID, "WHAT'S THE WORST THAT CAN HAPPEN?!?"
OOH, GIRL, YOU MESSED UP.
THIS'LL BE COOL, RIGHT?
HE'LL STILL BE AROUND.
HE HASN'T LEFT TOWN YET AND I CAN GIVE HIM THIS HELLBEAST #$@&! OF A CAT BACK TO HIM.
SURE. WITH A LITTLE GOOD LUCK.
SUPER HEROES HAVE GOOD LUCK, RIGHT?

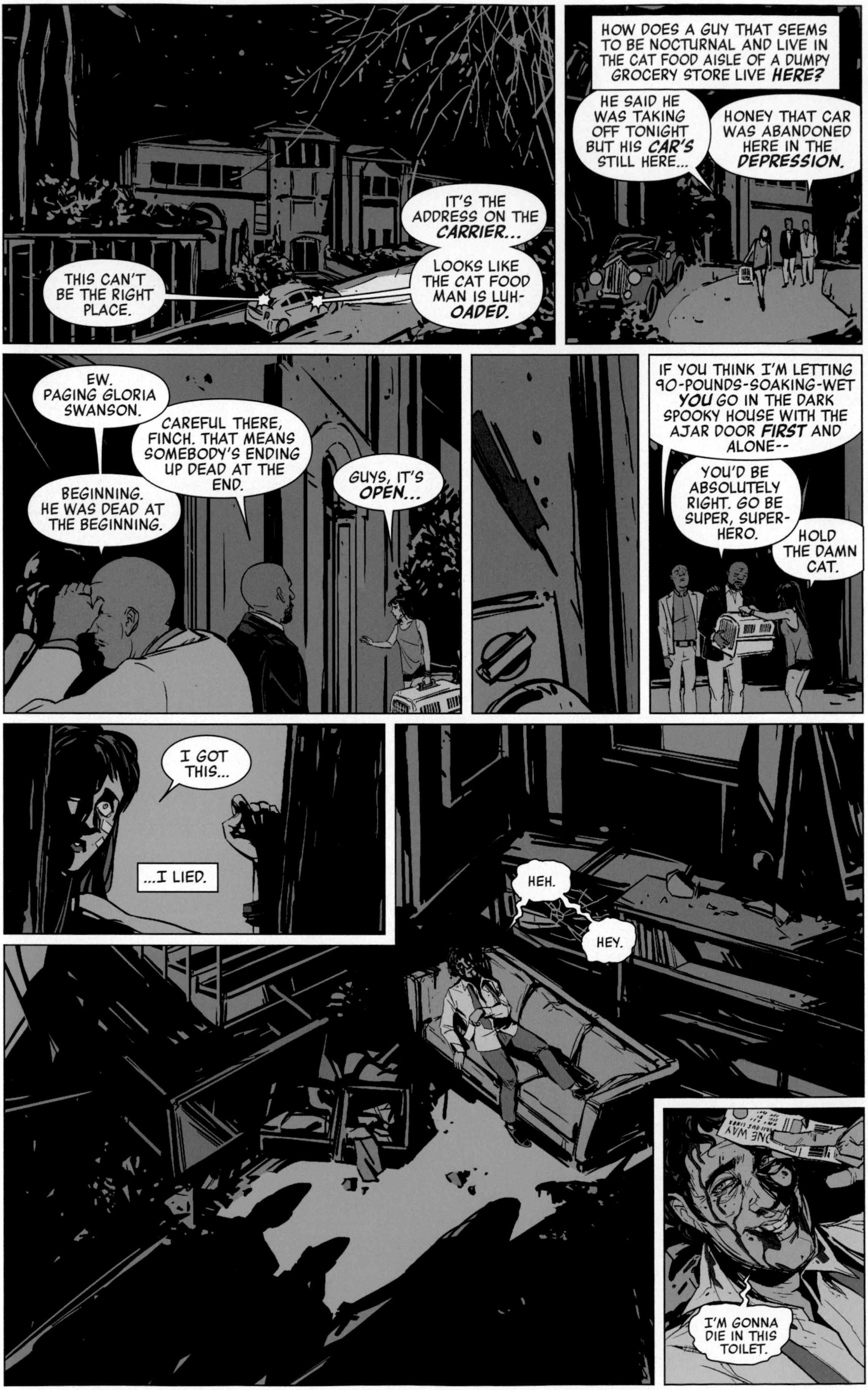
IT'S THE ADDRESS ON THE CARRIER...
LOOKS LIKE THE CAT FOOD MAN IS LUH-OADED.
THIS CAN'T BE THE RIGHT PLACE.
HOW DOES A GUY THAT SEEMS TO BE NOCTURNAL AND LIVE IN THE CAT FOOD AISLE OF A DUMPY GROCERY STORE LIVE HERE?
HE SAID HE WAS TAKING OFF TONIGHT BUT HIS CAR'S STILL HERE...
HONEY THAT CAR WAS ABANDONED HERE IN THE DEPRESSION.
EW. PAGING GLORIA SWANSON.
CAREFUL THERE, FINCH. THAT MEANS SOMEBODY'S ENDING UP DEAD AT THE END.
BEGINNING. HE WAS DEAD AT THE BEGINNING.
GUYS, IT'S OPEN...
IF YOU THINK I'M LETTING 90-POUNDS-SOAKING-WET YOU GO IN THE DARK SPOOKY HOUSE WITH THE AJAR DOOR FIRST AND ALONE--
YOU'D BE ABSOLUTELY RIGHT. GO BE SUPER, SUPER-HERO.
HOLD THE DAMN CAT.
I GOT THIS...
...I LIED.
HEH.
HEY.
ONE WAY
I'M GONNA DIE IN THIS TOILET.

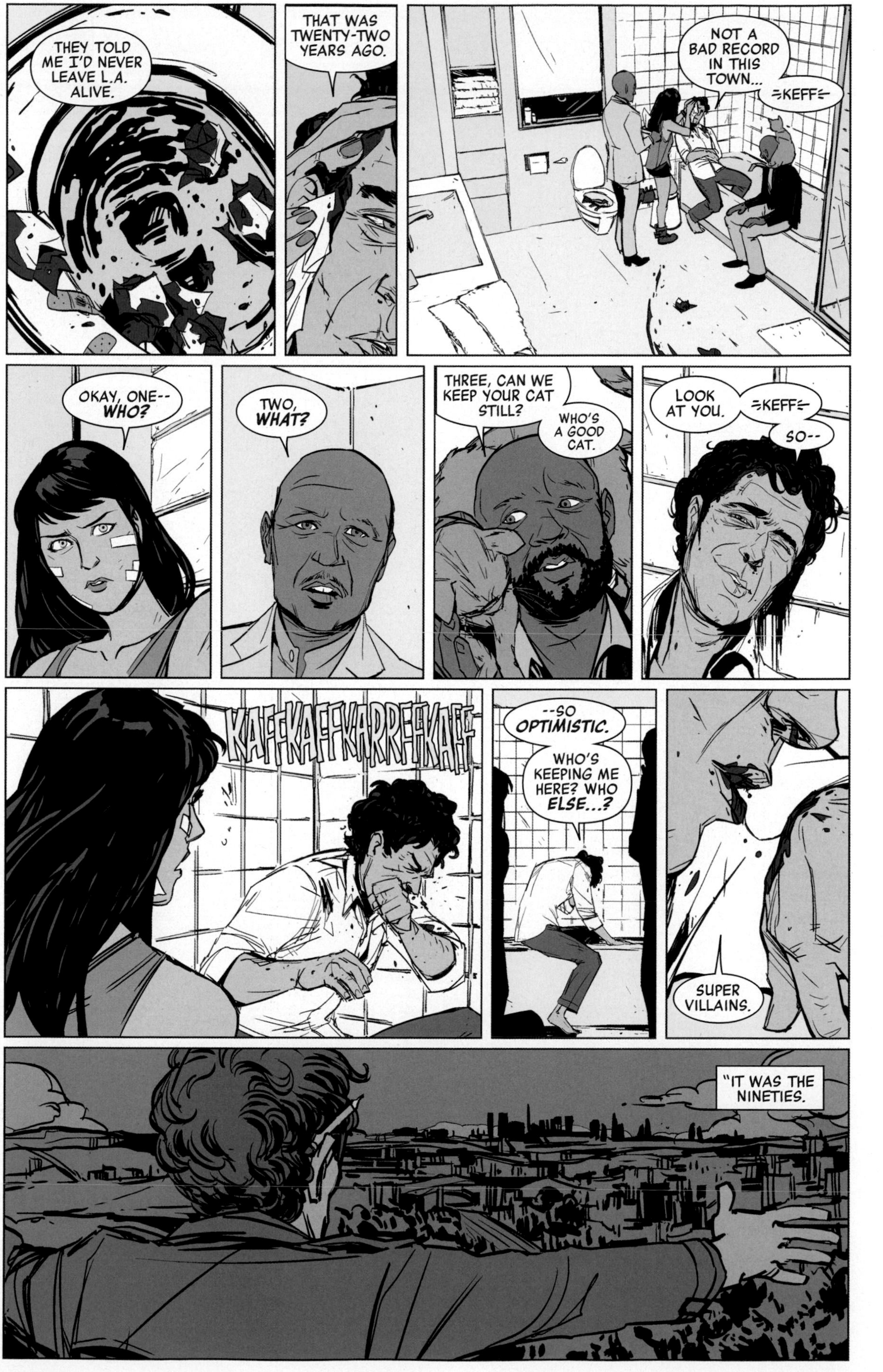
THEY TOLD ME I'D NEVER LEAVE L.A. ALIVE.
THAT WAS TWENTY-TWO YEARS AGO.
NOT A BAD RECORD IN THIS TOWN...
KEFF
OKAY, ONE-- WHO?
TWO, WHAT?
THREE, CAN WE KEEP YOUR CAT STILL?
WHO'S A GOOD CAT.
LOOK AT YOU.
KEFF
SO--
KAFFKAFFKARRFFKAFF
--SO OPTIMISTIC.
WHO'S KEEPING ME HERE? WHO ELSE...?
SUPER VILLAINS.
"IT WAS THE NINETIES.

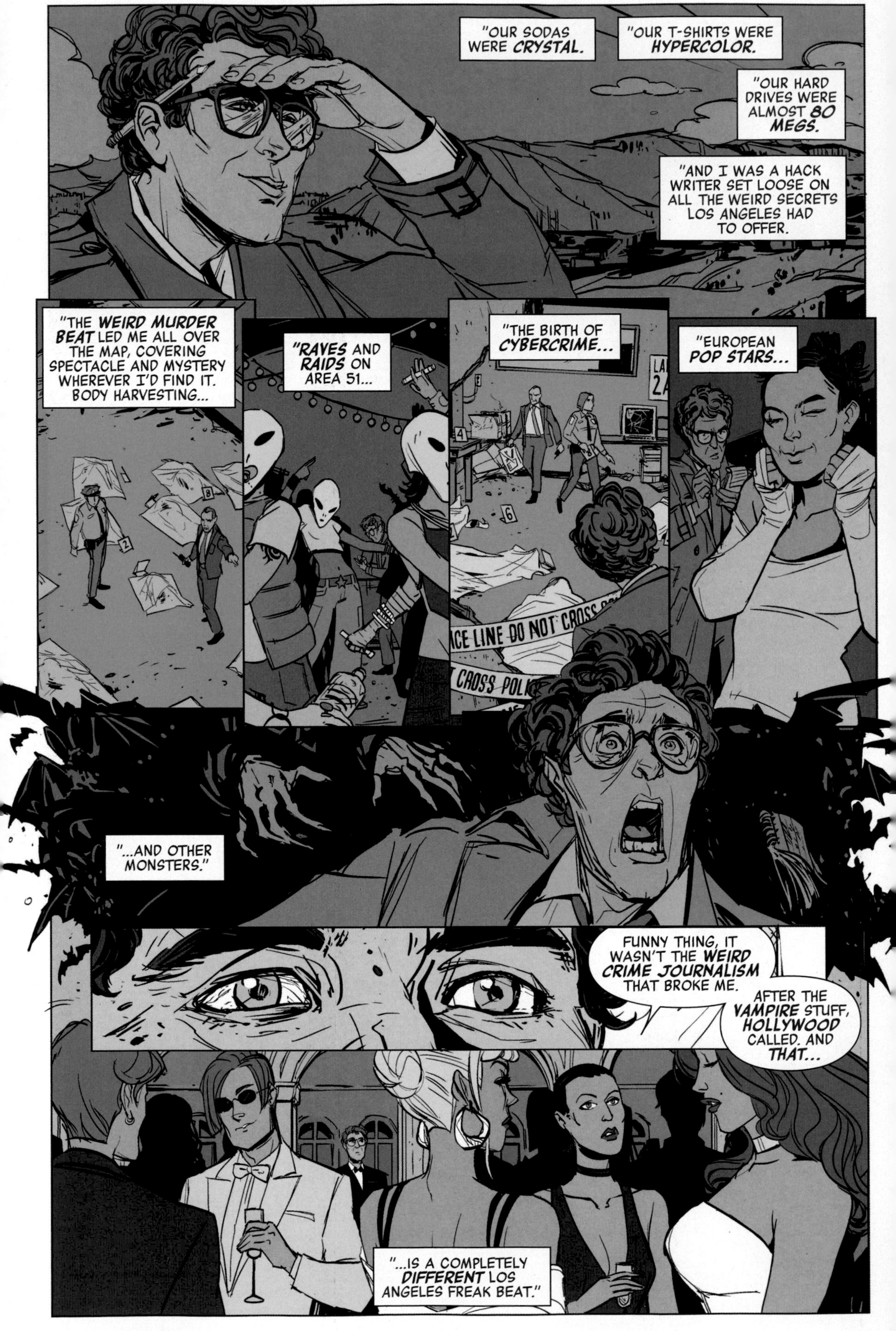
"OUR SODAS WERE CRYSTAL.
"OUR T-SHIRTS WERE HYPERCOLOR.
"OUR HARD DRIVES WERE ALMOST 80 MEGS.
"AND I WAS A HACK WRITER SET LOOSE ON ALL THE WEIRD SECRETS LOS ANGELES HAD TO OFFER.
"THE WEIRD MURDER BEAT LED ME ALL OVER THE MAP, COVERING SPECTACLE AND MYSTERY WHEREVER I'D FIND IT. BODY HARVESTING...
"RAVES AND RAIDS ON AREA 51...
"THE BIRTH OF CYBERCRIME...
"EUROPEAN POP STARS...
"...AND OTHER MONSTERS."
FUNNY THING, IT WASN'T THE WEIRD CRIME JOURNALISM THAT BROKE ME.
AFTER THE VAMPIRE STUFF, HOLLYWOOD CALLED. AND THAT...
"...IS A COMPLETELY DIFFERENT LOS ANGELES FREAK BEAT."

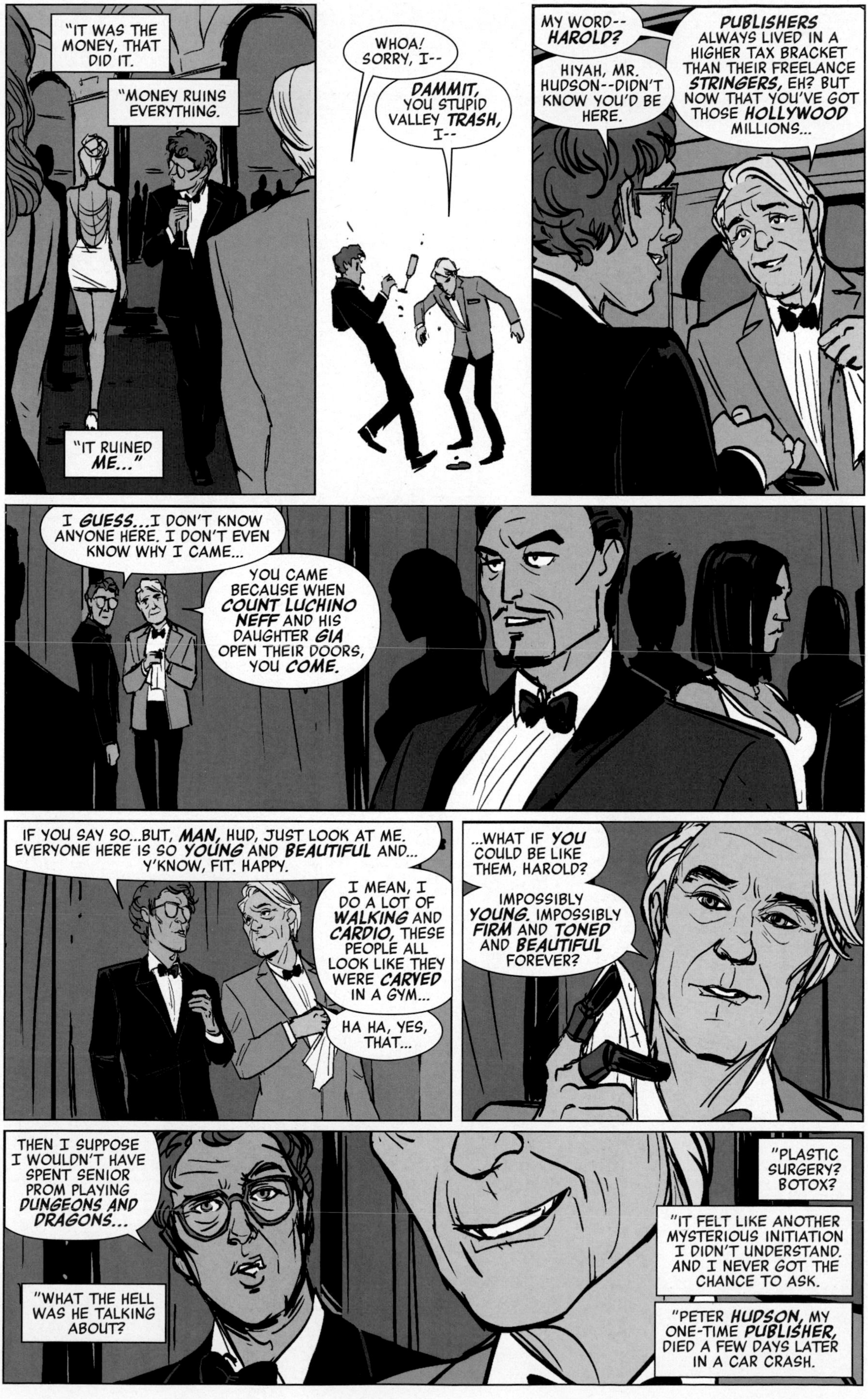
"IT WAS THE MONEY, THAT DID IT.
"MONEY RUINS EVERYTHING.
"IT RUINED ME..."
WHOA! SORRY, I--
DAMMIT, YOU STUPID VALLEY TRASH, I--
MY WORD-- HAROLD?
HIYAH, MR. HUDSON--DIDN'T KNOW YOU'D BE HERE.
PUBLISHERS ALWAYS LIVED IN A HIGHER TAX BRACKET THAN THEIR FREELANCE STRINGERS, EH? BUT NOW THAT YOU'VE GOT THOSE HOLLYWOOD MILLIONS...
I GUESS...I DON'T KNOW ANYONE HERE. I DON'T EVEN KNOW WHY I CAME...
YOU CAME BECAUSE WHEN COUNT LUCHINO NEFF AND HIS DAUGHTER GIA OPEN THEIR DOORS, YOU COME.
IF YOU SAY SO...BUT, MAN, HUD, JUST LOOK AT ME. EVERYONE HERE IS SO YOUNG AND BEAUTIFUL AND... Y'KNOW, FIT. HAPPY.
I MEAN, I DO A LOT OF WALKING AND CARDIO, THESE PEOPLE ALL LOOK LIKE THEY WERE CARVED IN A GYM...
HA HA, YES, THAT...
...WHAT IF YOU COULD BE LIKE THEM, HAROLD?
IMPOSSIBLY YOUNG. IMPOSSIBLY FIRM AND TONED AND BEAUTIFUL FOREVER?
THEN I SUPPOSE I WOULDN'T HAVE SPENT SENIOR PROM PLAYING DUNGEONS AND DRAGONS...
"WHAT THE HELL WAS HE TALKING ABOUT?
"PLASTIC SURGERY? BOTOX?
"IT FELT LIKE ANOTHER MYSTERIOUS INITIATION I DIDN'T UNDERSTAND. AND I NEVER GOT THE CHANCE TO ASK.
"PETER HUDSON, MY ONE-TIME PUBLISHER, DIED A FEW DAYS LATER IN A CAR CRASH.

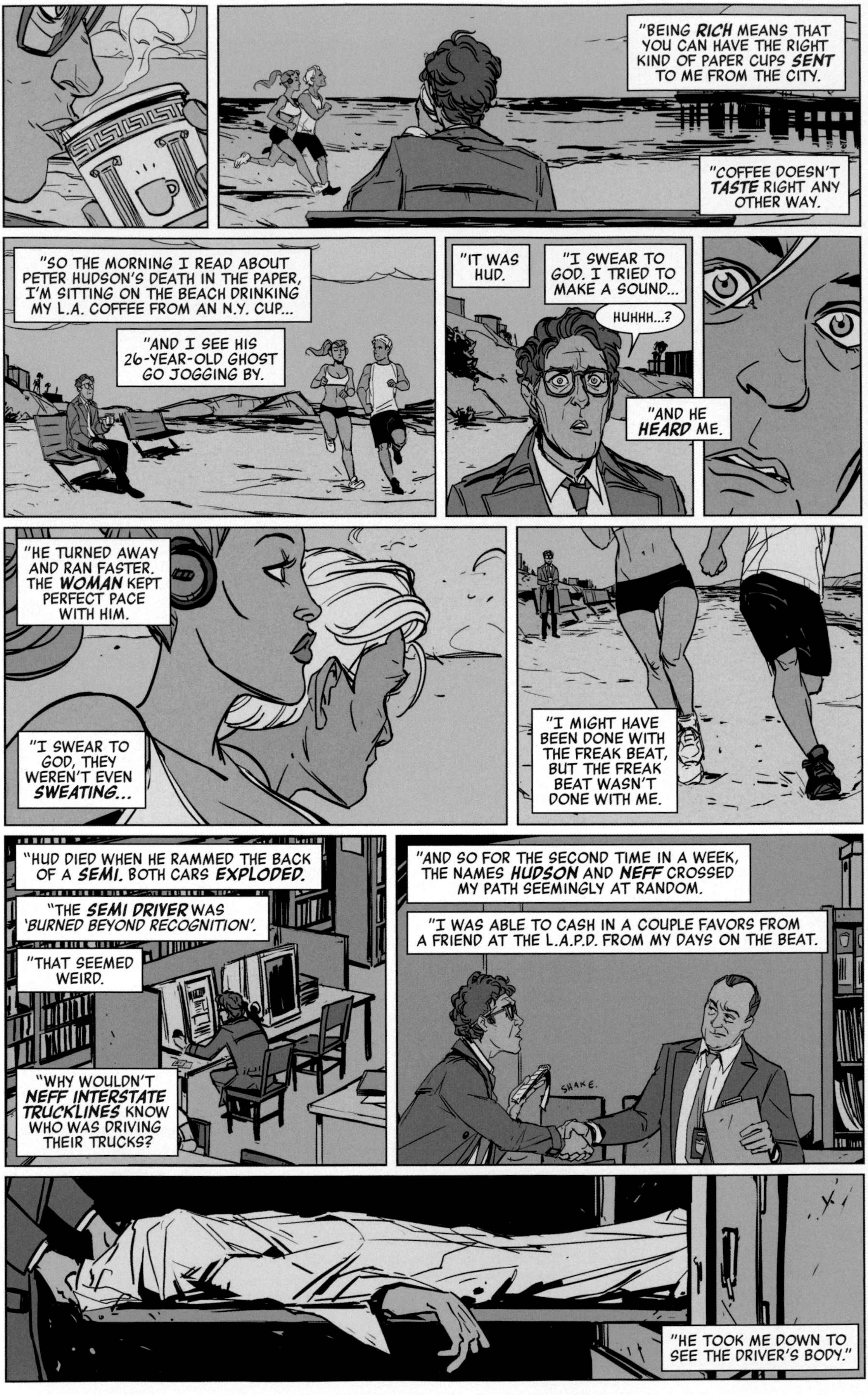
"BEING RICH MEANS THAT YOU CAN HAVE THE RIGHT KIND OF PAPER CUPS SENT TO ME FROM THE CITY.
"COFFEE DOESN'T TASTE RIGHT ANY OTHER WAY.
"SO THE MORNING I READ ABOUT PETER HUDSON'S DEATH IN THE PAPER, I'M SITTING ON THE BEACH DRINKING MY L.A. COFFEE FROM AN N.Y. CUP...
"AND I SEE HIS 26-YEAR-OLD GHOST GO JOGGING BY.
"IT WAS HUD.
"I SWEAR TO GOD. I TRIED TO MAKE A SOUND...
HUHHH...?
"AND HE HEARD ME.
"HE TURNED AWAY AND RAN FASTER. THE WOMAN KEPT PERFECT PACE WITH HIM.
"I SWEAR TO GOD, THEY WEREN'T EVEN SWEATING...
"I MIGHT HAVE BEEN DONE WITH THE FREAK BEAT, BUT THE FREAK BEAT WASN'T DONE WITH ME.
"HUD DIED WHEN HE RAMMED THE BACK OF A SEMI. BOTH CARS EXPLODED.
"THE SEMI DRIVER WAS 'BURNED BEYOND RECOGNITION'.
"THAT SEEMED WEIRD.
"WHY WOULDN'T NEFF INTERSTATE TRUCKLINES KNOW WHO WAS DRIVING THEIR TRUCKS?
"AND SO FOR THE SECOND TIME IN A WEEK, THE NAMES HUDSON AND NEFF CROSSED MY PATH SEEMINGLY AT RANDOM.
"I WAS ABLE TO CASH IN A COUPLE FAVORS FROM A FRIEND AT THE L.A.P.D. FROM MY DAYS ON THE BEAT.
SHAKE.
"HE TOOK ME DOWN TO SEE THE DRIVER'S BODY."

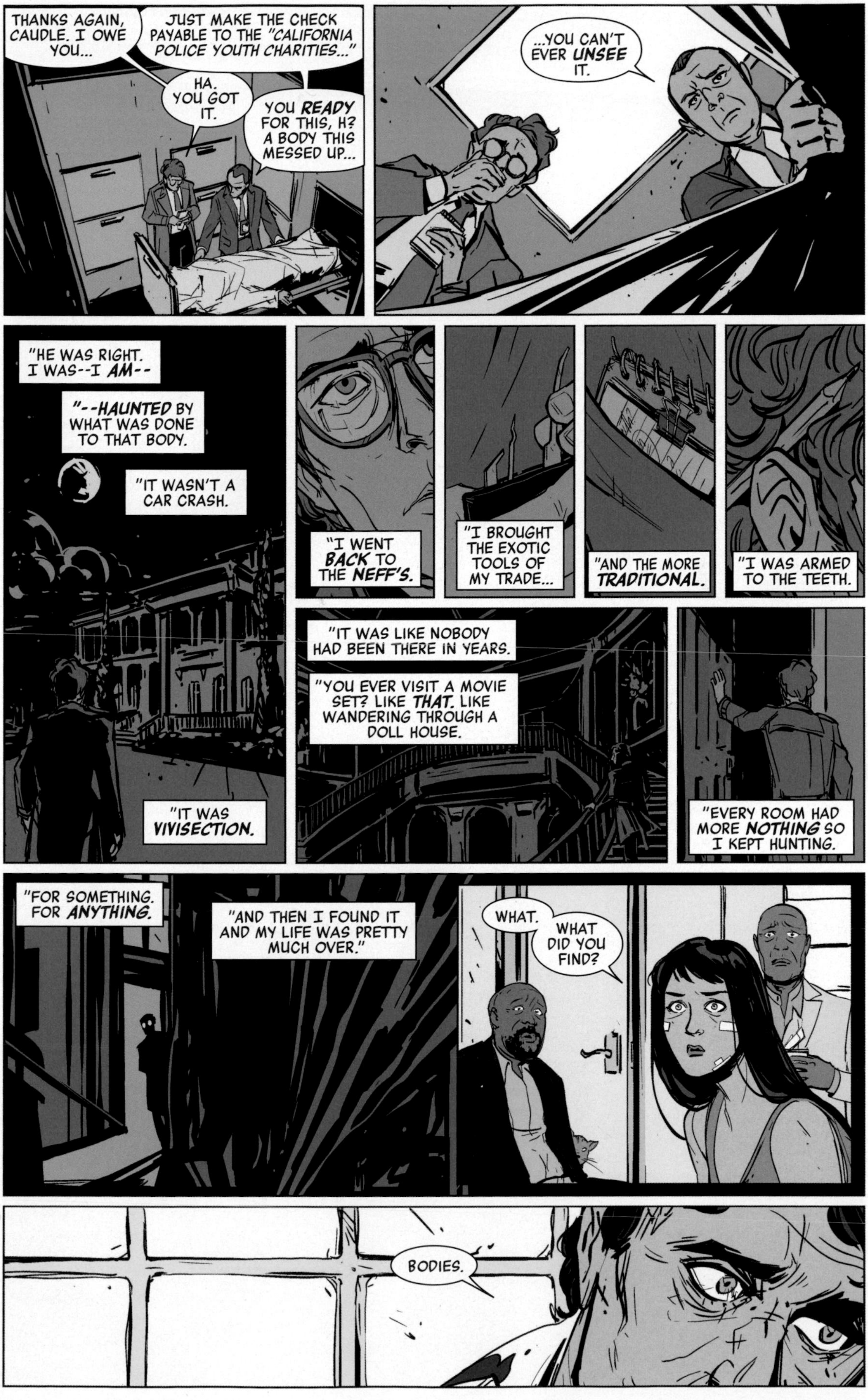
THANKS AGAIN, CAUDLE. I OWE YOU...
JUST MAKE THE CHECK PAYABLE TO THE "CALIFORNIA POLICE YOUTH CHARITIES..."
HA. YOU GOT IT.
YOU READY FOR THIS, H? A BODY THIS MESSED UP...
...YOU CAN'T EVER UNSEE IT.
"HE WAS RIGHT. I WAS--I AM--
"--HAUNTED BY WHAT WAS DONE TO THAT BODY.
"IT WASN'T A CAR CRASH.
"IT WAS VIVISECTION.
"I WENT BACK TO THE NEFF'S.
"I BROUGHT THE EXOTIC TOOLS OF MY TRADE...
"AND THE MORE TRADITIONAL.
"I WAS ARMED TO THE TEETH.
"IT WAS LIKE NOBODY HAD BEEN THERE IN YEARS.
"YOU EVER VISIT A MOVIE SET? LIKE THAT. LIKE WANDERING THROUGH A DOLL HOUSE.
"EVERY ROOM HAD MORE NOTHING SO I KEPT HUNTING.
"FOR SOMETHING. FOR ANYTHING.
"AND THEN I FOUND IT AND MY LIFE WAS PRETTY MUCH OVER."
WHAT.
WHAT DID YOU FIND?
BODIES.

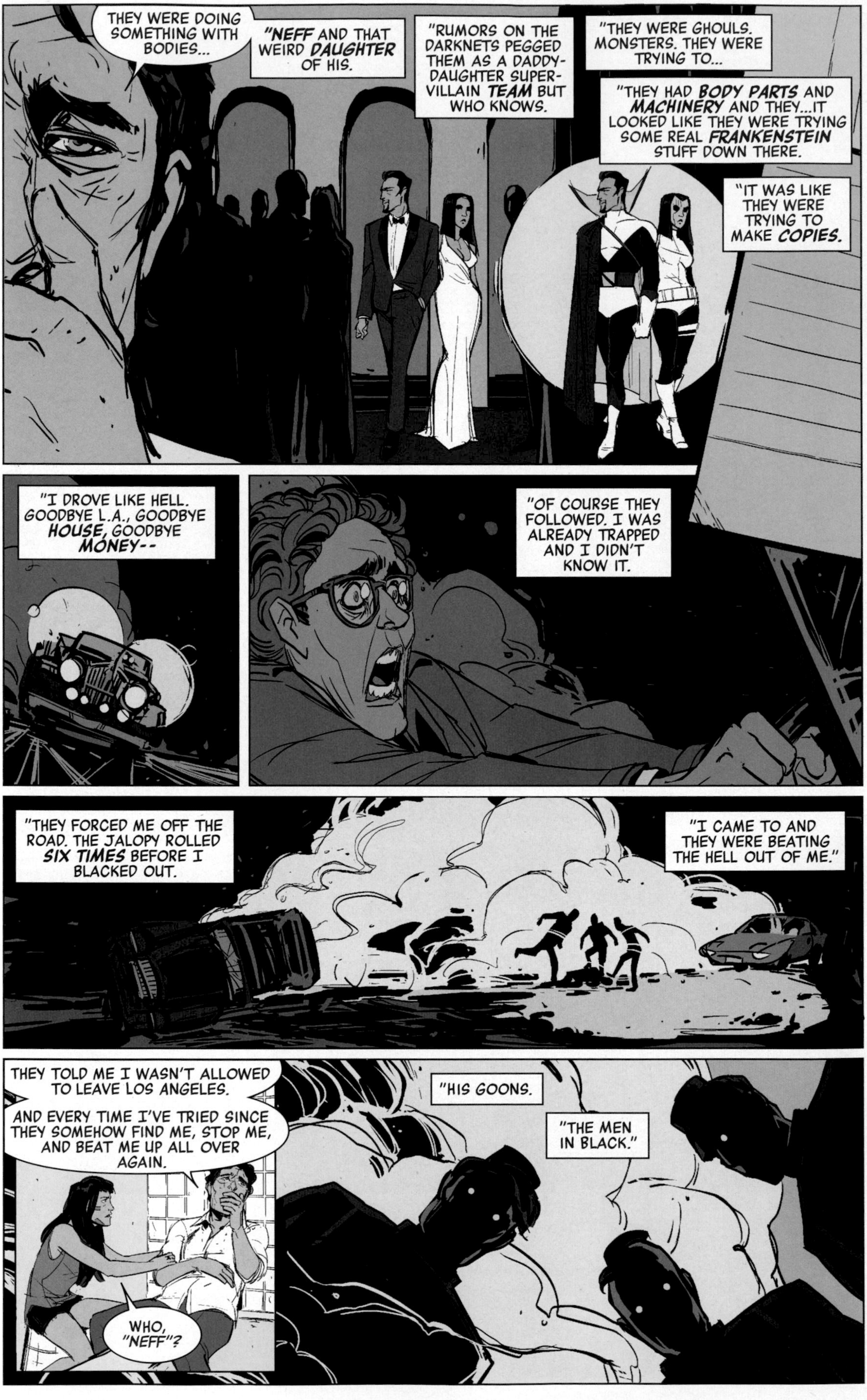

THEY WERE DOING SOMETHING WITH BODIES...
"NEFF AND THAT WEIRD DAUGHTER OF HIS.
"RUMORS ON THE DARKNETS PEGGED THEM AS A DADDY-DAUGHTER SUPER-VILLAIN TEAM BUT WHO KNOWS.
"THEY WERE GHOULS. MONSTERS. THEY WERE TRYING TO...
"THEY HAD BODY PARTS AND MACHINERY AND THEY...IT LOOKED LIKE THEY WERE TRYING SOME REAL FRANKENSTEIN STUFF DOWN THERE.
"IT WAS LIKE THEY WERE TRYING TO MAKE COPIES.
"I DROVE LIKE HELL. GOODBYE L.A., GOODBYE HOUSE, GOODBYE MONEY--
"OF COURSE THEY FOLLOWED. I WAS ALREADY TRAPPED AND I DIDN'T KNOW IT.
"THEY FORCED ME OFF THE ROAD. THE JALOPY ROLLED SIX TIMES BEFORE I BLACKED OUT.
"I CAME TO AND THEY WERE BEATING THE HELL OUT OF ME."
THEY TOLD ME I WASN'T ALLOWED TO LEAVE LOS ANGELES.
AND EVERY TIME I'VE TRIED SINCE THEY SOMEHOW FIND ME, STOP ME, AND BEAT ME UP ALL OVER AGAIN.
"HIS GOONS.
"THE MEN IN BLACK."
WHO, "NEFF"?

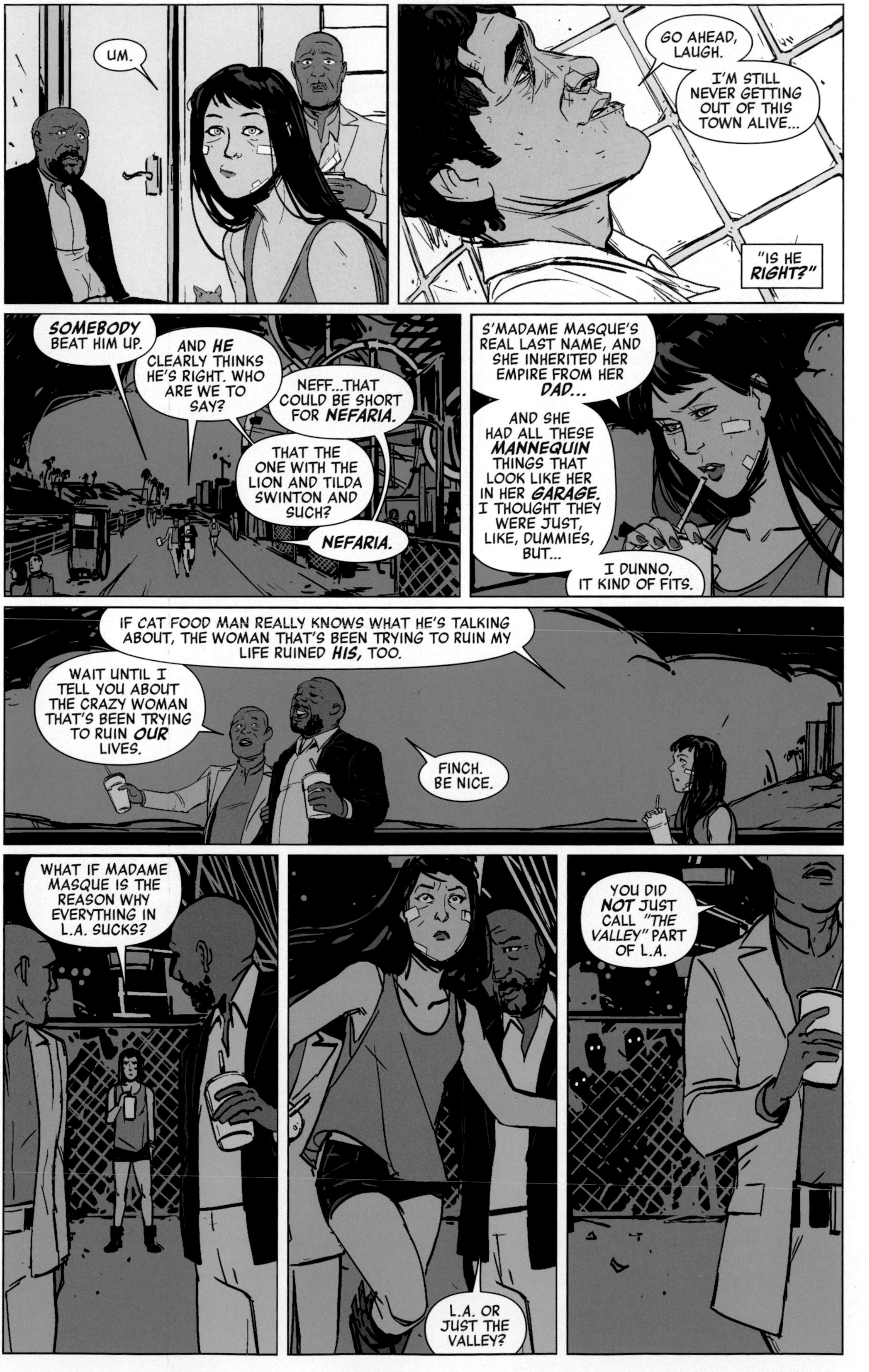
UM.
GO AHEAD, LAUGH.
I'M STILL NEVER GETTING OUT OF THIS TOWN ALIVE...
"IS HE RIGHT?"
SOMEBODY BEAT HIM UP.
AND HE CLEARLY THINKS HE'S RIGHT. WHO ARE WE TO SAY?
NEFF...THAT COULD BE SHORT FOR NEFARIA.
THAT THE ONE WITH THE LION AND TILDA SWINTON AND SUCH?
NEFARIA.
S'MADAME MASQUE'S REAL LAST NAME, AND SHE INHERITED HER EMPIRE FROM HER DAD...
AND SHE HAD ALL THESE MANNEQUIN THINGS THAT LOOK LIKE HER IN HER GARAGE. I THOUGHT THEY WERE JUST, LIKE, DUMMIES, BUT...
I DUNNO, IT KIND OF FITS.
IF CAT FOOD MAN REALLY KNOWS WHAT HE'S TALKING ABOUT, THE WOMAN THAT'S BEEN TRYING TO RUIN MY LIFE RUINED HIS, TOO.
WAIT UNTIL I TELL YOU ABOUT THE CRAZY WOMAN THAT'S BEEN TRYING TO RUIN OUR LIVES.
FINCH. BE NICE.
WHAT IF MADAME MASQUE IS THE REASON WHY EVERYTHING IN L.A. SUCKS?
L.A. OR JUST THE VALLEY?
YOU DID NOT JUST CALL "THE VALLEY" PART OF L.A.

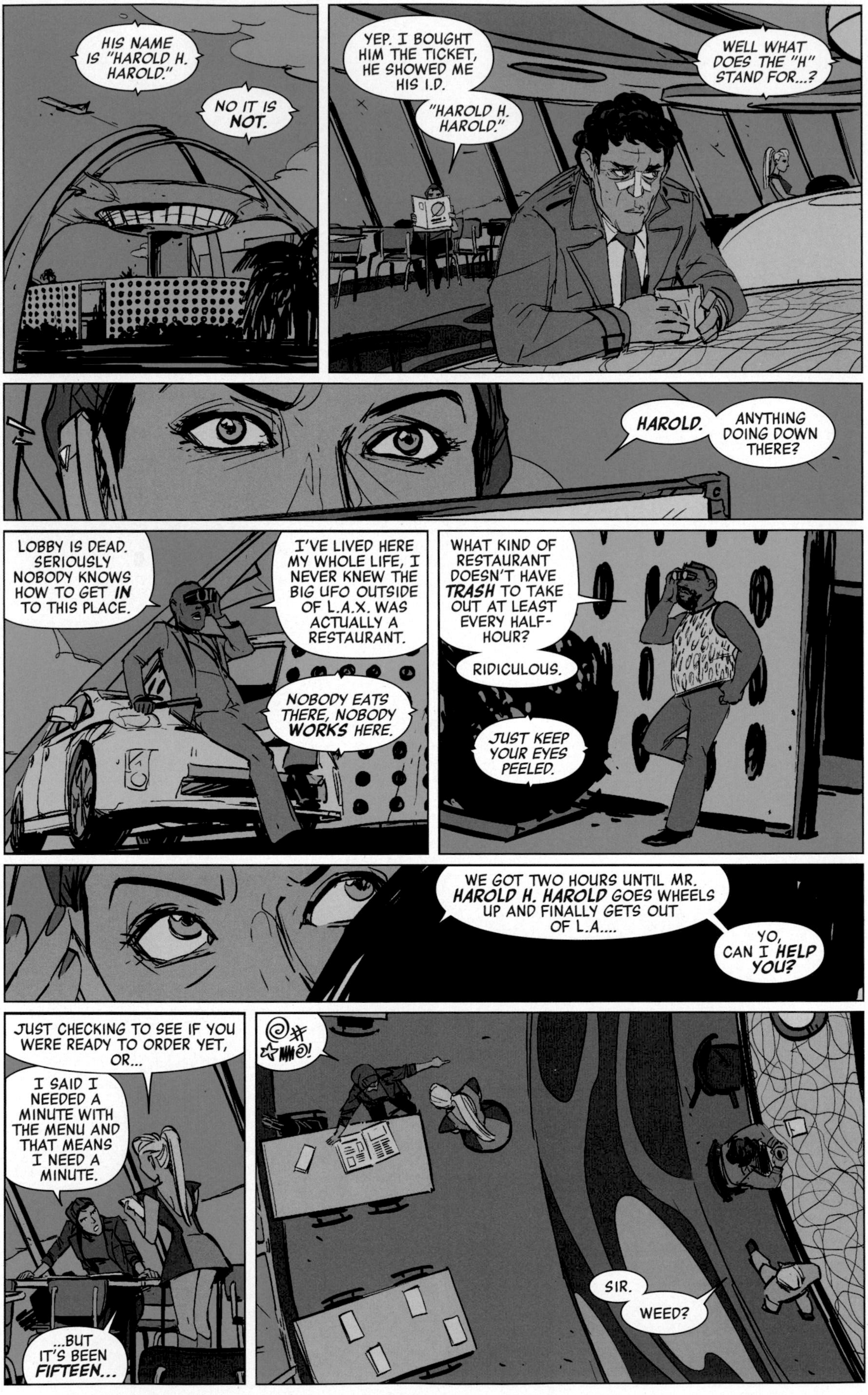
HIS NAME IS "HAROLD H. HAROLD."
NO IT IS NOT.
YEP. I BOUGHT HIM THE TICKET, HE SHOWED ME HIS I.D.
"HAROLD H. HAROLD."
WELL WHAT DOES THE "H" STAND FOR...?
HAROLD.
ANYTHING DOING DOWN THERE?
LOBBY IS DEAD. SERIOUSLY NOBODY KNOWS HOW TO GET IN TO THIS PLACE.
I'VE LIVED HERE MY WHOLE LIFE, I NEVER KNEW THE BIG UFO OUTSIDE OF L.A.X. WAS ACTUALLY A RESTAURANT.
NOBODY EATS THERE, NOBODY WORKS HERE.
WHAT KIND OF RESTAURANT DOESN'T HAVE TRASH TO TAKE OUT AT LEAST EVERY HALF-HOUR?
RIDICULOUS.
JUST KEEP YOUR EYES PEELED.
WE GOT TWO HOURS UNTIL MR. HAROLD H. HAROLD GOES WHEELS UP AND FINALLY GETS OUT OF L.A....
YO, CAN I HELP YOU?
JUST CHECKING TO SEE IF YOU WERE READY TO ORDER YET, OR...
I SAID I NEEDED A MINUTE WITH THE MENU AND THAT MEANS I NEED A MINUTE.
...BUT IT'S BEEN FIFTEEN...
SIR.
WEED?

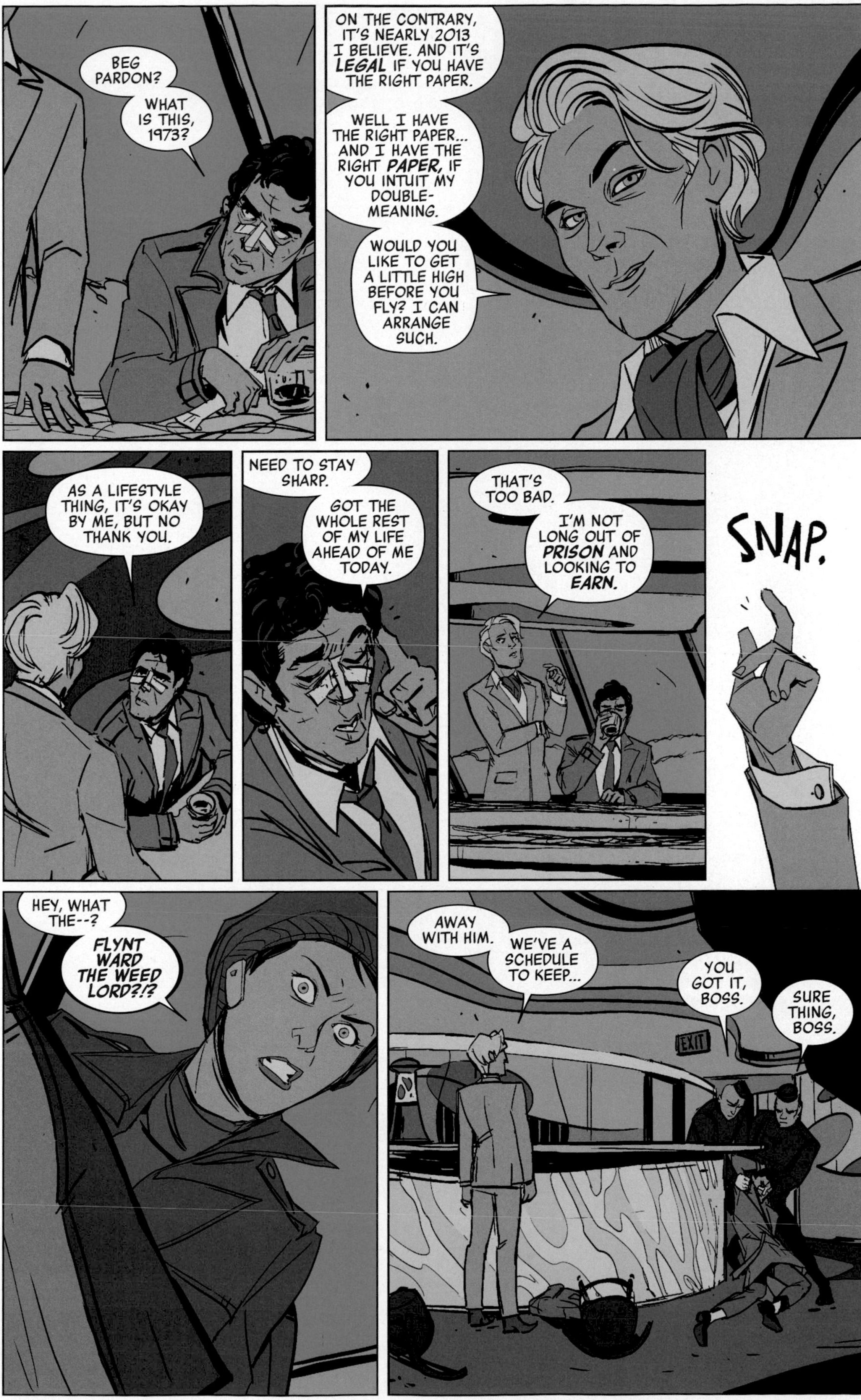
BEG PARDON?
WHAT IS THIS, 1973?
ON THE CONTRARY, IT'S NEARLY 2013 I BELIEVE. AND IT'S LEGAL IF YOU HAVE THE RIGHT PAPER.
WELL I HAVE THE RIGHT PAPER... AND I HAVE THE RIGHT PAPER, IF YOU INTUIT MY DOUBLE-MEANING.
WOULD YOU LIKE TO GET A LITTLE HIGH BEFORE YOU FLY? I CAN ARRANGE SUCH.
AS A LIFESTYLE THING, IT'S OKAY BY ME, BUT NO THANK YOU.
NEED TO STAY SHARP.
GOT THE WHOLE REST OF MY LIFE AHEAD OF ME TODAY.
THAT'S TOO BAD.
I'M NOT LONG OUT OF PRISON AND LOOKING TO EARN.
SNAP.
HEY, WHAT THE--?
FLYNT WARD THE WEED LORD?!?
AWAY WITH HIM.
WE'VE A SCHEDULE TO KEEP...
YOU GOT IT, BOSS.
SURE THING, BOSS.
EXIT

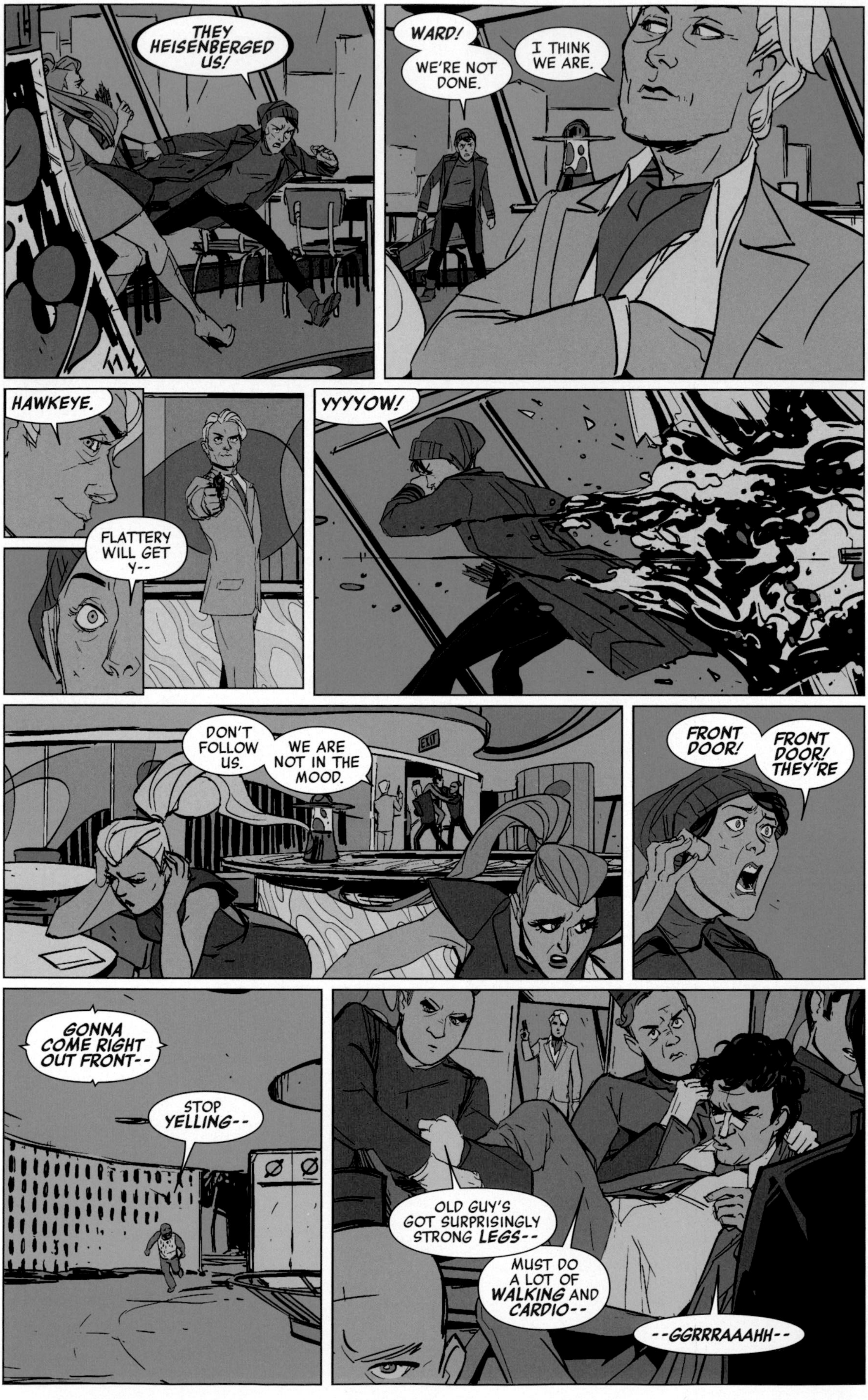
THEY HEISENBERGED US!
WARD!
WE'RE NOT DONE.
I THINK WE ARE.
HAWKEYE.
FLATTERY WILL GET Y--
YYYYOW!
DON'T FOLLOW US.
WE ARE NOT IN THE MOOD.
EXIT
FRONT DOOR!
FRONT DOOR! THEY'RE
GONNA COME RIGHT OUT FRONT--
STOP YELLING--
OLD GUY'S GOT SURPRISINGLY STRONG LEGS--
MUST DO A LOT OF WALKING AND CARDIO--
--GGRRRAAAHH--

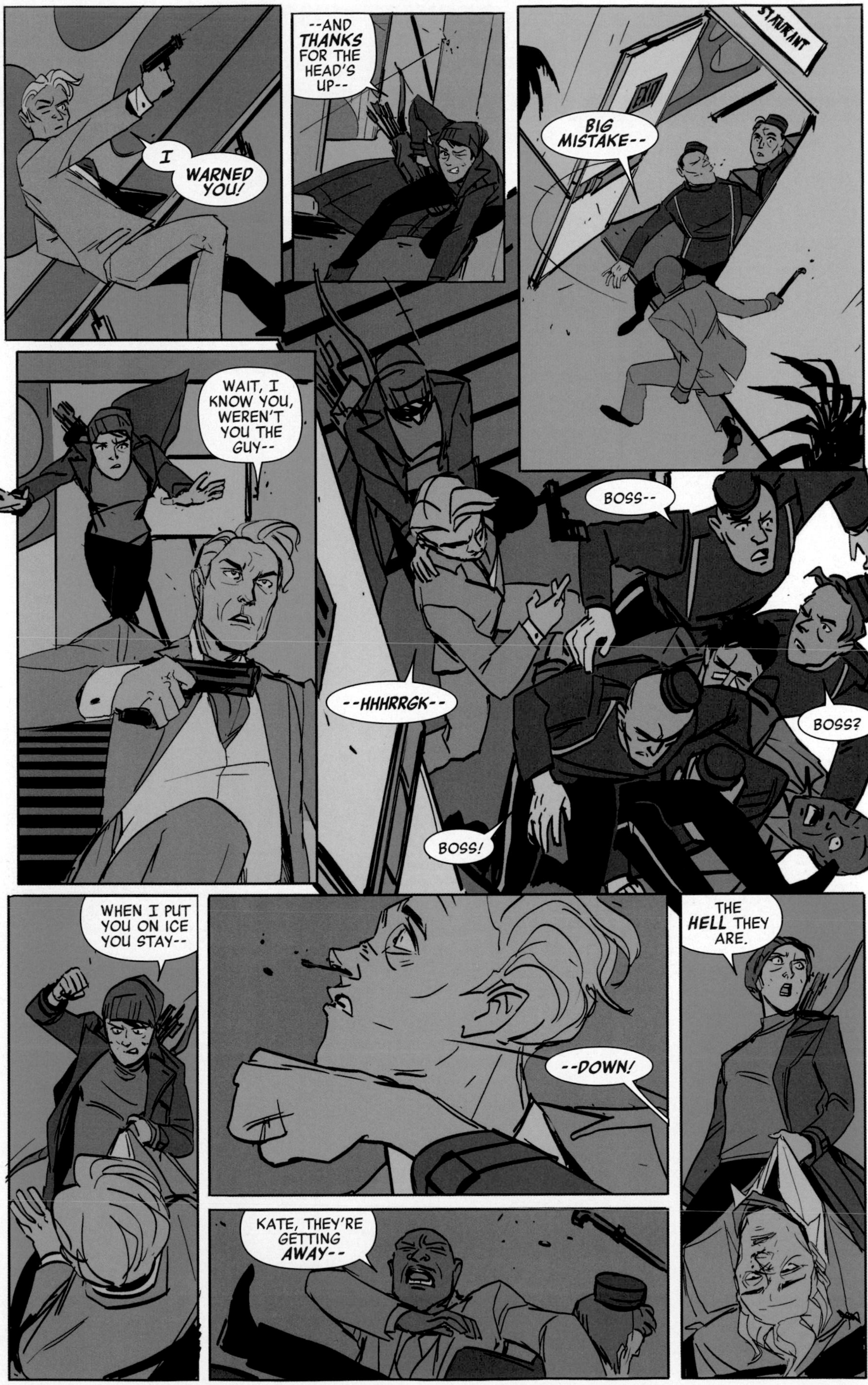
I WARNED YOU!
--AND THANKS FOR THE HEAD'S UP--
BIG MISTAKE--
WAIT, I KNOW YOU, WEREN'T YOU THE GUY--
BOSS--
--HHHRRGK--
BOSS?
BOSS!
WHEN I PUT YOU ON ICE YOU STAY--
--DOWN!
THE HELL THEY ARE.
KATE, THEY'RE GETTING AWAY--

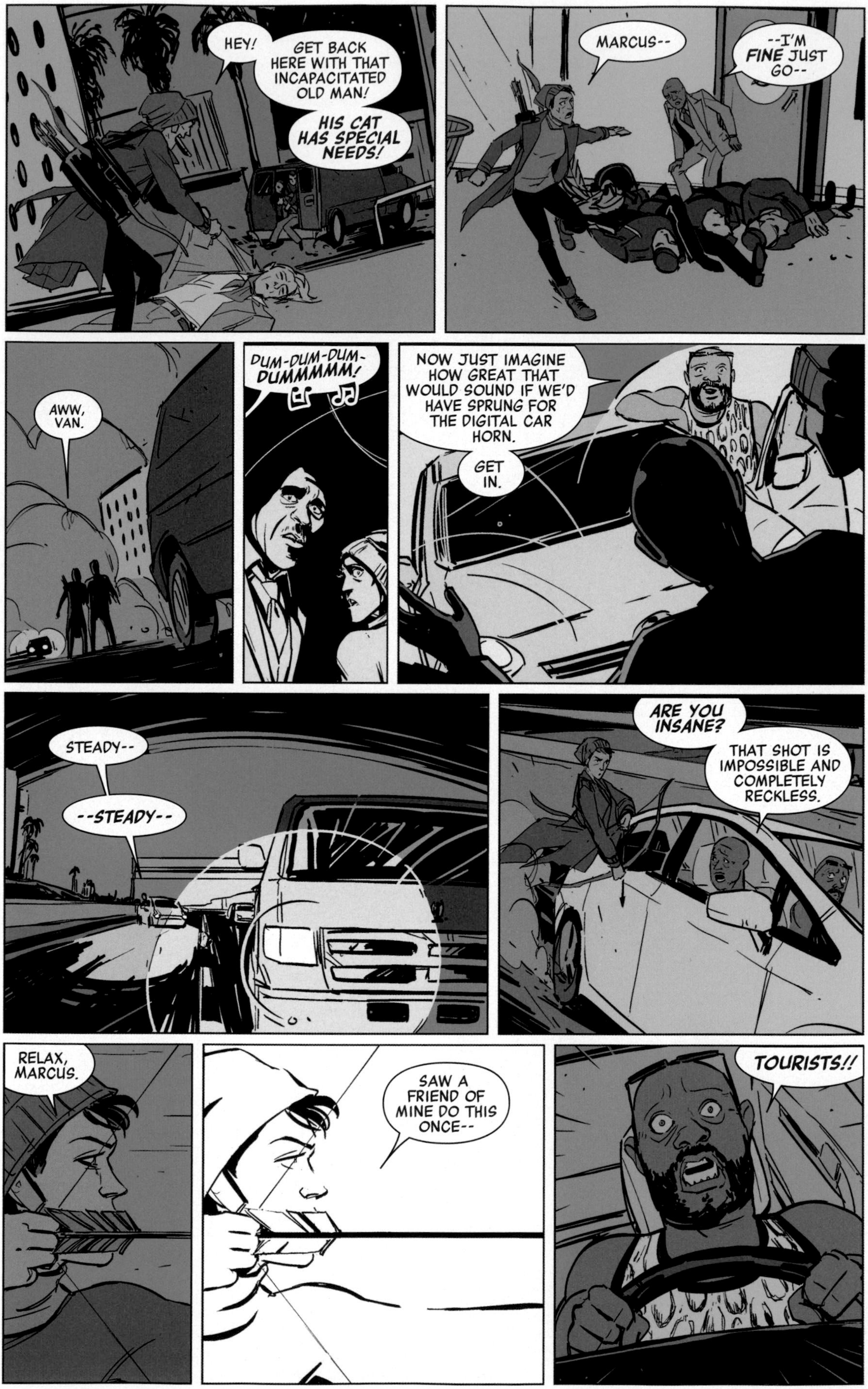
HEY!
GET BACK HERE WITH THAT INCAPACITATED OLD MAN!
HIS CAT HAS SPECIAL NEEDS!
MARCUS--
--I'M FINE JUST GO--
AWW, VAN.
DUM-DUM-DUM-DUMMMMM!
NOW JUST IMAGINE HOW GREAT THAT WOULD SOUND IF WE'D HAVE SPRUNG FOR THE DIGITAL CAR HORN.
GET IN.
STEADY--
--STEADY--
ARE YOU INSANE?
THAT SHOT IS IMPOSSIBLE AND COMPLETELY RECKLESS.
RELAX, MARCUS.
SAW A FRIEND OF MINE DO THIS ONCE--
TOURISTS!!

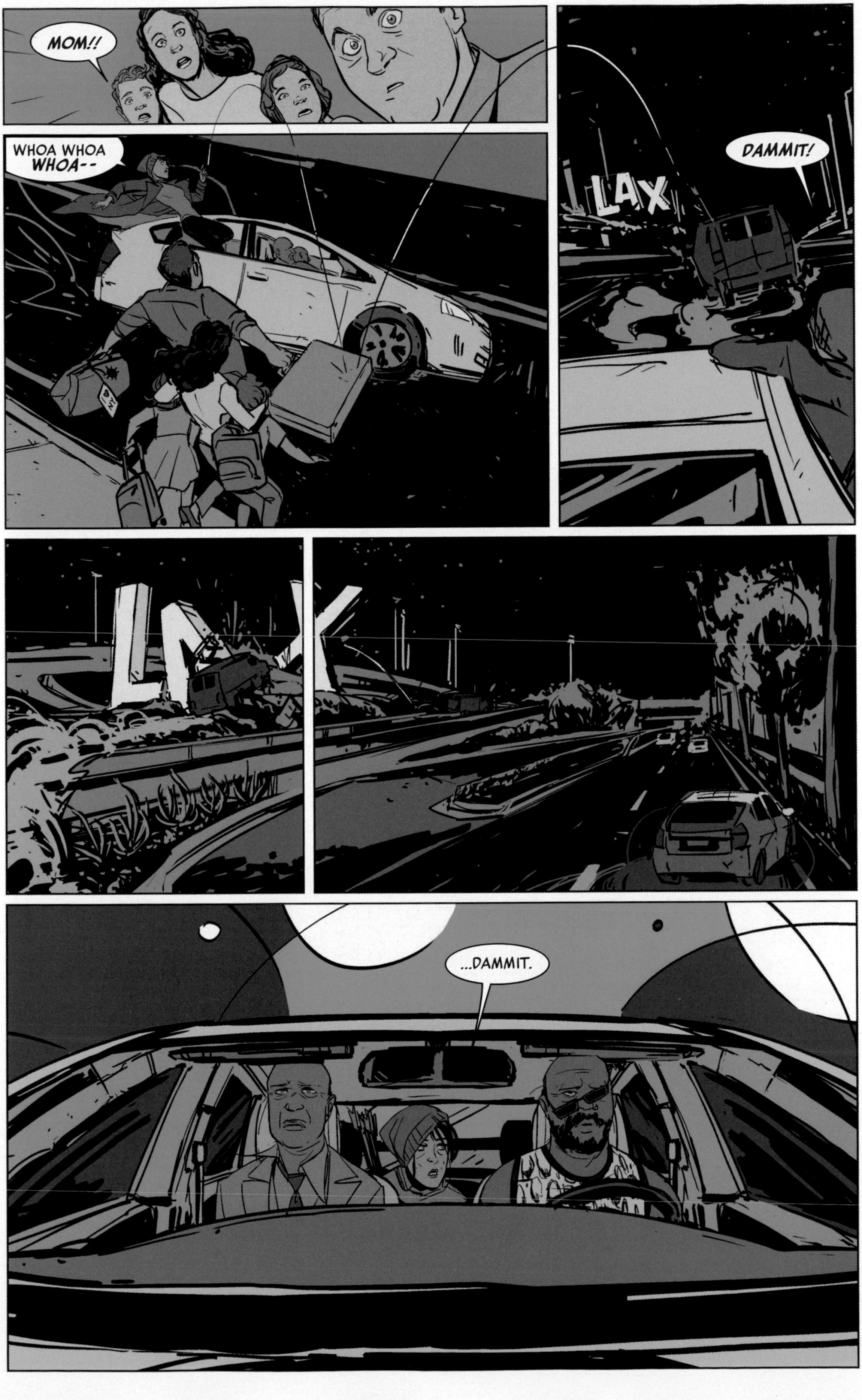
MOM!!
WHOA WHOA WHOA--
DAMMIT!
LAX
...DAMMIT.

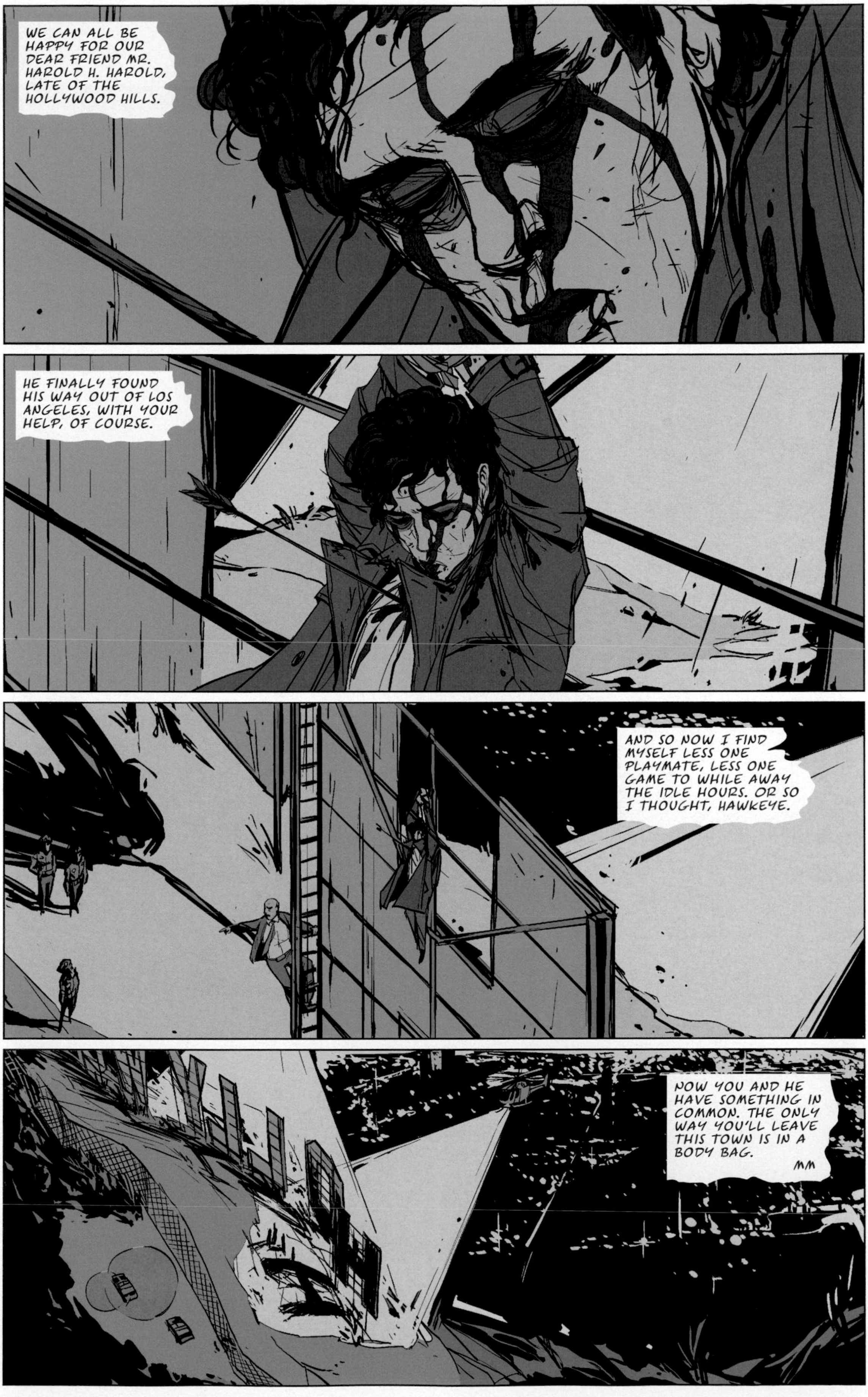
WE CAN ALL BE HAPPY FOR OUR DEAR FRIEND MR. HAROLD H. HAROLD, LATE OF THE HOLLYWOOD HILLS.
HE FINALLY FOUND HIS WAY OUT OF LOS ANGELES, WITH YOUR HELP, OF COURSE.
AND SO NOW I FIND MYSELF LESS ONE PLAYMATE, LESS ONE GAME TO WHILE AWAY THE IDLE HOURS. OR SO I THOUGHT, HAWKEYE.
NOW YOU AND HE HAVE SOMETHING IN COMMON. THE ONLY WAY YOU'LL LEAVE THIS TOWN IS IN A BODY BAG.
MM

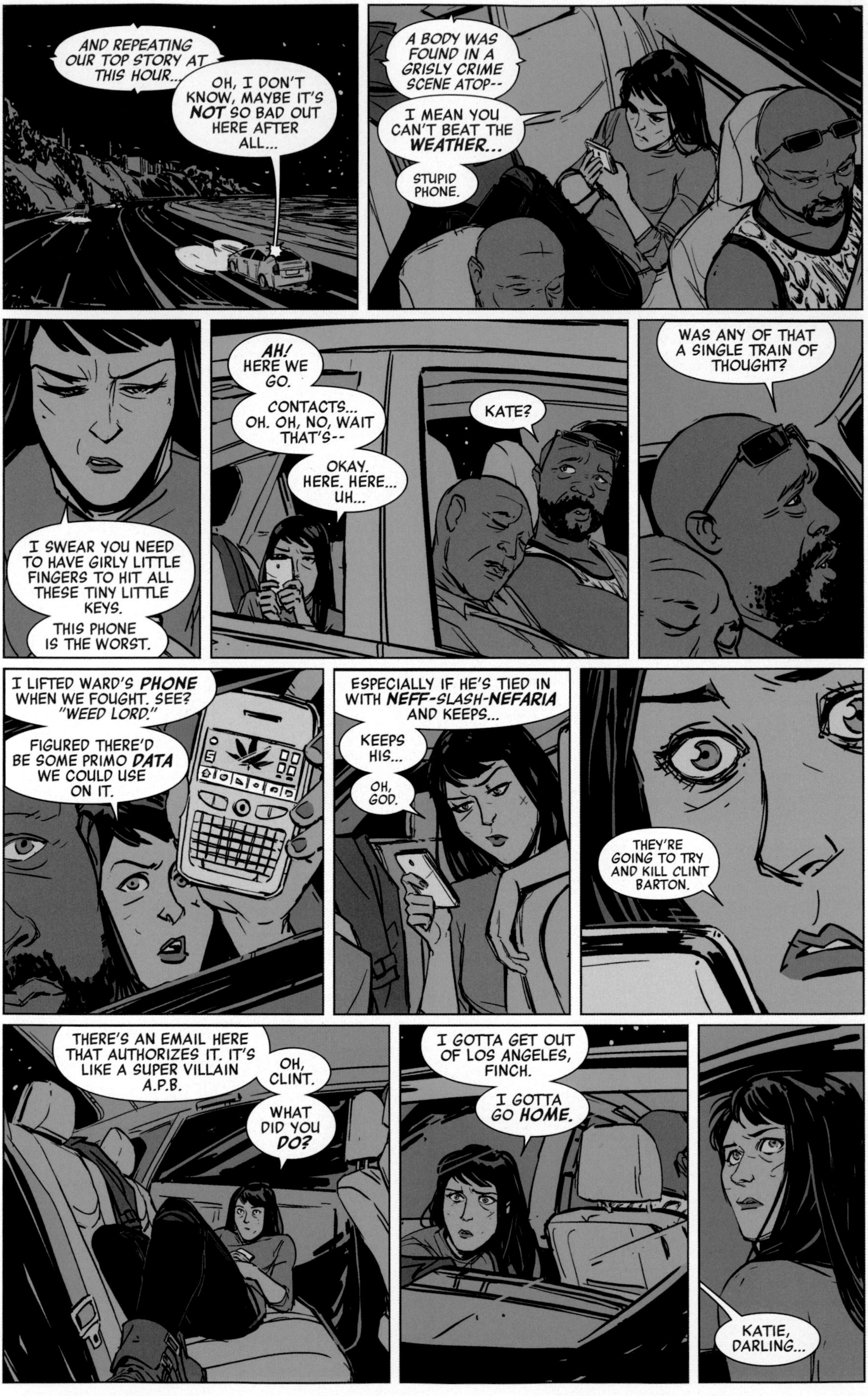
AND REPEATING OUR TOP STORY AT THIS HOUR...
OH, I DON'T KNOW, MAYBE IT'S NOT SO BAD OUT HERE AFTER ALL...
A BODY WAS FOUND IN A GRISLY CRIME SCENE ATOP--
I MEAN YOU CAN'T BEAT THE WEATHER...
STUPID PHONE.
I SWEAR YOU NEED TO HAVE GIRLY LITTLE FINGERS TO HIT ALL THESE TINY LITTLE KEYS.
THIS PHONE IS THE WORST.
AH! HERE WE GO.
CONTACTS... OH. OH, NO, WAIT THAT'S--
OKAY. HERE. HERE... UH...
KATE?
WAS ANY OF THAT A SINGLE TRAIN OF THOUGHT?
I LIFTED WARD'S PHONE WHEN WE FOUGHT. SEE? "WEED LORD."
FIGURED THERE'D BE SOME PRIMO DATA WE COULD USE ON IT.
ESPECIALLY IF HE'S TIED IN WITH NEFF-SLASH-NEFARIA AND KEEPS...
KEEPS HIS...
OH, GOD.
THEY'RE GOING TO TRY AND KILL CLINT BARTON.
THERE'S AN EMAIL HERE THAT AUTHORIZES IT. IT'S LIKE A SUPER VILLAIN A.P.B.
OH, CLINT.
WHAT DID YOU DO?
I GOTTA GET OUT OF LOS ANGELES, FINCH.
I GOTTA GO HOME.
KATIE, DARLING...

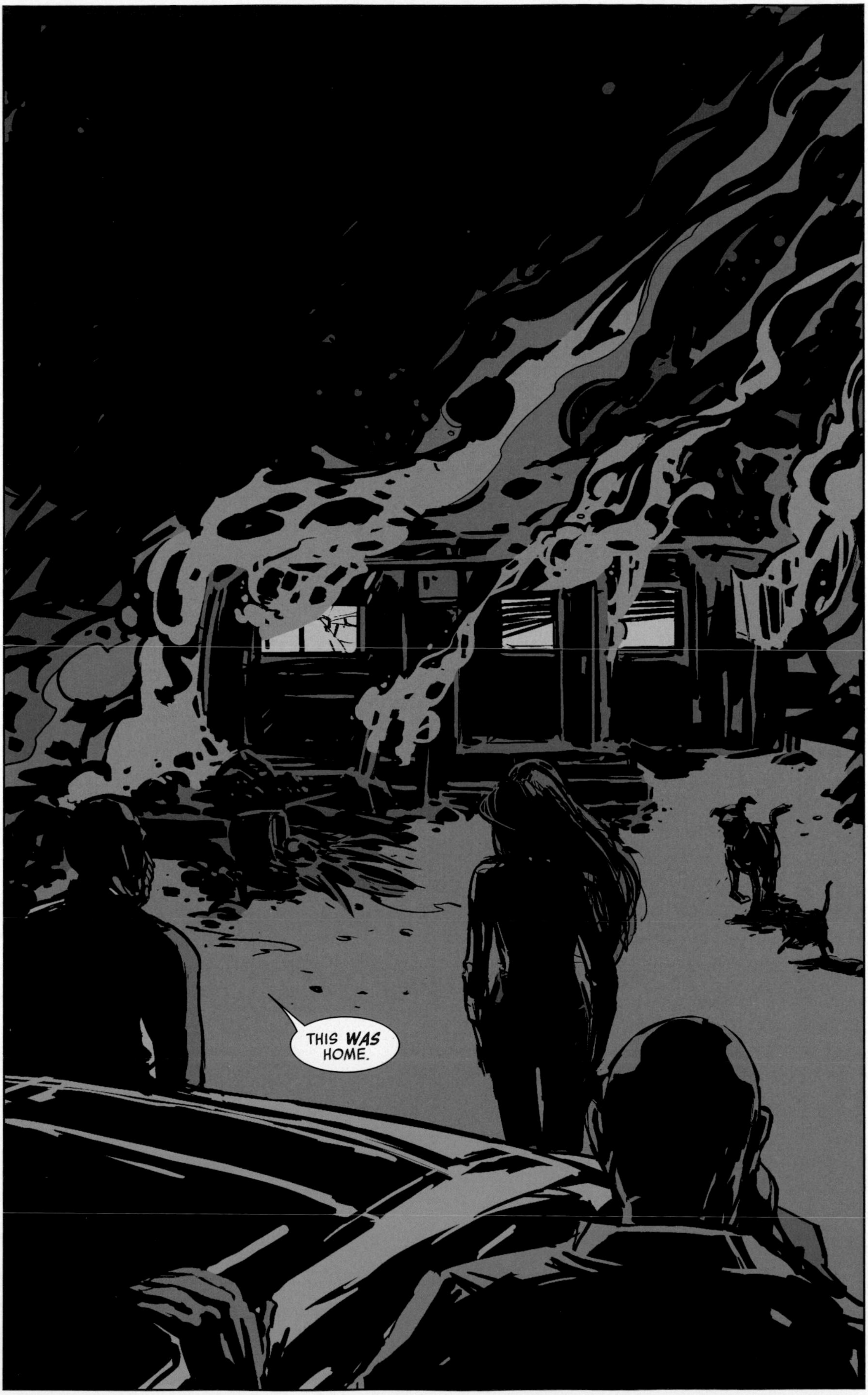
THIS WAS HOME.

20

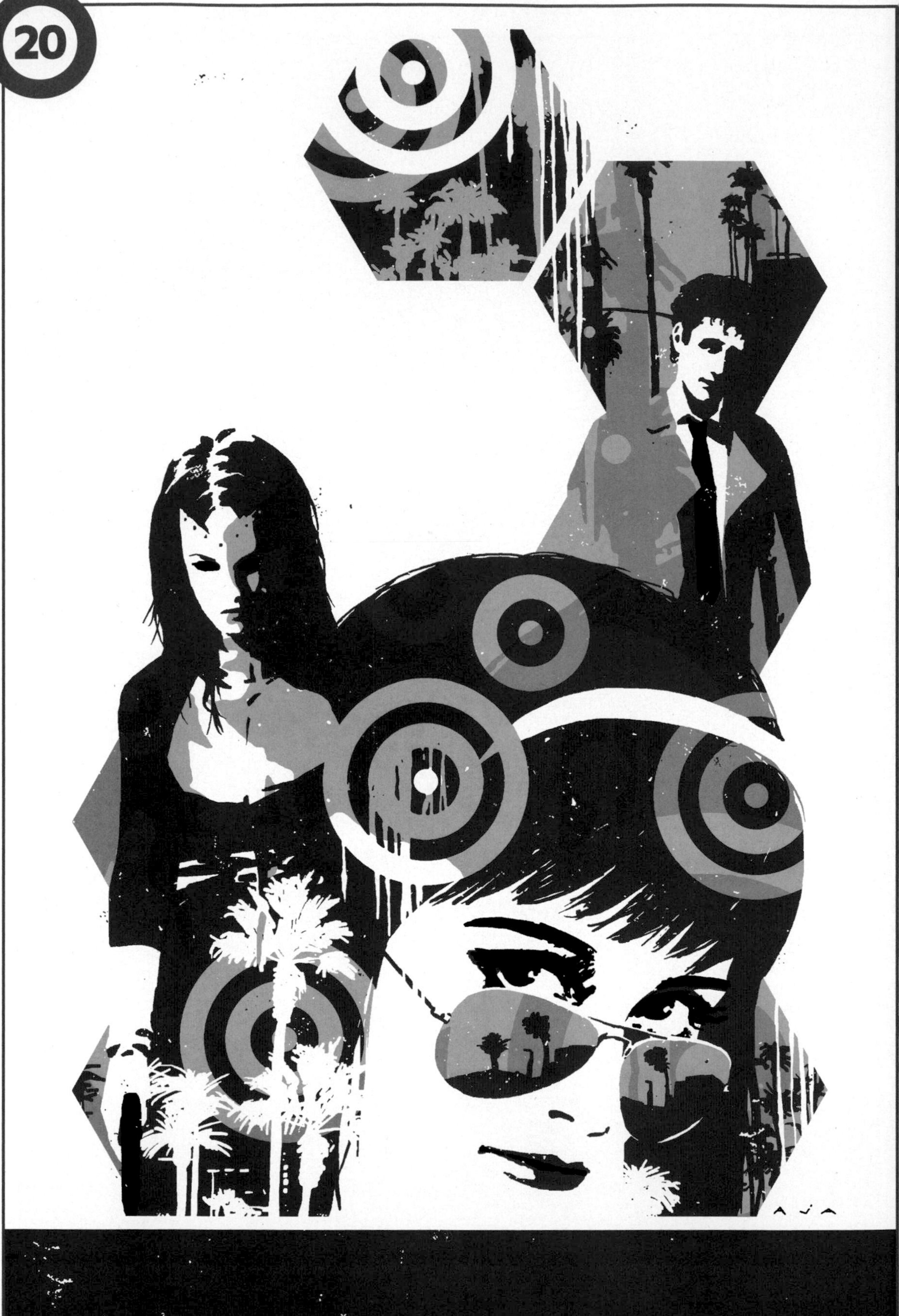
AJA

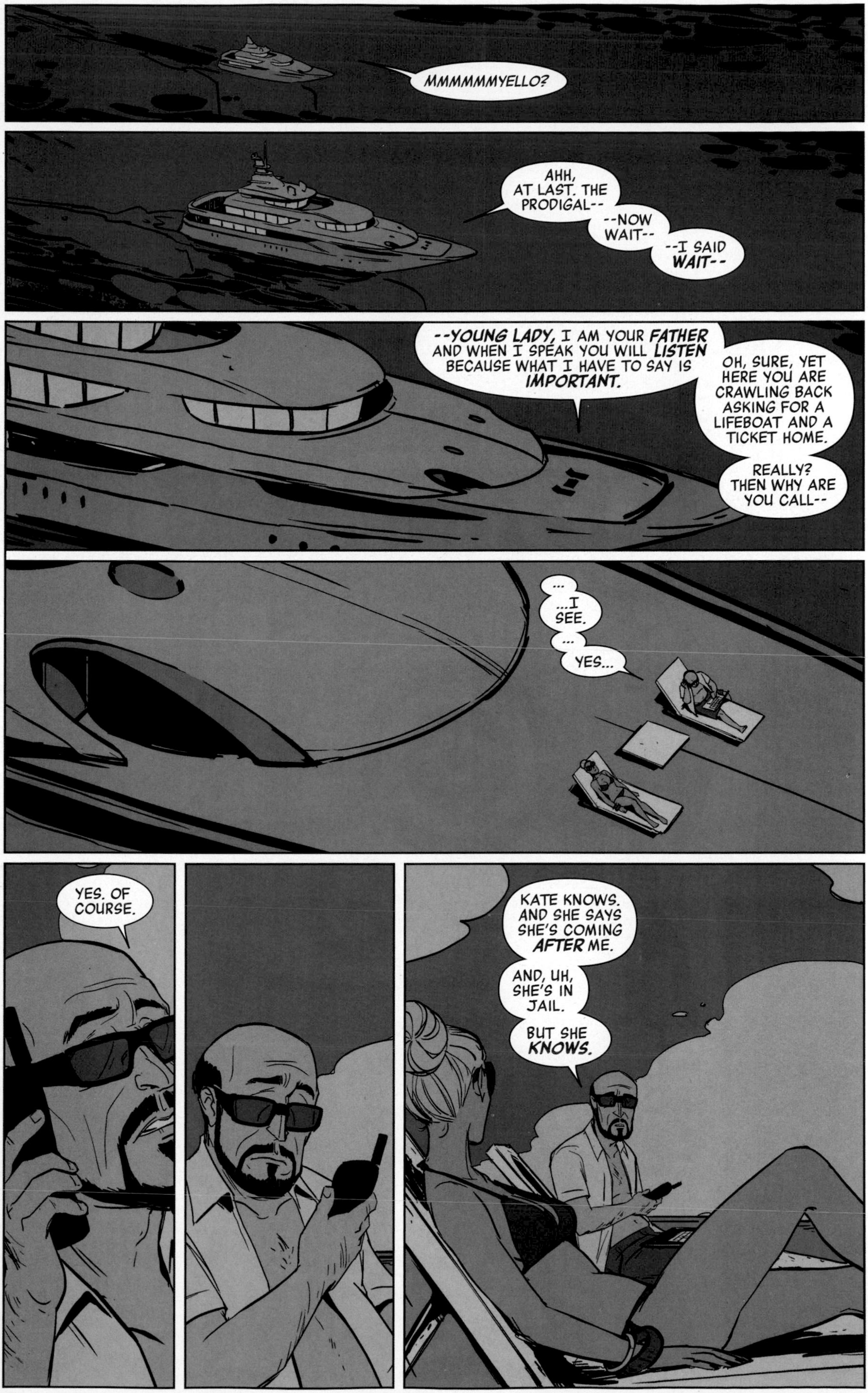
MMMMMMYELLO?
AHH, AT LAST. THE PRODIGAL--
--NOW WAIT--
--I SAID WAIT--
--YOUNG LADY, I AM YOUR FATHER AND WHEN I SPEAK YOU WILL LISTEN BECAUSE WHAT I HAVE TO SAY IS IMPORTANT.
OH, SURE, YET HERE YOU ARE CRAWLING BACK ASKING FOR A LIFEBOAT AND A TICKET HOME.
REALLY? THEN WHY ARE YOU CALL--
...
...I SEE.
...
YES...
YES. OF COURSE.
KATE KNOWS. AND SHE SAYS SHE'S COMING AFTER ME.
AND, UH, SHE'S IN JAIL.
BUT SHE KNOWS.

"WHEN DO I GET MY *PHONE CALL?*"

"PLEASE TURN *BACK--*"

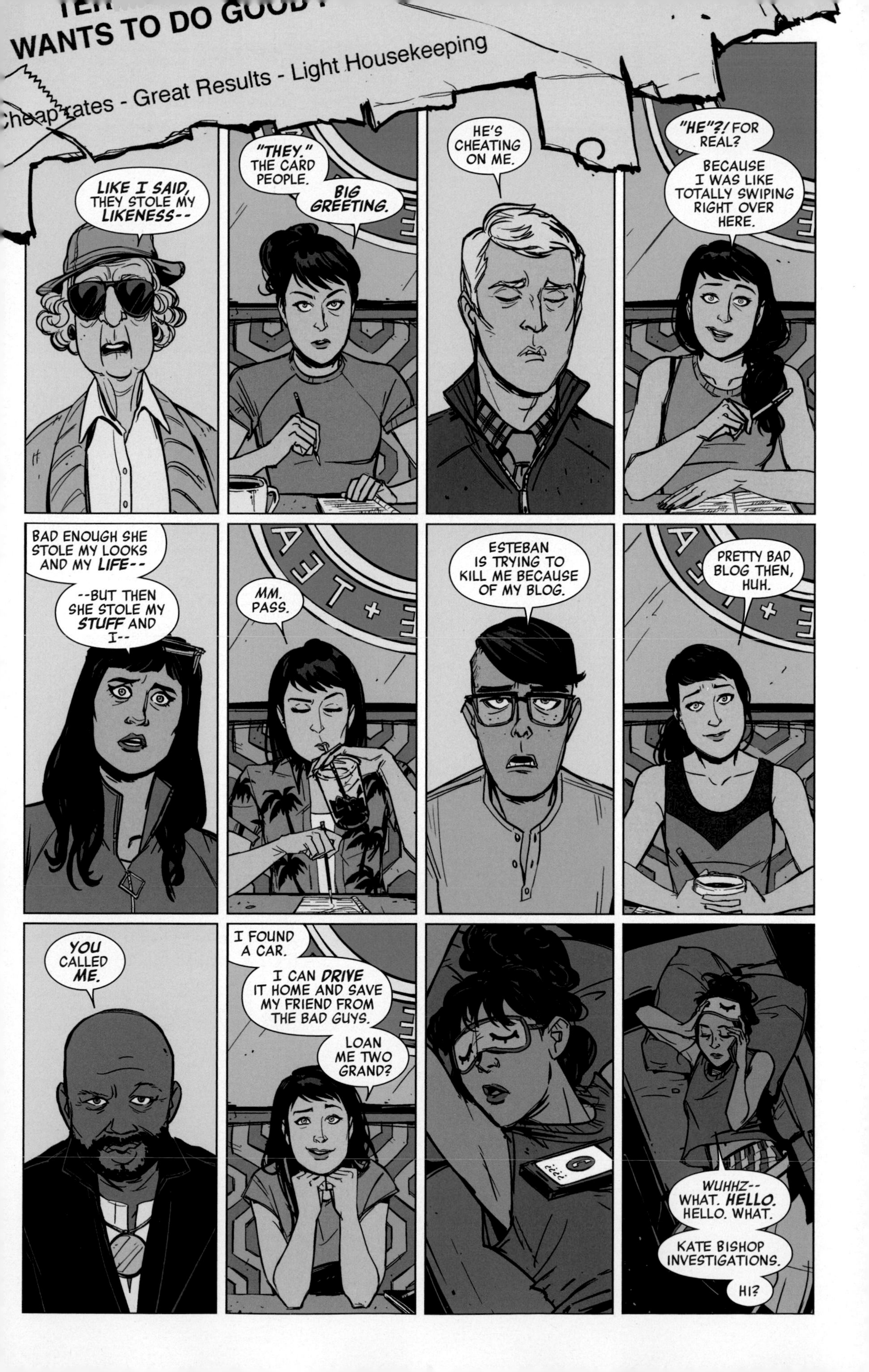
WANTS TO DO GOOD
Cheap rates - Great Results - Light Housekeeping
LIKE I SAID, THEY STOLE MY LIKENESS--
"THEY." THE CARD PEOPLE.
BIG GREETING.
HE'S CHEATING ON ME.
"HE"?! FOR REAL?
BECAUSE I WAS LIKE TOTALLY SWIPING RIGHT OVER HERE.
BAD ENOUGH SHE STOLE MY LOOKS AND MY LIFE--
--BUT THEN SHE STOLE MY STUFF AND I--
MM. PASS.
ESTEBAN IS TRYING TO KILL ME BECAUSE OF MY BLOG.
PRETTY BAD BLOG THEN, HUH.
YOU CALLED ME.
I FOUND A CAR.
I CAN DRIVE IT HOME AND SAVE MY FRIEND FROM THE BAD GUYS.
LOAN ME TWO GRAND?
WUHHZ-- WHAT. HELLO. HELLO. WHAT.
KATE BISHOP INVESTIGATIONS.
HI?

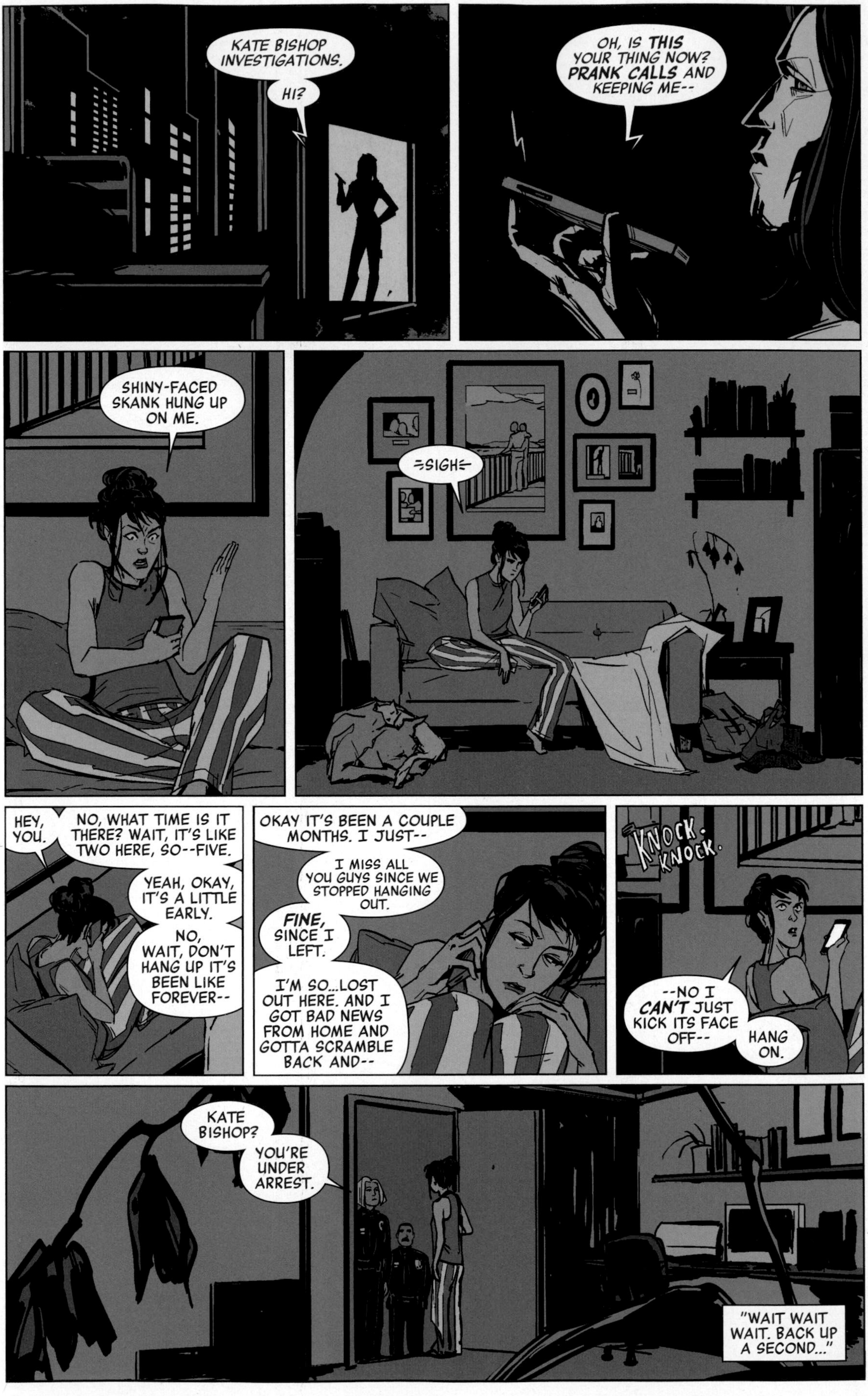

KATE BISHOP INVESTIGATIONS.
HI?
OH, IS THIS YOUR THING NOW? PRANK CALLS AND KEEPING ME--
SHINY-FACED SKANK HUNG UP ON ME.
=SIGH=
HEY, YOU.
NO, WHAT TIME IS IT THERE? WAIT, IT'S LIKE TWO HERE, SO--FIVE.
YEAH, OKAY, IT'S A LITTLE EARLY.
NO, WAIT, DON'T HANG UP IT'S BEEN LIKE FOREVER--
OKAY IT'S BEEN A COUPLE MONTHS. I JUST--
I MISS ALL YOU GUYS SINCE WE STOPPED HANGING OUT.
FINE, SINCE I LEFT.
I'M SO...LOST OUT HERE. AND I GOT BAD NEWS FROM HOME AND GOTTA SCRAMBLE BACK AND--
KNOCK KNOCK
--NO I CAN'T JUST KICK ITS FACE OFF--
HANG ON.
KATE BISHOP?
YOU'RE UNDER ARREST.
"WAIT WAIT WAIT. BACK UP A SECOND..."

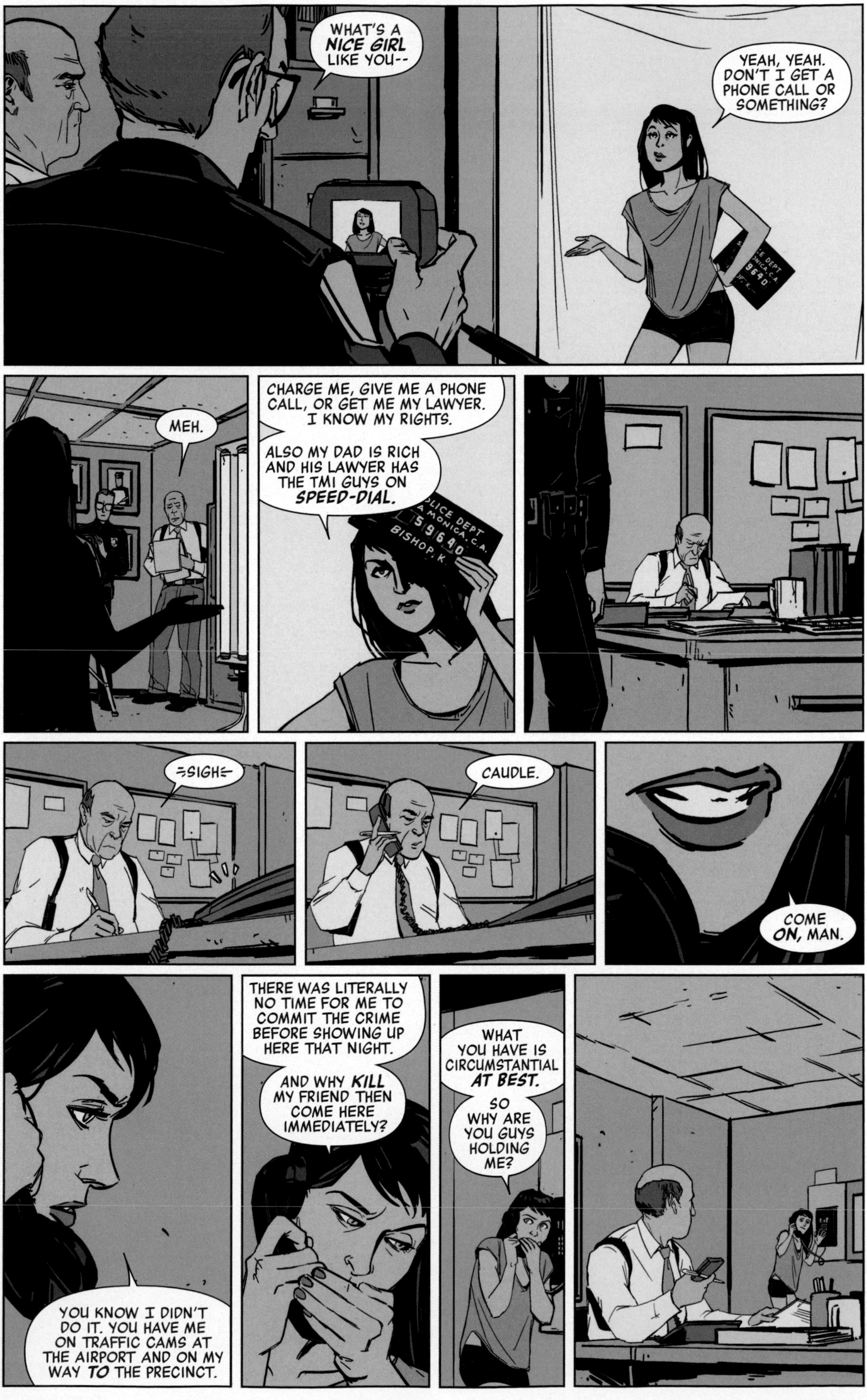

WHAT'S A NICE GIRL LIKE YOU--
YEAH, YEAH. DON'T I GET A PHONE CALL OR SOMETHING?
MEH.
CHARGE ME, GIVE ME A PHONE CALL, OR GET ME MY LAWYER. I KNOW MY RIGHTS.
ALSO MY DAD IS RICH AND HIS LAWYER HAS THE TMI GUYS ON SPEED-DIAL.
POLICE DEPT
A MONICA, C.A.
159640
BISHOP, K.
=SIGH=
CAUDLE.
COME ON, MAN.
YOU KNOW I DIDN'T DO IT. YOU HAVE ME ON TRAFFIC CAMS AT THE AIRPORT AND ON MY WAY TO THE PRECINCT.
THERE WAS LITERALLY NO TIME FOR ME TO COMMIT THE CRIME BEFORE SHOWING UP HERE THAT NIGHT.
AND WHY KILL MY FRIEND THEN COME HERE IMMEDIATELY?
WHAT YOU HAVE IS CIRCUMSTANTIAL AT BEST.
SO WHY ARE YOU GUYS HOLDING ME?

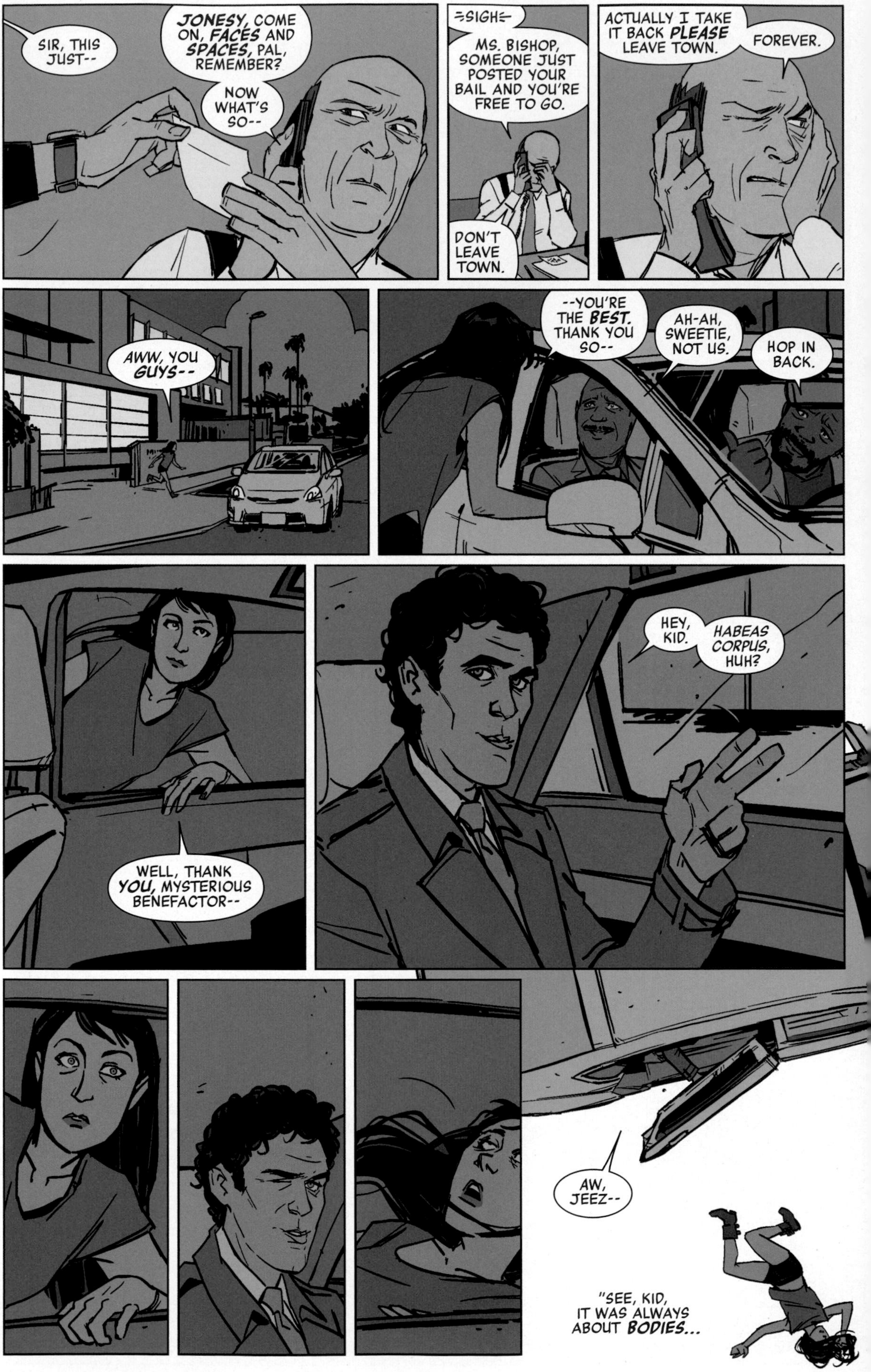
SIR, THIS JUST--
JONESY, COME ON, FACES AND SPACES, PAL, REMEMBER?
NOW WHAT'S SO--
=SIGH=
MS. BISHOP, SOMEONE JUST POSTED YOUR BAIL AND YOU'RE FREE TO GO.
DON'T LEAVE TOWN.
ACTUALLY I TAKE IT BACK PLEASE LEAVE TOWN.
FOREVER.
AWW, YOU GUYS--
--YOU'RE THE BEST. THANK YOU SO--
AH-AH, SWEETIE, NOT US.
HOP IN BACK.
WELL, THANK YOU, MYSTERIOUS BENEFACTOR--
HEY, KID.
HABEAS CORPUS, HUH?
AW, JEEZ--
"SEE, KID, IT WAS ALWAYS ABOUT BODIES...

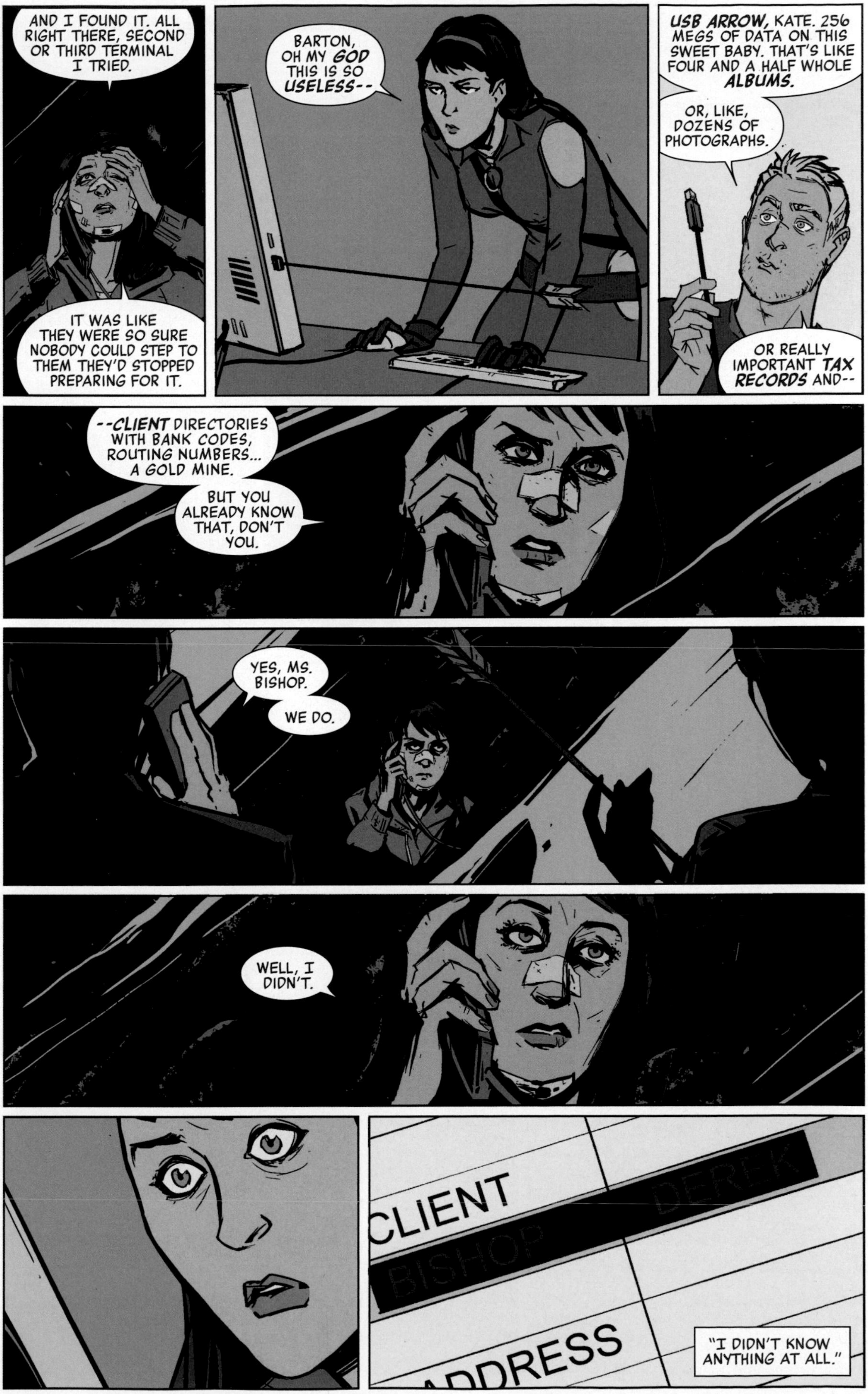
AND I FOUND IT. ALL RIGHT THERE, SECOND OR THIRD TERMINAL I TRIED.
IT WAS LIKE THEY WERE SO SURE NOBODY COULD STEP TO THEM THEY'D STOPPED PREPARING FOR IT.
BARTON, OH MY GOD THIS IS SO USELESS--
USB ARROW, KATE. 256 MEGS OF DATA ON THIS SWEET BABY. THAT'S LIKE FOUR AND A HALF WHOLE ALBUMS.
OR, LIKE, DOZENS OF PHOTOGRAPHS.
OR REALLY IMPORTANT TAX RECORDS AND--
--CLIENT DIRECTORIES WITH BANK CODES, ROUTING NUMBERS... A GOLD MINE.
BUT YOU ALREADY KNOW THAT, DON'T YOU.
YES, MS. BISHOP.
WE DO.
WELL, I DIDN'T.
CLIENT
DEREK
BISHOP
ADDRESS
"I DIDN'T KNOW ANYTHING AT ALL."

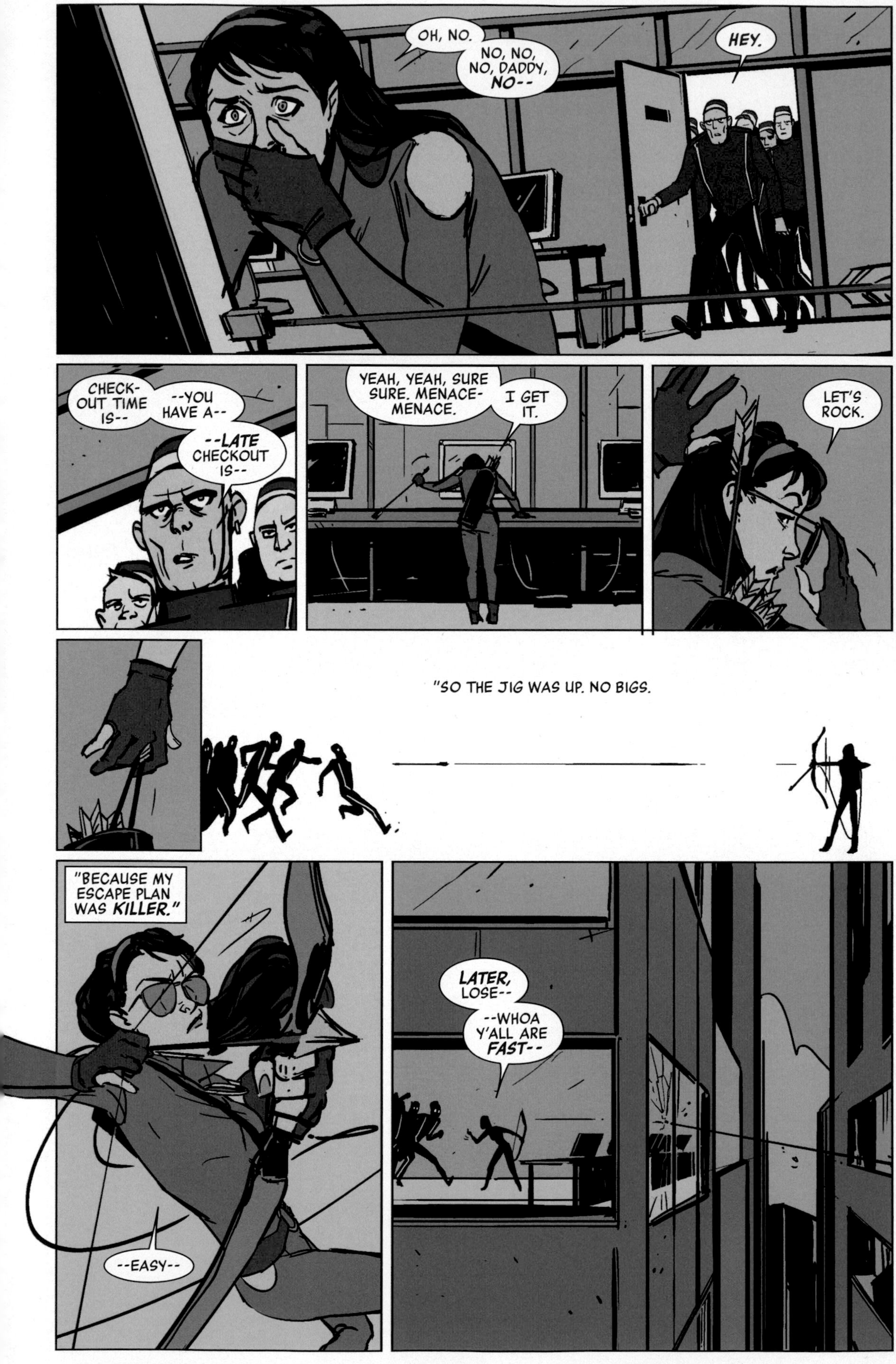
OH, NO.
NO, NO, NO, DADDY, NO--
HEY.
CHECK-OUT TIME IS--
--YOU HAVE A--
--LATE CHECKOUT IS--
YEAH, YEAH, SURE SURE. MENACE-MENACE.
I GET IT.
LET'S ROCK.
"SO THE JIG WAS UP. NO BIGS.
"BECAUSE MY ESCAPE PLAN WAS KILLER."
--EASY--
LATER, LOSE--
--WHOA Y'ALL ARE FAST--

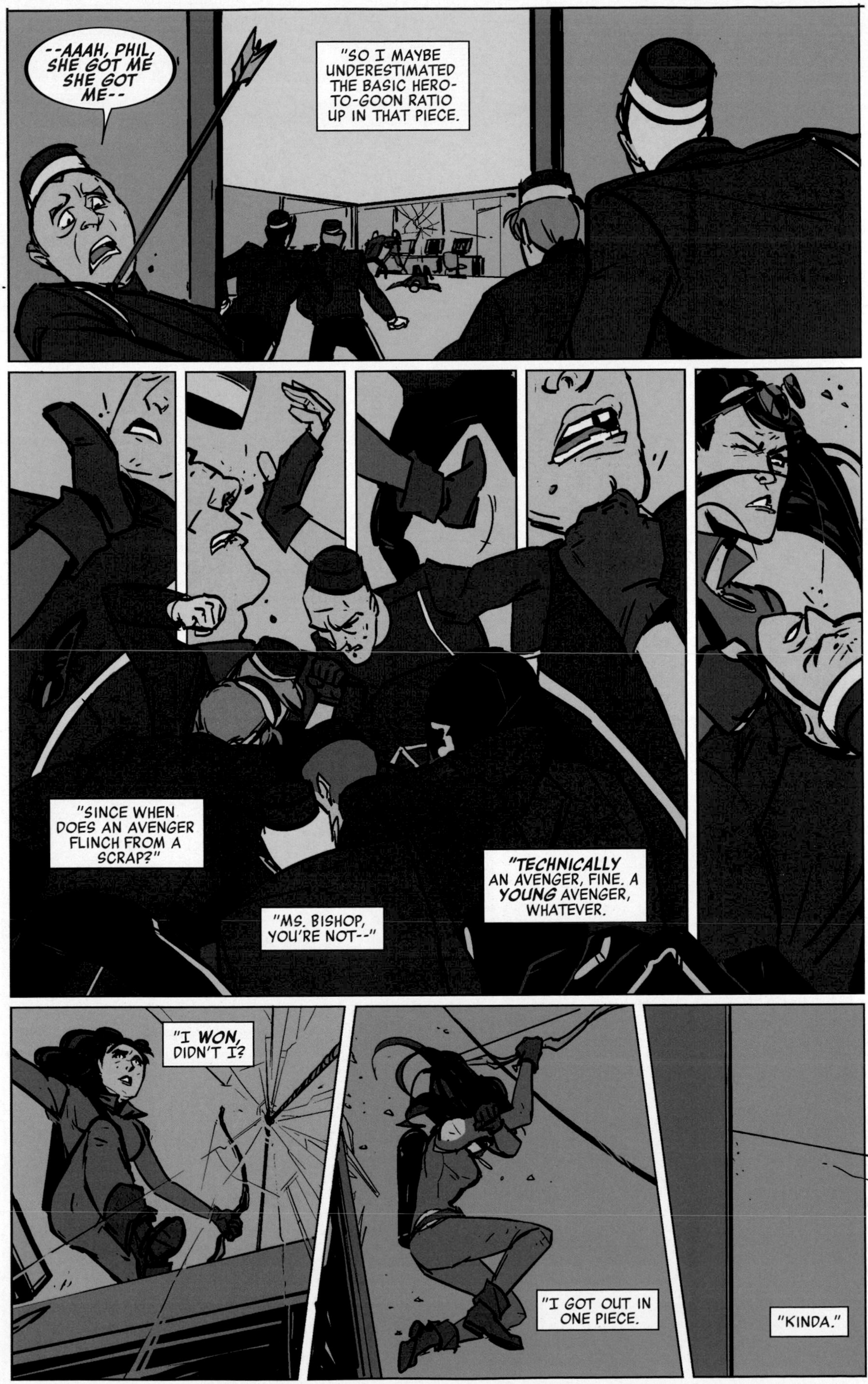
--AAAH, PHIL, SHE GOT ME SHE GOT ME--
"SO I MAYBE UNDERESTIMATED THE BASIC HERO-TO-GOON RATIO UP IN THAT PIECE.
"SINCE WHEN DOES AN AVENGER FLINCH FROM A SCRAP?"
"MS. BISHOP, YOU'RE NOT--"
"TECHNICALLY AN AVENGER, FINE. A YOUNG AVENGER, WHATEVER.
"I WON, DIDN'T I?
"I GOT OUT IN ONE PIECE.
"KINDA."

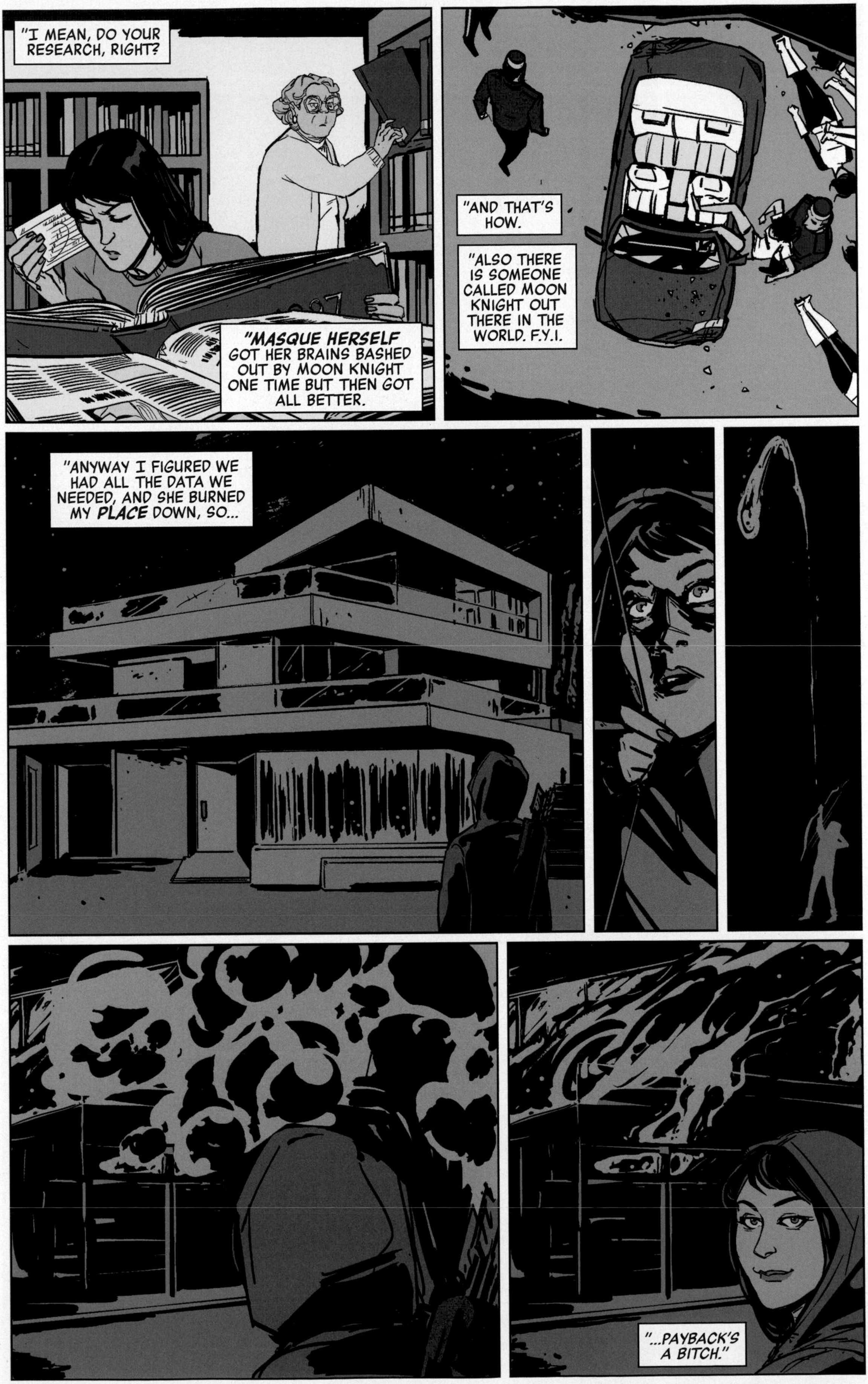
"I MEAN, DO YOUR RESEARCH, RIGHT?
"MASQUE HERSELF GOT HER BRAINS BASHED OUT BY MOON KNIGHT ONE TIME BUT THEN GOT ALL BETTER.
"AND THAT'S HOW.
"ALSO THERE IS SOMEONE CALLED MOON KNIGHT OUT THERE IN THE WORLD. F.Y.I.
"ANYWAY I FIGURED WE HAD ALL THE DATA WE NEEDED, AND SHE BURNED MY PLACE DOWN, SO...
"...PAYBACK'S A BITCH."

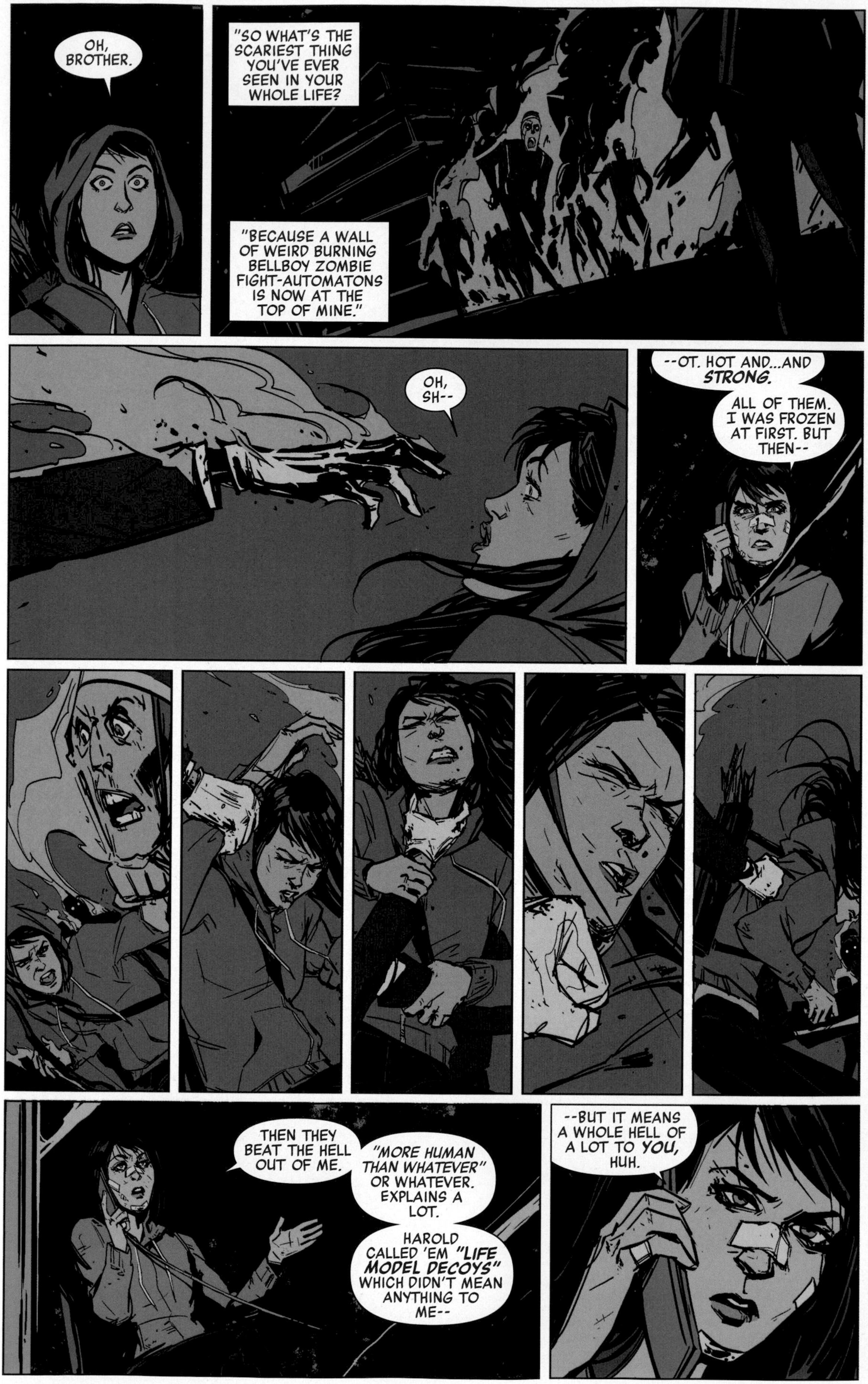
OH, BROTHER.
"SO WHAT'S THE SCARIEST THING YOU'VE EVER SEEN IN YOUR WHOLE LIFE?
"BECAUSE A WALL OF WEIRD BURNING BELLBOY ZOMBIE FIGHT-AUTOMATONS IS NOW AT THE TOP OF MINE."
OH, SH--
--OT. HOT AND...AND **STRONG.**
ALL OF THEM. I WAS FROZEN AT FIRST. BUT THEN--
THEN THEY BEAT THE HELL OUT OF ME.
"MORE HUMAN THAN WHATEVER" OR WHATEVER. EXPLAINS A LOT.
HAROLD CALLED 'EM ***"LIFE MODEL DECOYS"*** WHICH DIDN'T MEAN ANYTHING TO ME--
--BUT IT MEANS A WHOLE HELL OF A LOT TO ***YOU,*** HUH.

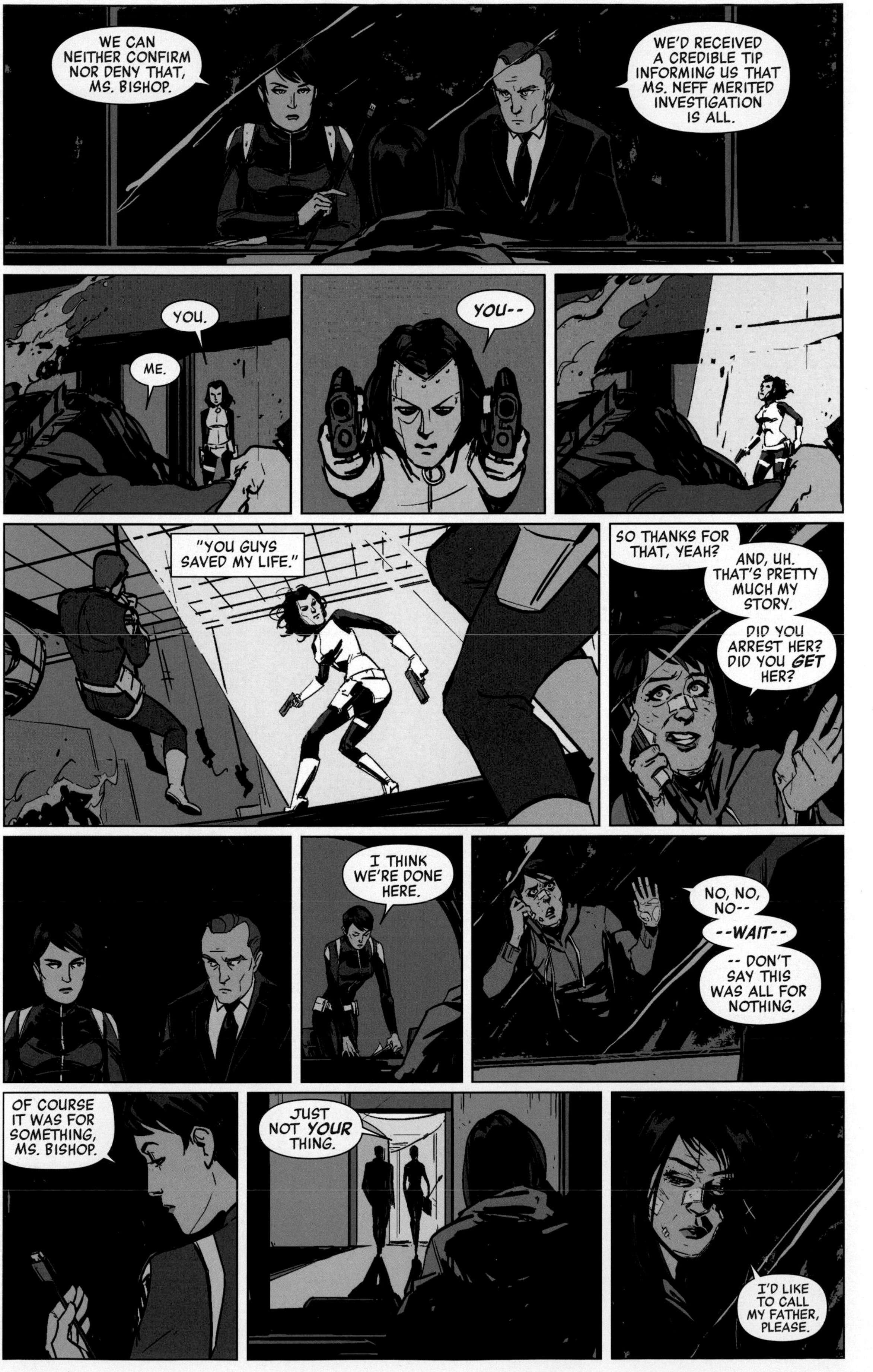
WE CAN NEITHER CONFIRM NOR DENY THAT, MS. BISHOP.
WE'D RECEIVED A CREDIBLE TIP INFORMING US THAT MS. NEFF MERITED INVESTIGATION IS ALL.
YOU.
ME.
YOU--
"YOU GUYS SAVED MY LIFE."
SO THANKS FOR THAT, YEAH?
AND, UH. THAT'S PRETTY MUCH MY STORY.
DID YOU ARREST HER? DID YOU GET HER?
I THINK WE'RE DONE HERE.
NO, NO, NO--
--WAIT--
-- DON'T SAY THIS WAS ALL FOR NOTHING.
OF COURSE IT WAS FOR SOMETHING, MS. BISHOP.
JUST NOT YOUR THING.
I'D LIKE TO CALL MY FATHER, PLEASE.

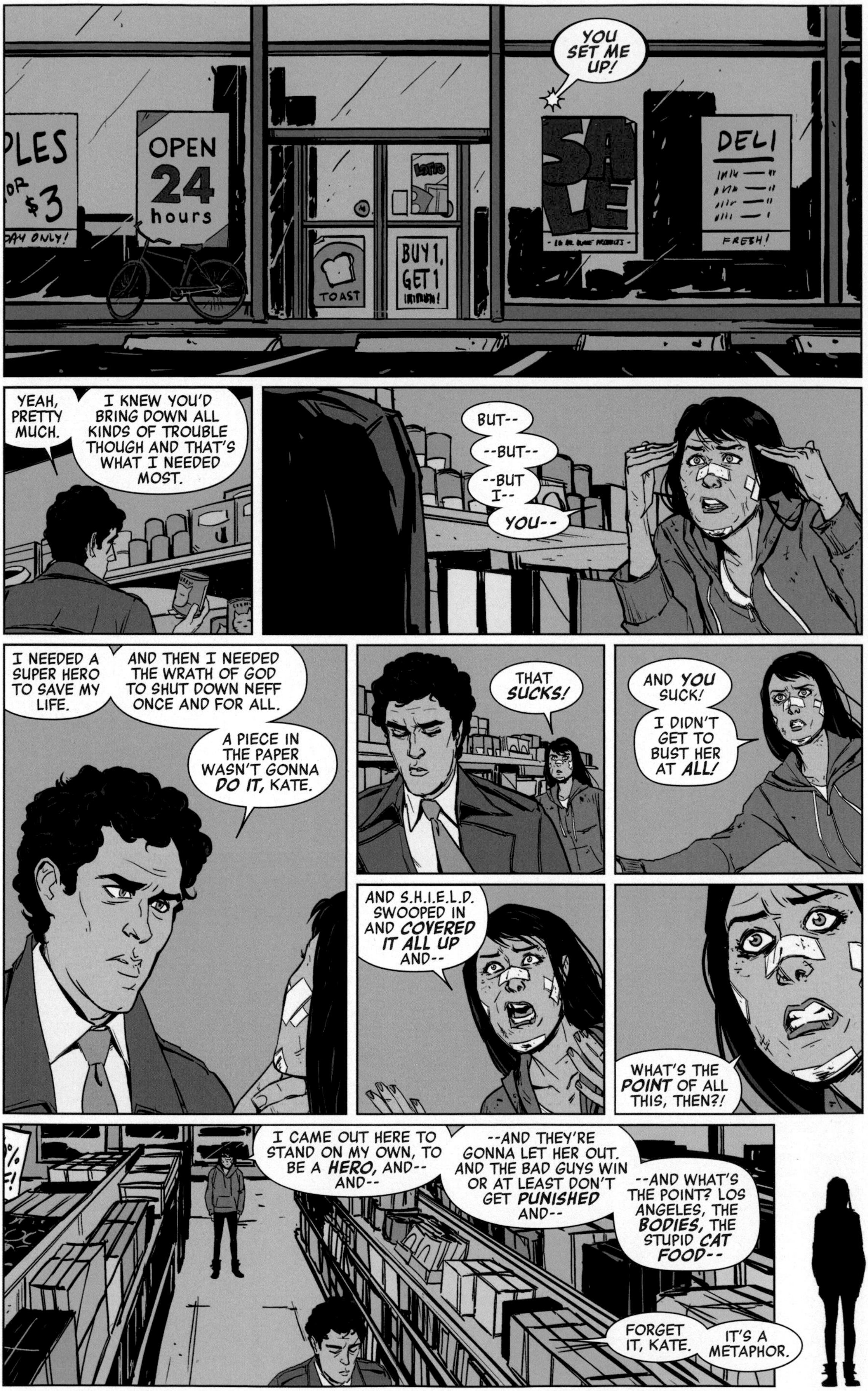
PLES
OR $3
DAY ONLY!
OPEN 24 hours
TOAST
BUY 1, GET 1
SALE
DELI
FRESH!
YOU SET ME UP!
YEAH, PRETTY MUCH.
I KNEW YOU'D BRING DOWN ALL KINDS OF TROUBLE THOUGH AND THAT'S WHAT I NEEDED MOST.
BUT--
--BUT--
--BUT I--
YOU--
I NEEDED A SUPER HERO TO SAVE MY LIFE.
AND THEN I NEEDED THE WRATH OF GOD TO SHUT DOWN NEFF ONCE AND FOR ALL.
A PIECE IN THE PAPER WASN'T GONNA DO IT, KATE.
THAT SUCKS!
AND YOU SUCK!
I DIDN'T GET TO BUST HER AT ALL!
AND S.H.I.E.L.D. SWOOPED IN AND COVERED IT ALL UP AND--
WHAT'S THE POINT OF ALL THIS, THEN?!
I CAME OUT HERE TO STAND ON MY OWN, TO BE A HERO, AND-- AND--
--AND THEY'RE GONNA LET HER OUT. AND THE BAD GUYS WIN OR AT LEAST DON'T GET PUNISHED AND--
--AND WHAT'S THE POINT? LOS ANGELES, THE BODIES, THE STUPID CAT FOOD--
FORGET IT, KATE.
IT'S A METAPHOR.

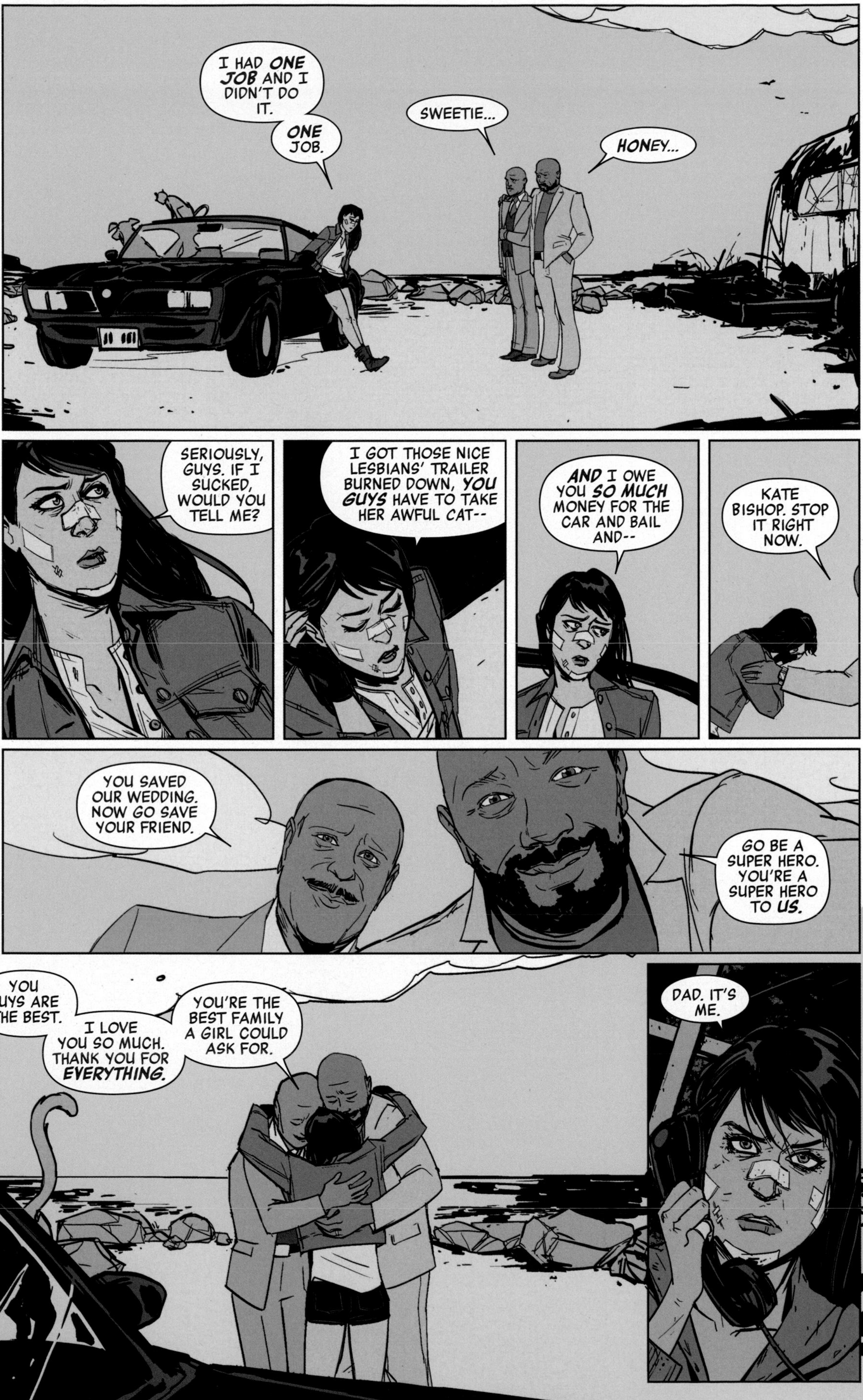
I HAD ONE JOB AND I DIDN'T DO IT.
ONE JOB.
SWEETIE...
HONEY...
SERIOUSLY, GUYS. IF I SUCKED, WOULD YOU TELL ME?
I GOT THOSE NICE LESBIANS' TRAILER BURNED DOWN, YOU GUYS HAVE TO TAKE HER AWFUL CAT--
AND I OWE YOU SO MUCH MONEY FOR THE CAR AND BAIL AND--
KATE BISHOP. STOP IT RIGHT NOW.
YOU SAVED OUR WEDDING. NOW GO SAVE YOUR FRIEND.
GO BE A SUPER HERO. YOU'RE A SUPER HERO TO US.
YOU GUYS ARE THE BEST.
I LOVE YOU SO MUCH. THANK YOU FOR EVERYTHING.
YOU'RE THE BEST FAMILY A GIRL COULD ASK FOR.
DAD. IT'S ME.

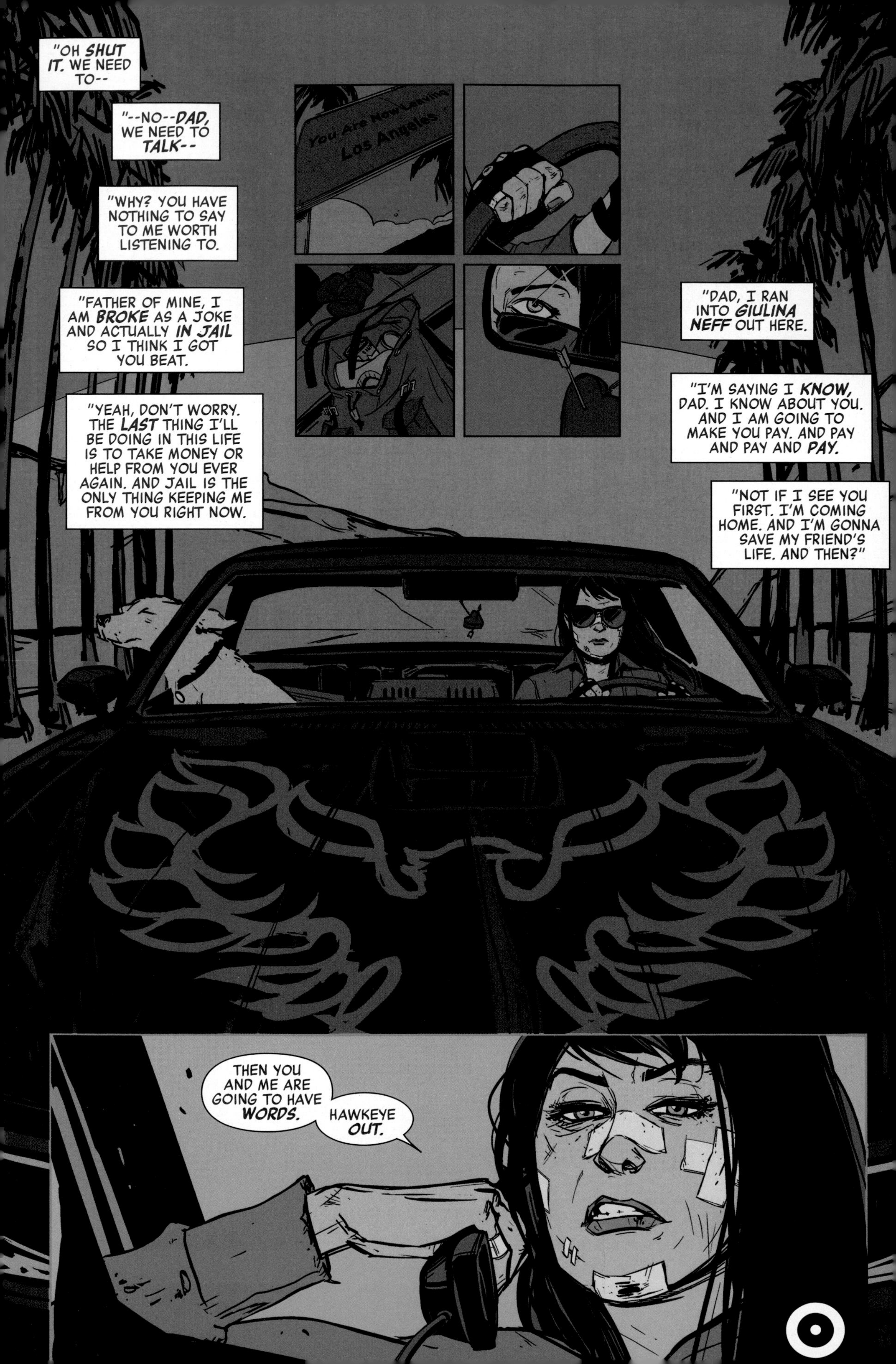

"OH SHUT IT. WE NEED TO--
"--NO--DAD, WE NEED TO TALK--
"WHY? YOU HAVE NOTHING TO SAY TO ME WORTH LISTENING TO.
"FATHER OF MINE, I AM BROKE AS A JOKE AND ACTUALLY IN JAIL SO I THINK I GOT YOU BEAT.
"YEAH, DON'T WORRY. THE LAST THING I'LL BE DOING IN THIS LIFE IS TO TAKE MONEY OR HELP FROM YOU EVER AGAIN. AND JAIL IS THE ONLY THING KEEPING ME FROM YOU RIGHT NOW.
You Are Now Leaving Los Angeles
"DAD, I RAN INTO GIULINA NEFF OUT HERE.
"I'M SAYING I KNOW, DAD. I KNOW ABOUT YOU. AND I AM GOING TO MAKE YOU PAY. AND PAY AND PAY AND PAY.
"NOT IF I SEE YOU FIRST. I'M COMING HOME. AND I'M GONNA SAVE MY FRIEND'S LIFE. AND THEN?"
THEN YOU AND ME ARE GOING TO HAVE WORDS.
HAWKEYE OUT.

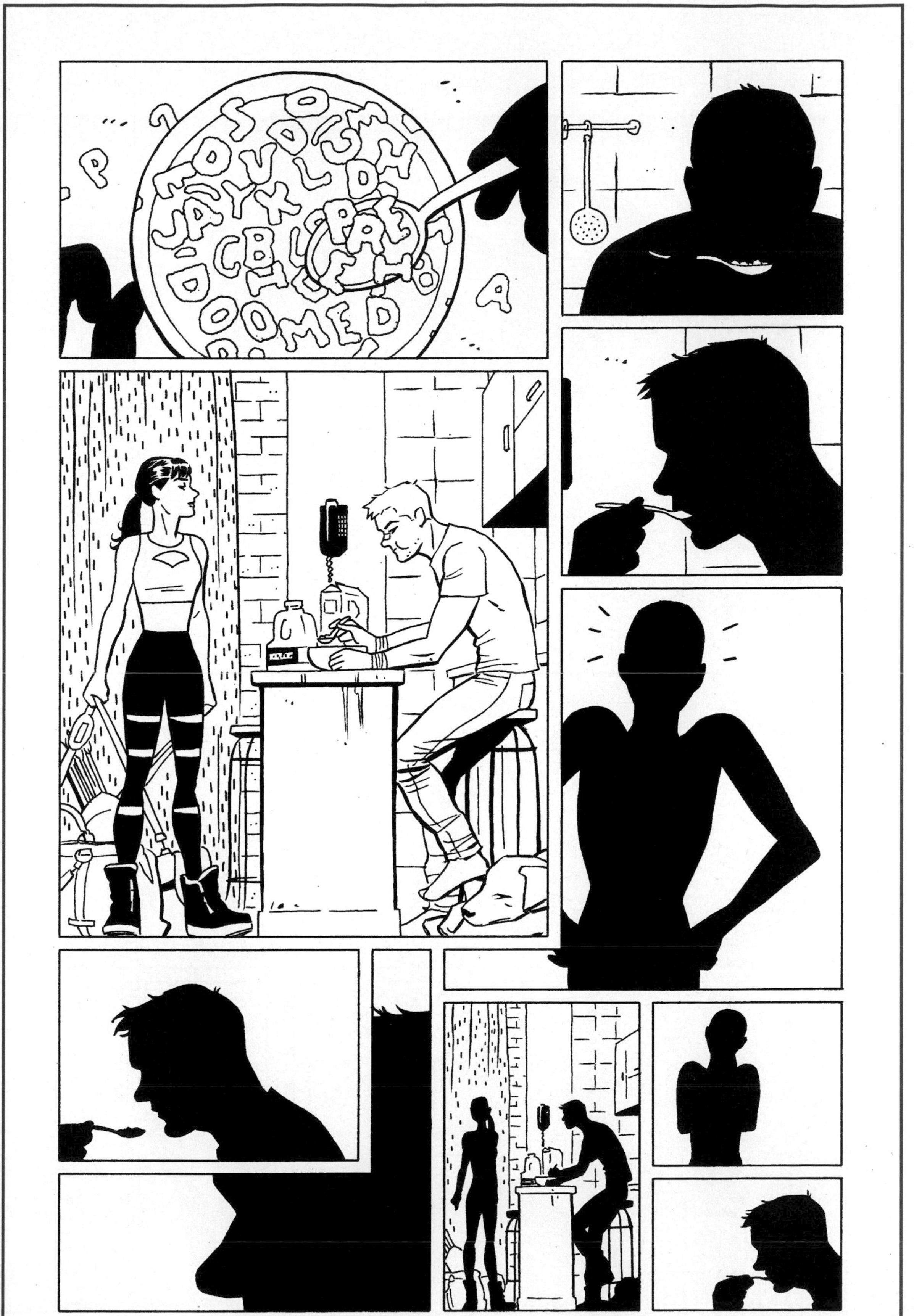
DOOMED

HAWKEYE ANNUAL #1, PAGE 1 INKS
BY JAVIER PULIDO

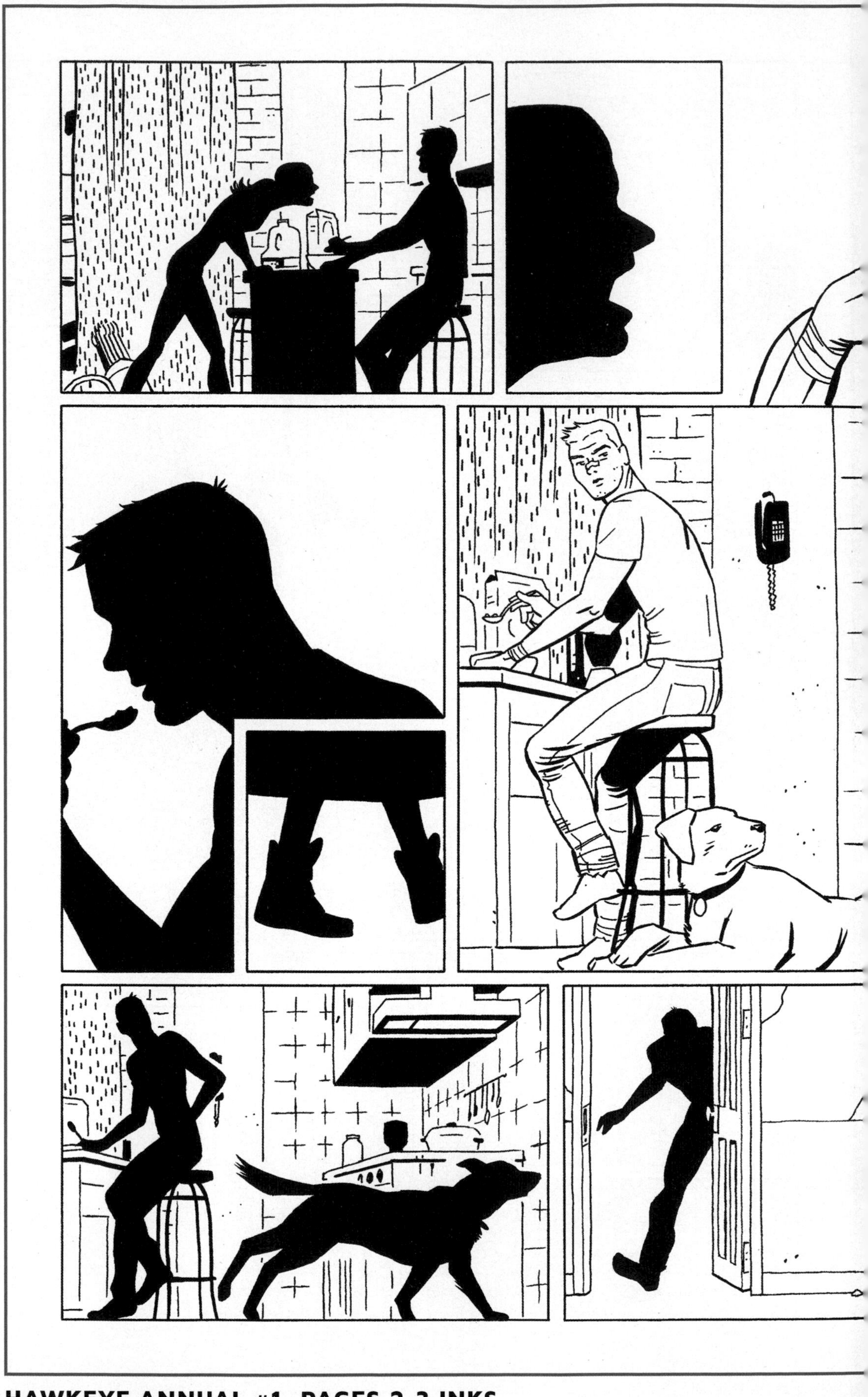

HAWKEYE ANNUAL #1, PAGES 2-3 INKS
BY JAVIER PULIDO

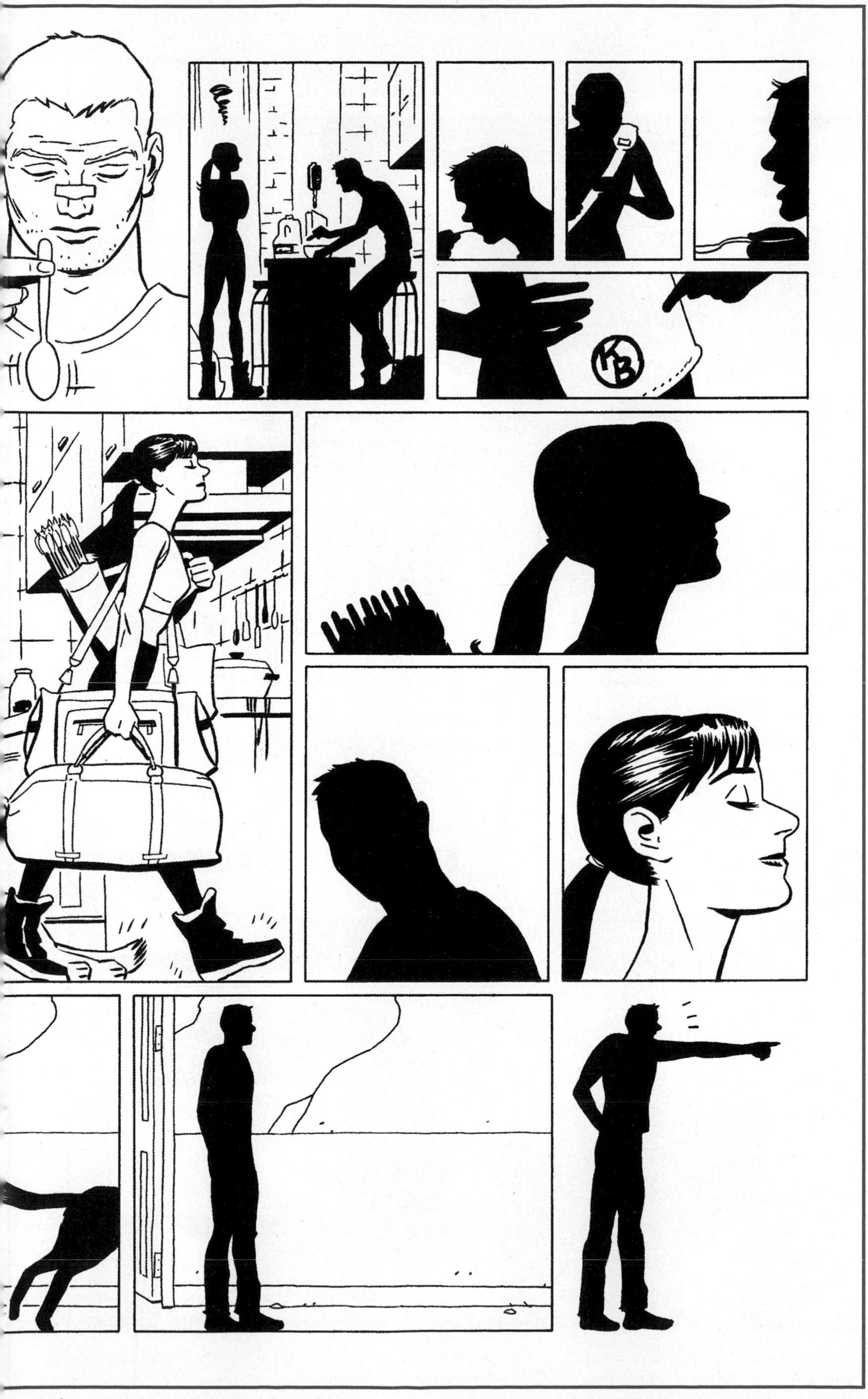
KB

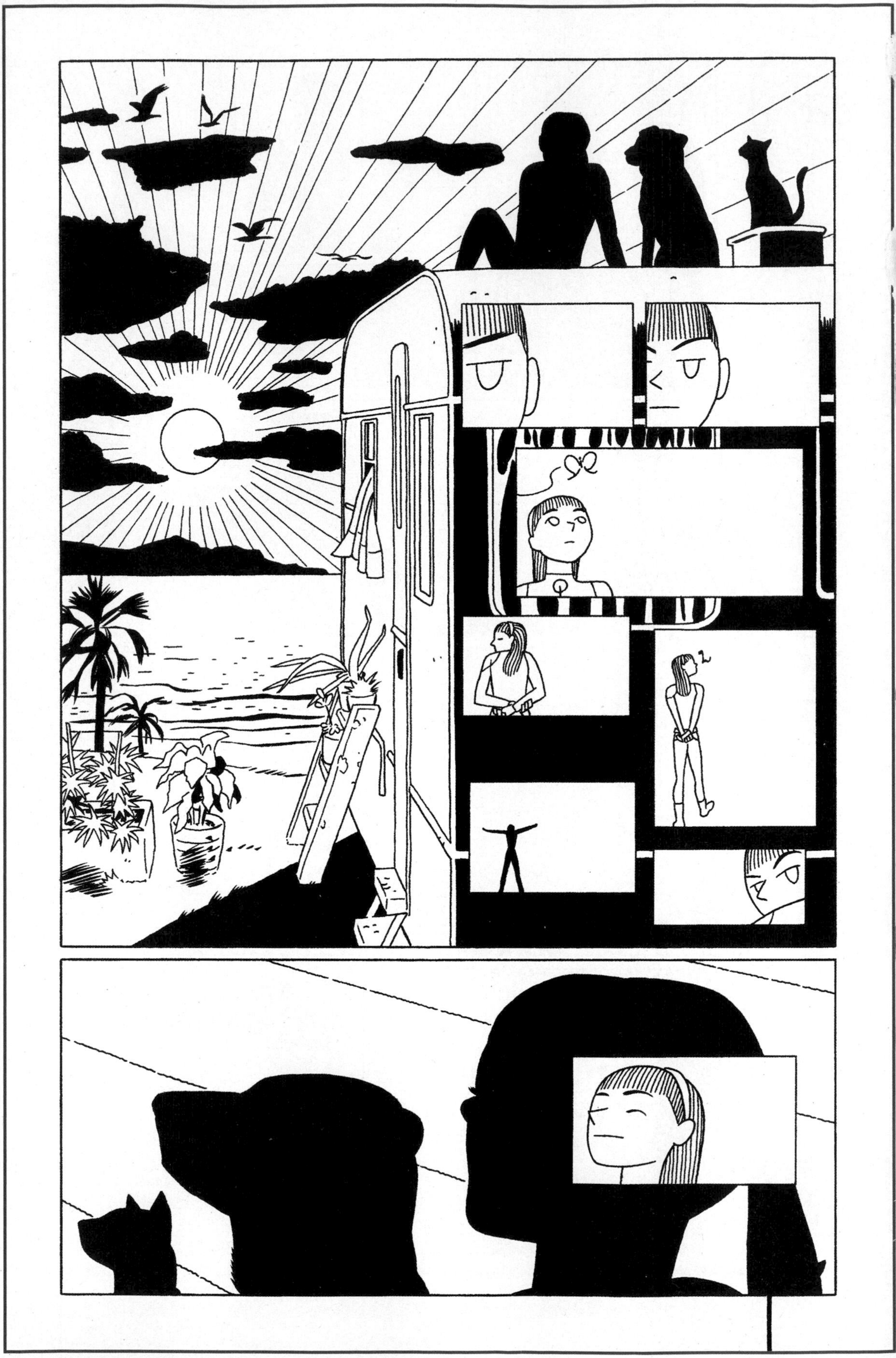

HAWKEYE ANNUAL #1, PAGE 28 INKS
BY JAVIER PULIDO